SEDUCED

Center Point
Large Print

Also by Randy Wayne White and available from Center Point Large Print:

Doc Ford Series:
  Night Moves
  Bone Deep
  Cuba Straits
  Deep Blue

Hannah Smith Series:
  Haunted

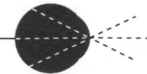

SEDUCED

Randy Wayne White

CENTER POINT LARGE PRINT
THORNDIKE, MAINE

This Center Point Large Print edition is published in the year 2016 by arrangement with G. P. Putnam's Sons, an imprint of Penguin Publishing Group, a division of Penguin Random House LLC.

The text of this Large Print edition is unabridged. In other aspects, this book may vary from the original edition. Printed in the United States of America on permanent paper. Set in 16-point Times New Roman type.

ISBN: 978-1-68324-193-5

Library of Congress Cataloging-in-Publication Data

Names: White, Randy Wayne, author.
Title: Seduced / Randy Wayne White.
Description: Center Point Large Print edition. | Thorndike, Maine : Center Point Large Print, 2016.
Identifiers: LCCN 2016042519 | ISBN 9781683241935 (hardcover : alk. paper)
Subjects: LCSH: Large type books. | GSAFD: Mystery fiction. | Suspense fiction.
Classification: LCC PS3573.H47473 S43 2016b | DDC 813/.54—dc23
LC record available at https://lccn.loc.gov/2016042519

For J. D. M.

When the woman saw that the tree was good for food, and that it was pleasant to the eyes, and a tree to be desired to make one wise, she took of the fruit thereof, and did eat, and gave also unto her husband with her; and he did eat.

—GENESIS 3:6

Seduction begins with a fantasy that, pending a willing partner and a safe place, choreographs its own dangerous reality.

—H. M. TOMLINSON

[Disclaimer]

Sanibel and Captiva Islands are real places, faithfully described, but used fictitiously in this novel. The same is true of certain businesses, marinas, bars, and other places frequented by Doc Ford, Tomlinson, and pals.

In all other respects, however, this novel is a work of fiction. Names (unless used by permission), characters, places, and incidents are either the product of the author's imagination or are used fictitiously. Any resemblance to actual persons, living or dead, or to actual events or locales is unintentional and coincidental.

Contact Mr. White at www.docford.com.

Author's Note

The summer before I started this novel, on a day of ninety-degree heat, two pals and I landed a Maule seaplane in a remote bay and waded ashore to explore the only chunk of high ground for many, many miles. Common sense dictated that a spot such as this would also attract snakes—pythons, in fact—but we were too busy sinking in muck and battling mosquitoes to worry about trifles.

Our intent was to photograph artifacts left by Florida's pre-Columbian settlers, which we did, but we also came away with a bag full of "wild" oranges. These were gathered off the ground because the hammock—an island, of sorts—was such a tangle of thorns and vines, we could not find the tree.

Difficult to imagine? We considered it odd, too, but not until later when we were safely home and had properly rehydrated after a dip in the pool. The oranges, freshly squeezed, helped. Never had we tasted juice like this—superbly sour yet sweet, with a lime-lemon tang. Very different from feral oranges found on islands that had once been farmed. And light-years better than pasteurized juice.

As we rallied, more oddities were jogged from

our heat-addled brains. The place we'd been was surrounded by mangrove swamp, fourteen miles from the next chunk of high ground and twenty-one miles to the nearest road. The island, which wasn't much of an island (three hundred feet long, two hundred feet wide), hadn't been inhabited since pre-Columbian times, and it had been decades, possibly centuries, since anyone had been boneheaded enough to hack their way into the interior.

What was an orange tree doing there? How had it survived beneath a forest canopy that had obviously won the battle for sunlight? How had it reproduced in isolation? More to the point, why couldn't we find the damn thing?

There was one troubling detail we'd all noticed, but only subliminally: aside from a big alligator, we had seen no wildlife—no tracks, no scat—in what should have been an animal haven.

Instead, we pondered only citrus-related oddities. We researched every facet of the subject. Well . . . a couple of us did. My friends, Capt. Mark Futch and Jeff Carter, are unusual men. Mark is an eighth-generation Floridian, a pilot/fishing guide, whose roots are tangled in piracy via the Bahamas and Boca Grande. He has connections in the citrus industry, too. Jeff is a fine writer and historian. His knowledge about all sorts of things, including botany, is beyond my depth, which is why I stick to instigating dangerous trips.

A month of research and much texting ensued. What we learned provided the foundation for this book. What we experienced on our second trip provided a pivotal character in it.

Yes, we returned to that miserable place.

It was August. The temperature was already pushing one hundred degrees by the time we landed. Twenty yards of water separated us from shore, but this time, by god, we were prepared. We'd bought special "mud shoes" (designed to mimic the splaying of a duck's feet) to skate us over the thigh-deep muck.

Two of us were heavier than ducks. We sank, tried to recover, and sank deeper. One of us might be there yet had we not drawn upon crawling skills learned as a child. Mark veered left, convinced he'd spotted an easier entrance into the mangroves. Jeff veered right, and I followed, which was duck-like behavior, but on my belly, not my feet.

Half an hour later, after hacking our way through mangroves, Jeff and I stopped because one of us was exhausted, and Jeff didn't look good, either. That's when we heard Mark scream. A *serious* scream—some of you will know the difference. Garbled profanities followed.

Jeff, who is from Georgia, looked at me and drawled, "That boy's hurt bad."

I feared it was true. Mark was our pilot.

We bulled our way inland through foliage so

dense, there was no sunlight. By now Mark was bellowing, "Python . . . A big f-ing python. It's chasing me!"

It was true. Well, maybe not chasing him, but it was a great big f-ing python. Two of us were carrying sidearms. When we finally located Mark, one of us shot the thing, but the snake slid off and disappeared. (How my second shot missed is a mystery—the damn thing was thicker than my thigh.)

We spent the next hour moving as quietly as prey, our eyes darting from branches above to the ground below, all because of what, by then, had become a group obsession: an orange tree that, one way or another, dated back to the 1500s and the Spanish Conquistadors.

The tree exists. In this novel, Hannah Smith finds a larger version, but it grows in the same bizarre configuration.

A dark, strange place, that island. It, too, is described accurately in this novel. A third trip confirmed that wildlife there has been decimated by the snake population, but there was one less snake when we left. The skin of a twelve-foot Burmese python now hangs on the wall of my son Rogan's office—a story I will save for another book.

Before thanking those who contributed their expertise or good humor during the writing of *Seduced*, I want to make clear that all errors, exaggerations, or misstatements of fact are entirely my fault, not theirs. This applies particularly to those I consulted about orange trees, and the terrible citrus greening disease (HLB).

These generous people include Pamela D. Roberts, Professor, Department of Plant Pathology, University of Florida, who invested her time and trust by helping me throughout this project.

Steve Smith of Babcock Ranch helped a great deal via his primers on citrus farming. Biochemist Gregg Fergus and patent attorney Vern Norviel provided guidance and assistance regarding biotech patents. John Stark, Ph.D., University of California, Davis, and Peggy Sieburth, Ph.D., Florida Department of Agriculture, were also helpful.

Equally as generous were Michael and Margie Bennette, and Brian and Denise Cobb. Their devotion to Florida, and Florida archaeology, are much appreciated. Ms. Liesa Priddy, Collier County native, and a respected board member of the Florida Wildlife Commission, once again provided advice and information on the fascinating area that is her home. The fine ladies of the Arcadia, Florida, Book Club kindly suggested where Hannah and Roberta should converse over lunch and tea.

Insights, ideas, and medical advice were provided by doctors Brian Hummel, my brother Dan White, Marybeth B. Saunders, and Peggy C.

Kalkounos, and my amazing nephew, Justin White, Ph.D.

Pals, advisers, and/or teammates are always a help because they know firsthand that writing and writers are a pain in the ass. They are Gary Terwilliger, Ron Iossi, Jerry Rehfuss, Stu Johnson, Victor Candalaria, Gene Lamont, Nick Swartz, Kerry Griner, Mike Shevlin, Jon Warden, Dr. Mike Tucker, Davey Johnson, Barry Rubel, Mike Westhoff, and behavioral guru Don Carman.

My wife, singer/songwriter Wendy Webb, provides not just support and understanding but is a trusted adviser. Bill Lee, and his orbiting star, Diana, as always, have guided me, safely, into the strange but fun and enlightened world of our mutual friend, the Reverend Sighurdhr M. Tomlinson. Equal thanks go to Albert Randall, Donna Terwilliger, Rachael Ketterman, Stephen Grendon, my devoted SOB, the angelic Mrs. Iris Tanner, and my partners and pals, Mark Marinello, Marty and Brenda Harrity.

Much of this novel was written at corner tables before and after hours at Doc Ford's Rum Bar and Grille, where staff were tolerant beyond the call of duty. Thanks go to: Liz Harris Barker, Greg and Bryce Barker, Madonna Donna Butz, Jeffery Kelley, Chef Rene Ramirez, Amanda Rodriguez, Kim McGonnell, Ashley Rhoeheffer, the Amazing Cindy Porter, Desiree

Olsen, Gabby Moschitta, Rachael Okerstrom, Rebecca Harris, Sarah Carnithian, Tyler Wussler, Tall Sean Lamont, Motown Rachel Songalewski, Boston Brian Cunningham, and Cardinals Fan Justin Harris.

At Doc Ford's on Fort Myers Beach: Lovely Kandice Salvador, Johnny G, Meliss Alleva, Rickards and Molly Brewer, Reyes Ramon Jr., Reyes Ramon Sr., Netta Kramb, Sandy Rodriquez, Mark Hines, Stephen Hansman, Nora Billheimer, Eric Hines, Dave Werner, Daniel Troxell, Kelsey King, Jenna Hocking, Adam Stocco, Brandon Cashatt, Dani Peterson, Tim Riggs, Elijah Blue Jansen, Jessica Del Gandio, Douglas Martens, Jacob Krigbaum, Jeff Bright, Derek Aubry, Chase Uhl, Carly Purdy, Nikki Sarros, Bre Cagnoli, Carly Cooper, Andrew Acord, Diane Bellini, Jessie Fox, Justin Voskuhl, Lalo Contreras, Nick Howes, Rich Capo, Zeke Pietrzyk, Reid Pietrzyk, Ryan Fowler, Dan Mumford, Kelly Bugaj, Taylor Darby, Jaqueline Engh, Carmen Reyes, Karli Goodison, Kaitlyn Wolfe, Alex and Eric Munchel, Zach Leon, Alex Hall.

At Doc Ford's on Captiva Island: Big Papa Mario Zanolli, Lovely Julie Grzeszak, Shawn Scott, Joy Schawalder, Alicia Rutter, Adam Traum, Alexandra Llanos, Antonio Barragan, Chris Orr, Daniel Leader, Dylan Wussler, Edward Bowen, Erica DeBacker, Irish Heather Walk,

Jon Economy, Josh Kerschner, Katie Kovacs, Ryan Body, Ryan Cook, Sarah Collins, Shelbi Muske, Scott Hamilton, Tony Foreman, Yakhyo Yakubov, Yamily Fernandez, Cheryl Radar Erickson, Heather Hartford, Stephen Snook Man Day, Anastasia Moiseyev, Chelsea Bennett, and Shokruh "Shogun" Akhmedov.

Finally, thanks to my amazing sons Lee and Rogan for helping finish another book.

—*Randy Wayne White*
Casa Blanca
Cojimar, Cuba

One

I was enjoying the conversation with a man I used to date, a biologist named Marion Ford, until the subject swung from Florida oranges to a giant snake. He'd seen it crossing a bay south of the island where I grew up and still occasionally reside.

"How far south?"

"A ways. We were flying back from Key West."

"That's where you disappeared to?"

"I've been traveling," he said, which was typical. "It was a Burmese python—twelve, maybe fifteen feet long. Too big for a boa. Hard to be sure of the size because it was swimming, but that's not the point."

"It is to me," I said. "If you're trying to scare me into moving closer to your lab, I'm flattered, but I'd prefer the particulars first. There are better ways than inventing snakes."

"Invent?" He was mystified. Marion has warmth, if you get to know him, but he is slow to recognize playful humor.

"I don't doubt you saw it, but there's a hundred miles of coast between here and the Keys. Was the snake closer to Naples or Sanibel Island?"

"Let me finish. I was making a connection between the parasites killing your orange trees and higher-profile exotics like pythons, boas, a whole long list of reptiles that are taking over the state. Not just reptiles, of course. Fire ants have all but destroyed the quail population. Brazilian pepper trees are another example, but they were intentionally introduced by state biologists, so—"

"Marion," I said patiently, "you know I'm not fond of snakes, and you know why. Please stick to the subject."

"I thought I was."

"You were for a while. Now you're not."

I was aboard a tidy Marlow cabin cruiser that is my home, neatening up the galley, with the phone to my ear. As we talked, I could look out the cabin door and see the family dock built by my late Uncle Jake as it wobbled through the mangroves. Across the road, atop an Indian mound, was an old yellow-pine Cracker house with a tin roof and a wraparound porch. Veiled by screening were ceiling fans, a summer kitchen, and a hammock where, as a child, I had often slept on hot summer nights.

What I chose not to notice was a black Lincoln Town Car parked in the shade. For more than an hour, I'd been trying to ignore the thing. It belonged to an old-time Florida millionaire who, twenty years ago, had been my mother's secret lover. Two brain surgeries and a fondness for smoking pot have not improved her memory, nor pacified her mood swings and sometimes wild behavior.

Better, I'd decided, to call a friend rather than fixate on what might be going on up there. Inside, it was just the two of them: my mother, Loretta, and eighty-year-old Harney Chatham, the former lieutenant governor of Florida, who was also a married man.

Not that anyone remembers lieutenant governors. Even Mr. Chatham's recent prostate surgery had not made the news.

Ford asked, "Are you still there?"

I realized my attention had drifted. "I'm not one to interrupt, but that doesn't mean I'm not listening. How big was the snake?"

Apparently, he had already covered that ground. Instead of sighing, as a normal person would, he calmly repeated the details—a quality that was admirable, I suppose, but also rankled me. It was as if he were a professor tutoring one of his slower students.

"Hannah," he added, "I haven't heard from you in more than three weeks—"

"You disappeared a month ago, so what do you expect?"

"I didn't disappear, I was traveling," he reminded me. "Now, out of the blue, you call to tell me the oranges in your citrus grove are dying. Why ask me for advice?"

"They're *withering*," I corrected, "with a sort

of green mold on the skins, and the fruit's bitter."

"The entire grove?"

"The ones I care about. The honeybells and grapefruit, all my favorites. You can tell by the leaves. They start to curl up, with yellow streaks."

"But not all?"

"I didn't think to check."

"You should. If some of the trees aren't infected, I'd step back and ask myself what's different about them? Less shade, more sun— a different soil or rootstock? But if the entire grove is diseased—"

I said, "It's not big enough to be called a grove; not really. Just a few dozen trees my grandfather planted way, way back."

"I know. All I'm saying is, you must have ties to people in the citrus business who can give you better advice than me."

Again, my eyes moved to the black limousine. "Some of the biggest," I replied, "but I do miss our talks. You're a biologist, and it's been a while, so I thought maybe you'd heard something new."

This, he found humorous. "The parasites that spread citrus greening don't have fins, and they don't swim. I'm a *marine* biologist. All I know is, they're exotics, and they've damn near ruined a billion-dollar industry. Is that really the reason you called?"

I was about to cover my deception by shifting

topics when I saw Loretta charge out of the house wearing a housecoat and fluffy pink slippers. Her mannerisms were frantic as if she were being chased, or had suffered a second brain aneurysm. She bounced on her toes and flapped her hands in my direction, then charged back onto the porch.

"Something's wrong," I said.

"Nothing we can't fix, Hannah, if you're willing to—"

"Not us, my crazy mother," I interrupted, and went out the cabin door in a hurry.

The former lieutenant governor was either dead or in a bad way. I knew it when Loretta blocked me from the porch, saying, "Even as a child you had a selfish streak. Now you refuse to do me this one little favor?"

The favor she had demanded was, "Go away, and, for god's sake, don't call the law. It's too late to save your mama from sinning . . . But you didn't hear that from me. I'm not gonna confess to anything."

I felt a little dizzy when I heard those words. "Where is he, Loretta?"

"Who?"

"You don't think I recognize his car? If Mr. Chatham is sick, we need to do something. Please tell me something terrible hasn't happened."

She stared at the Lincoln Town Car and hyperventilated.

"Loretta, move. If Reggie's sleeping in the backseat, go bang on the window and get him up here. I'll look for myself."

Reggie was Mr. Chatham's limo driver.

"Not until I think this through," she snapped, and squared herself in front of the door. Loretta isn't a large woman—not compared to me, her only child—but she has a magic way of puffing herself while her bright blue eyes catch fire. "For once in your life, do something to make me happy, Hannah. Just go away and leave us be."

"I'm not leaving until—"

"Do as you're told, young lady!" she hollered, and glared with those wild eyes of hers.

For an instant, I was a child again, standing in the same doorway of the same house that hadn't changed much since my mother had stung me with similar words many times, over many years. But that girl was long gone, along with her timid nature. "If you don't move, I'll go 'round to the back door. Or pick you up and carry you to the couch. Is that what you want? The two of us wrestling around like crazy people while we could be helping?" Then I called over the top of her head, "Mr. Chatham! Everything okay in there? It's me, Hannah Smith."

On the mantel above the fireplace is a cherry-wood clock my great-grandfather made when he wasn't fishing mullet, or selling rum and egret plumes. The clock's ticking was the only reply.

"My lord," I murmured. "Loretta, talk to me. Please tell me you did not do something crazy. You didn't stab him, did you?"

"Stab him! 'Course I didn't. In my own bed? What do you think I am?"

"My lord," I said again. "Is that where he is?"

With a dazed look, she turned toward the hall, her bedroom beyond, then appeared to wilt and stepped away. "When the law comes, I suppose you'll tell them the governor ain't the first man I killed."

Kilt is the way the word is pronounced in the small fishing communities of Southwest Florida.

"He's *dead?*"

"I believe he is," was her cryptic reply, "but Harney's not the type to give up all at once." She began to sob.

I rushed into the house to where Loretta's recliner faced the TV, which wasn't blaring soap operas for a change. Nearby was her walker. It was covered with a caftan as a vanity. Aside from confiding to a few women friends, she won't admit she needs help getting around, not even to our handsome UPS man, let alone a former lover. I slid the walker within reach and hurried down the hall, calling the governor's name.

The door to my old room was open, nothing I recognized on the walls or desk. Loretta's door was shut tight, which was normal. As always, I could feel the privacy of shadows and forbidden drawers radiating from within. Twice I knocked, then bumped the door open. After a look, I hollered, "Call nine-one-one. Hurry!" but didn't budge for a moment because my legs felt watery, like in a bad dream.

In life, Mr. Chatham was an imposing man with oversized accomplishments. He favored Western-cut suits, string bolo ties, and the only time he removed his hat was when entering a house, or greeting a lady, or before sliding into the back of his limo.

His cowboy hat—"my John Wayne Stetson," he called it—was the only reason I knew for certain the man who lay there, toes up and naked with vomit crusted on his chin, was the former lieutenant governor. My mother, despite her panic, had had the good manners to place the hat strategically over his pelvis. The Stetson tilted, as if on a peg, the man's two long, heavy legs sticking out. I charged in and did what I'd been taught in a CPR course I had to take when I'd upgraded my captain's license. Mr. Chatham's neck was as white and cool as clay when I felt for a pulse. Glassy eyes failed to respond to my shouting, nor when I hammered a fist on his chest.

Next step: clear the airway, then begin mouth-to-mouth. Practicing on a CPR dummy had not prepared me for the realities involved. But I did as I'd been taught. Billowed two breaths into his lungs, then shouted out the compressions in a robotic way while I pumped his chest. This helped stem a blooming nausea.

"Mama—you'd best be dialing that damn phone! Carry it outside while you talk, and bring Reggie fast as you can."

There was no need to add this because the chauffeur was suddenly beside me, hands on my shoulders, and cooing in his gentle Southern way. "You done what you could, Miz Hannah. Go on now, girl, an' leave the rest to me."

I stepped back and brushed hair from my face. "He's got no pulse. Did Loretta call nine-one-one?"

Reggie, a tiny, wiry man, was wearing the same blue cap he always wore. "All taken care of," he said. Then he removed his driving gloves and yelled, "Governor! Wake up, sir. This is ain't no place for this to be happening."

He plopped down, grabbed the man who'd been his employer for decades, shook him by the shoulders, and looked up at me with wide eyes. "Lord God, he's cold as death, Miz Hannah. His heart done stopped. I knew this was gonna happen."

"You can't be sure."

"Cold as he is? Honey, he's been gone a while."

"We have to keep doing compressions until—"

"I know, I know," the little man said, yet

sounded resigned. "I took that course for my chauffeur's license, but the governor wouldn't like it, you seeing what I gotta do first." He glanced at the Stetson, as if to convey his meaning, then hunched his back and continued CPR. Between breaths he told me, "Leave us alone, girl. It's what he'd want."

I was duty-bound to stay but suddenly in need of air. In the bathroom, I left the water running to cover the sound of my nausea, then washed my face and went searching for my mother. She was on the porch, rocking and staring past the mangroves that fringe our dock. It was a cool, bright afternoon in February, with the sky too low for soaring gulls and frigate birds. When I covered her legs with a blanket, she spoke in a monotone. "No need to badger me, I know it's my fault. He warned me often enough."

"Don't fret about that now."

"I'm being punished for doin' what I knew I shouldn't do. I, by god, deserve whatever hell has to offer, 'cause that's where I'm headed."

"Don't say such things. Do you mean Mr. Chatham mentioned he had heart problems? I think that's what happened. He had a heart attack."

"It wasn't him who warned me."

"What are you talking about?"

"Never mind. The governor's problems always started way south of his heart. We was both that way, God help us. That's why he had that thingamabob installed. I knew we was playing with fire but couldn't stop myself."

Rather than endure further details, I offered to make a pitcher of sweet tea. My mother rocked and stared.

"Earthly pleasures are a trap, Hannah. Chastity might seem its own punishment—until you accept a man from the spirit world. That's when our behavior is supposed to change. Oh, I knew what I was doing."

There is often no making sense of her babbling. I hugged my mother close as she cried, her shoulders bird-like. "I'll call the home health nurse and have her come early. Or would you rather I have the ladies come keep you company?"

I was referring to Loretta's friends from childhood, Epsey Hendry, Becky Darwin, and Jody Summerlin—all widows. Once a week, they would gather on the porch, with cookies, or a pie or brownies, and wait for the church shuttle to carry them to bingo.

There would be no bingo on this Friday night.

I gave her another hug, called Becky Darwin without explaining why she was needed, then went inside to check on Reggie. In the hall, I stopped out of respect. He was weeping, but in an angry way, and speaking in low tones to his former employer. Eavesdropping is not something I normally do, yet what I heard was so unexpected, I found myself drawn toward the open door.

I heard the chauffeur mutter, "Where the hell is the damn shutoff valve? I ain't gettin' paid to put my hands on your . . . no, I ain't. I warned you, Governor—by god, I warned you—now here we are. And who gonna explain this to that bitch you married if I can't . . . ? Shit fire! How's this damn contraption work?"

I peeked in and wished I hadn't. Mr. Chatham was faceup, no sheet over him, and his Stetson was on the floor. I'm not sure what I said—more of a gasp, I suppose—which caused Reggie to swing around and say, "I told him what would happen if a man his age got an implant, Miz Hannah. And takin' them damn blue pills of his, too. Please"—this was said with urgent deference—"we got to leak the air out of this damn thing and get the governor home before his wife finds out he's gone."

Again, I am uncertain of my response—another gasp, no doubt, albeit indignant, and something about waiting for the EMTs.

Reggie, who had tended to his employer's secrets for more than forty years, replied, "The governor ain't leaving here in an ambulance, and"—he motioned for emphasis—"he ain't going home lookin' like that. What would people think?"

What Loretta had termed a thingamabob was, indeed, a startling image to behold. Not that my eyes lingered. There is a sad, clinical starkness to an old man who lay as if staked to the bed by a porcine rod through his hips. A wicked thought darted through my mind regarding my mother, who, even in my childhood, had often walked around with a dazed expression on her face.

I backed into the hall. "What are you suggesting, Reggie? We can't move a dead body. That's against the law."

"The governor never cared nothing about the law. It's what he'd want."

"Are you telling me the ambulance isn't coming?"

The little man ignored that.

I said, "We should call Joel Ransler. He's an attorney."

He was also Mr. Chatham's illegitimate son by yet another mistress.

Reggie shook his head while leaning over the dead man. "Joel wouldn't help. Those two ain't shared a word since the fool almost got you killed. Besides, Joel moved to Jamaica for the winter—which proves he is a dang fool."

"We can't do this on our own," I said.

"Why not? There weren't nothing about transporting dead clients on the chauffeur's test. Doubt if the topic was mentioned in your captain's test, neither. Transportin' folks is what

29

folks like you and me are paid to do." Reggie's back was to me, a blessed screen from the explorations of his searching, uncertain hands.

"I'm not just a fishing guide," I argued. "My Uncle Jake's investigation agency is still doing business, and I'm licensed by the state. I took an oath, for heaven's sake."

Reggie, bending closer, replied, "Where the hell the doctors hide that thing? I'm running out of places."

I left the room, confirmed that Loretta was still on the porch, a rocking catatonic, then returned with my mind made up. "We're not moving him and that's that," I said. "I'd risk my license."

The little man's reply was a muffled question, which might have been a request for a flash-light.

"A what?"

"You can look now. I pulled a blanket over the both of us, but the lighting ain't good. Try the wall switch."

"No! I'm warning you, you can't do this. It's crazy. We have to contact the authorities."

"Don't pick at me so, Miz Hannah. Please. We can't let the governor be found in this condition. The coroner's gonna take one look and know what killed him. You ever met the governor's new wife? There'd be hell to pay, there purely would."

This was said with sinister implications, and a hint of fear.

"You don't really think a doctor would blame Loretta for—"

"How else you gonna explain it?" Reggie asked, then exclaimed, "Hey—found it, I think. Hear that hissing? But don't ask me where the air's goin'."

I peeked to see the little man exit what appeared to be a makeshift tent. He stood, bowed his head for a moment, then pulled the blanket over his former employer's face. "Gonna miss you, you ol' fool, I surely am," he murmured, then focused his red, watery eyes on me. "Miz Hannah, you telling me you ain't willing to keep a secret for an old friend like the governor? And with your mama's reputation at stake?"

"I'm bonded by the state of Florida," was all I could think to say. I was shaken by the chauffeur's sadness, and the prospect of Loretta somehow being dragged into this mess.

"What about if'n the governor was your client? In ol' Jake's agency. Was there something in that oath you took about protecting a client's privacy rights? I expect there was. *Confidentiality*—that's the word the governor always liked to use when reminding me to keep my mouth shut."

The wiry little man accurately interpreted my reluctance to speak. "Then it's true."

"Even if Mr. Chatham had hired me as a

31

private investigator, I'd have to check with an attorney. Do you realize how crazy it is, what you're suggesting?"

"You could pretend he'd hired you. Only us two would know."

"Me knowing is one too many," I countered.

"You are a stubborn woman, Miz Hannah. We got to hurry and get this thing done. Please . . . take this"—he produced car keys and some crumpled dollar bills from his pocket— "This'll make it all legal. The governor's good for whatever else we owe."

"I can't take your money."

"You already did," Reggie said, and gently squeezed the bills and the keys into my hands. "You're working for me now, and here's what your new client wants you to do. While I get him dressed, you pull the Lincoln up close to the rear of the house and open every door on that car. And not a word to nobody."

The little man's rheumy red eyes sharpened. "Doesn't that sound better than the governor and your mama making headlines on the television news?"

Two

We had crossed the Sematee county line and were into citrus-and-cattle country when, from a dirt road, a sheriff's vehicle, green on white, appeared in the rearview mirror, and came up fast, until it was a car length behind.

"Shit," I said, which is a profanity I often think, but seldom say aloud.

"I'll be go to hell," Reggie agreed. "God sure is testing us on this dark day. You're going too slow, Miz Hannah, I done told you. Cops ain't never seen the governor's car when it weren't speeding. Ain't that true, Governor?"

The little man had been doing that for thirty miles, speaking to his dead employer, often in a confidential way not meant for my ears.

"I'm going almost sixty as it is."

"That's what I'm saying! Honey, mash that pedal like you got nothing to fear or the deputy's gonna know something ain't right."

"This is nuts," I replied, but sped up a bit anyway.

I was driving because I had insisted on driving. The alternative was to sit in the back with the late Harney Chatham, who was belted into a reclining seat that didn't recline far enough. Our hope was, if his John Wayne Stetson stayed put, it would appear as if the big man were dozing, except his lifeless neck shifted with every turn in the road. So Reggie had to use a hand and his shoulder to maintain the desired effect. Thank god, the windows were tinted.

"Faster," he said, "and slouch yourself down a bit. You gotta drive faster, Miz Hannah, and sit way shorter, more relaxed, sort of let your top hand drape—know what I'm saying?—if that cop is to believe you're me. You're one tall drink of water, if you don't mind a compliment. It ain't too late to put on my driver's cap."

That wasn't going to happen.

Never had I ridden in a vehicle so large, so powerful and ghostly quiet. When the digital speedometer hit 70, I touched cruise control and checked the mirror. The squad car was still there, close enough I could see the deputy's silver sunglasses and bulldog jaw.

I heard Reggie spin around in the backseat. "That's good. He ain't talking on his microphone. They always do that before they use the siren. Oh yeah . . . we got nothing to worry about."

Nothing to worry about! I almost laughed. "Do you recognize the deputy? You'd better, because I went off and left my purse and my driver's license is in that purse. If he stops us, don't say a word. I'll do all the talking—unless you know him. Do you know him?" Jabbering like a fool is something else I seldom do.

"Miz Hannah, a driver's license ain't the first thing he's gonna ask about if he sees a dead body back here. So we ain't gonna stop even if he tries. Those toggles next to the radio? We got emergency lights installed front and back on this here Lincoln. We'll drive straight to the hospital and tell them the governor's sick, maybe had a heart attack. Only part we'll have to change is, we'll say you was sittin' back here when it happened."

Speaking to his former employer, he added, "It'll sound better if you died in the arms of a beautiful young woman instead of back here alone, with a man who's your own chauffeur. That'd look bad. Don't you think that'd look bad?"

"I think I'm about to fire you both as clients," I snapped, "but the hospital's not a bad idea." I thought for a moment. "Are you sure the deputies around here all know this car?"

"There ain't but one black stretch Town Car in all Sematee County," he replied, then spoke to Mr. Chatham. "I thought you said she was Florida-born, Governor? That there's a silly question, her not knowing your car."

I straightened the rearview mirror to make eye contact with the deputy and offered a casual wave. I didn't expect much, but that small gesture was enough. The man lifted his hand in response, then suddenly dropped back, did a U-turn, and sped off in the opposite direction.

"Didn't we tell her?" Reggie smiled. "She's got nothing to worry about, riding with us big dogs." This was punctuated with a child-like cackle. Tee-hee-hee.

It would have been wrong to say what I was thinking to a man his age, so I drove in silence, knuckles white on the wheel. Good manners began to fail me, however, when I slowed to turn into the double-winged security gate at the Chatham estate. It was a wall of ornate wrought iron attached to miles of fenced pasture where horses grazed. In the far distance, a barn was visible beneath domes of cypress and oaks.

"Uh-oh," Reggie said.

"Now what?"

"I forgot. Today's Miz Chatham's day off from the ranch. Don't slow down—keep going."

"You're kidding."

"Don't even look. Go on, now, drive right on past."

"You *wanted* his wife to be here?"

"I was counting on it. Mash that pedal."

"Reggie," I said, "I'm beginning to hope you're in shock instead of just slap-flat dumb and crazy. I've about had it with you."

"Honey, listen. That woman never leaves the third floor, or her office in the barn, normally. But Fridays is when the governor's daughters and grandkids come to ride and play around the ranch. See there"—he pointed, and I saw a line

36

of trail horses, children aboard—"and there's a bunch more somewhere, I guarantee, clomping around in the house, makin' a mess, getting peanut butter all over her upholstery. Lonnie Chatham purely hates them kids, but they love me and the governor like Santa Claus. See now why we can't stop?"

I hit the accelerator to jettison anger and held my tongue. A billboard that read *Chatham Lincoln-Mercury-Ford* flashed by before I slowed the limo to 60 and touched cruise control. "I'm going to park within a few blocks of the hospital and take a cab home, Reggie. After that, you're on your own."

"Please don't, Miz Hannah. I got an even better idea now."

"I bet."

"At least hear me out. I should'a thought of this first."

"My mind's made up," I said without looking around, or realizing I had made this claim before.

"You didn't work for this man for goin' on forty years. A man like the governor deserves to die in a respectable way."

"That's something you should take up with God, not me," I countered.

"Would love to do that, lord knows I would. What I'm saying is, the governor should die with the things he loves best around him—not that he didn't love your mama. He purely did.

That's why we can't let him be hauled off on a gurney from a hospital parking lot. Most of the people who work there are too young to remember who he is or all he did for the folks in this county. Remember who ponied up the money for that museum near your mama's home?"

This was true. Mr. Chatham had been generous when it came to helping fishermen in the area, and many illegal aliens as well, although some might argue that giving away cash earned by smuggling drugs could also be regarded as hush money.

I gripped the wheel tighter to keep myself from weakening. "Please leave Loretta out of this," I said. "Go ahead. What's your idea?"

"Oh, you're gonna like it, 'cause this is a good one. Not ten minutes from here is the governor's quail camp—Salt Creek Gun Club, way back in one of his citrus groves, a quarter mile on the Peace River. You've never seen a more beautiful spot."

"I can't believe this," I muttered.

"Oh, you will when we get there. There's a nice log cabin with shelves full of books, and a kennel for the shorthair pointers he used to run. They all dead now, too"—the little man's voice cracked—"ain't they, old friend? And all buried right there. Duke, and Buddy Rough, and ol' Elvis. I sure do miss that Elvis. He was some kind'a dog, weren't he, Harney?"

Harney was Mr. Chatham's given name. I'd never heard Reggie speak to his boss in such an informal, affectionate way. Listing the dogs got to me, too. I was near tears.

"Yep, the gun club, that's the place for you. It's gonna get chilly tonight, so I'll put you in the recliner and build a fire to keep you and them old dogs warm. Then later, when it's safe, I'll come back and find you already dead. Ain't that smart? Make it all official-like."

That broke the spell—almost. I'm no fool, but the little man wasn't acting. The depth of his remorse bespoke the transience of life, and of love and loyalty. I could hardly trust myself to speak. "Reggie, I'm not going to be seen doing what you're asking me to do. What about a caretaker? There has to be someone looking after the place. Someone who might, you know . . . come snooping around and offer to help with the heavy lifting?"

"Nope, just me. I got me a little cottage not far from there. Oh . . . and the new gentleman who manages the groves, Kermit Bigalow. He's there sometimes during the week but never on weekends, and never this late. Miz Hannah, long as I live, I'll never ask for another favor."

It was a little after five. It would be dark in an hour.

I said, "Are you absolutely sure there's no chance anyone will see us?"

"There's only one road in, and the same road out. They'd have to come on horseback, once we lock the gate behind us."

"There're riding trails? You don't mean public riding trails. If that's the case—"

"They're private, hardly ever used. They's from back in the quail-hunting days. You got nothing to worry your head about. I promise."

This time, I did laugh, a sarcastic chuckle. How many times had the chauffeur said that? All my instincts told me to drive to the nearest hospital and deal with the situation honestly. Yet I heard myself respond, "How far did you say the camp is?"

"Take the next right, that's Bronco Road. Honey"—Reggie's boyish cackle again—"we're almost there already."

Tee-hee-hee.

Parked outside a smaller wrought-iron gate, crested with the Triple C brand—Chatham Cattle & Citrus—the chauffeur hopped out, saying, "See how the chain's locked? No one here but us," then leaned into the backseat. "Relax yourself, Governor. I won't be long."

I drove through, waited until the gate was locked and Reggie was in the backseat again. "You said the cabin was set way back. How far?"

I was concerned because the road we'd been on, State Route 74, hadn't been overly busy, but there was a steady flow of semis, many of them open-bedded trucks piled high with oranges.

"No, ma'am, we still got a ways to go."

I hit the gas.

An asphalt lane arrowed through wide-open pasture that reminded me of photos of Africa. Humpbacked cattle with horns grazed in isolated islands of shade created by oaks with canopies the size of rain clouds. White ibis, on stilt legs, perched atop the dozing animals and ambushed flies, while one massive Brangus bull stood guard next to a windmill that pumped water.

"That's Jessie James," Reggie said. "He's famous in these parts. Weighs most of a ton, and he's serviced every kind'a cow there is. Rumor is, he has a taste for Thoroughbred horses, too. Even a truck or two, if they don't move quick enough. No sir, you don't want to turn your back on Mr. Jessie James."

"Is that the sort of crude story you share with all women visitors?" I asked. I didn't mean it to come out as sharp as it did.

"Sorry, dear. Truth is, ma'am, I feel like laughing and crying all at the same time. Guess my emotions got the best of my manners."

Through another gate, which was open, a mile of orange trees crowded in close. There was row after row, their odor fragrant, with the window down, yet they were a sad sight to behold. The disease, citrus greening, had curled and severed the leaves like a killer storm. The fruit, which should have been ripe on the branches, lay withered and bitter on the ground.

"Are all Mr. Chatham's groves like this? He should be harvesting now."

"That ain't a happy topic," Reggie responded.

"He lost the entire crop?"

"You'd have to ask Mr. Bigalow that question."

"Our trees have it, too. Most of them anyway." As I said it, I reminded myself of Marion Ford's advice to check the entire orchard.

On both sides of the road, the citrus grove ended as abruptly as a cliff. There was a third gate, also locked, a log mantel above with a large lacquered sign:

Salt Creek Gun Club

Members Only

"We didn't really sell memberships," Reggie said, after opening the gate. "It was built more for socializing when the governor was running for election. 'Shakin' hands is good,' he'd say, 'but three fingers of scotch is better.' You'd be surprised, Miz Hannah, at some of the famous names been here. Two U.S. presidents, I can think of, and Walt Disney hisself. Remember what you said about Mr. Disney?" (Reggie was speaking to his boss, I realized.) "You said, 'That there man is up to something.' He ain't laid a card on the table, but you knew, yes you did. This was back when the Disney folks was buying up land under different names all around Orlando but keepin' it secret. Only man in this state wasn't surprised is sitting right here next to me."

Not since the sheriff's car had I risked a look in the mirror but did now: two old friends huddled shoulder to shoulder, one tiny and frail, the other big, with a lolling, chalk-white face, the Stetson no longer a necessary part of the charade.

A strange feeling came over me. I hadn't known Mr. Chatham well, and didn't approve of his affair with my mother, which I'd told him to his face. Yet the man had been kind to me. He'd treated me with respect—as an equal, in fact, which was rare for men of his age, or men of wealth and power no matter their age.

Even rarer, he had entrusted me with the truth regarding the affair with my mother, and also about his early drug-smuggling years. The man had owned three shrimp boats and kept them busy running between what he called Pay Day Road, which was south of Sarasota, to the Yucatán, and sometimes Panama. Rather than spend the bundles of cash, Chatham had had the foresight to live poor during that period and take his time converting the cash into silver and gold, which he'd hidden away. A small part of the profit was filtered into buying a car dealership, the first of several in Sematee County. The cattle ranch and citrus groves came later, as did his two-term lieutenant governorship.

His affair with Loretta had continued through-out those decades and survived Chatham's two wives, three children, many grandchildren. It had also weathered at least one murder, several funerals, a brain aneurysm and two surgeries, after which the man, without me knowing, had privately, and sometimes anonymously, tended to my mother's every need.

Once again, I had to wonder, *Why had they never married?*

I wasn't Mr. Chatham's daughter, as I knew for certain, but my biological father had aban-doned us early on. As a child, this was a painful mystery until I had aged enough to understand that Loretta, even before her stroke, was wildly unpredictable and near impossible to live with. Yet, the famous man in the limousine's mirror had, in his way, been devoted to her all these years.

Why?

I had never understood, nor had I summoned the ill manners to ask the man. Now the oppor-tunity was gone.

Asphalt melted into a winding shell drive edged by oaks and shady moss. A wooden bridge clattered beneath our tires; cattails battled palmettos on both sides of the road, flattening into pine forest acreage. Beyond the rise of an archaic sand dune, a section of river and a two-story cabin appeared, each log layered by white caulking, beneath a pitched tin roof that flared to shade a porch with a view of the river. Through the trees were outbuildings, a barn and a corrugated-steel maintenance shed, with farm machinery, much of it rusty, sitting out beneath a warm winter sky. In a triple carport floored with sand was a beat-up truck that, according to Reggie, Mr. Chatham sometimes used to shuttle back and forth to his home.

It would be a way of explaining how the great man had arrived here alone.

"Don't you think?" the aging chauffeur asked softly.

I wasn't sure he was speaking to me, but replied, "About what?"

"Such a pretty ol' Florida sort of place," he said, "the way Florida used to be. Roasted many a hog in that fire pit yonder, and quail was thick along the river; they'd flush into the palmettos. Our pointers had them a time dealing with snakes. See that stretch of wire grass and river oats? That was a good place, too."

This made little sense. "Should I park near the back porch or the front?"

He answered. "Either one, but pull up close. I'll fetch a handcart. I ain't as stout as I used to be."

Then he got back to his original question, which was, "Miz Hannah . . . don't you think this is where you'd want to die?"

Three

I was returning from the limo with the cowboy Stetson in my hand when I stopped, listened for a moment, then listened a while longer.

"I think I hear voices," I called through the doorway. "We've got to get out of here."

Reggie was tending to Mr. Chatham, who sat as if asleep in a recliner said to be his favorite. Within reach was a wall of books, a floor lamp, and a newly opened bottle of liquor. Whiskey, possibly. It was tea-colored, in a glass that refused to balance itself in the dead man's hands.

"Shit fire . . . Sorry, sir, sorry . . . Spilt this good scotch all over your suit and bolo tie."

"Reggie. Come on."

"Who do you hear?"

"I don't know, but I did. Someone's coming."

The little man was too busy finding a towel to be concerned. "Canoes paddle past the dock sometimes. That's probably what it was. Why don't you walk yourself down to the river and see while I finish up here. Hope you don't mind, ma'am, but I still got my good-byes to say and I'd like to say them in private. Oh"—he hefted the liquor bottle—"how about a little taste of this for your nerves? You appear to be skittish."

As he reached for another glass, I declined,

and turned from the door. No point leaving fingerprints.

I crossed the yard to an old pump with a handle, stopping every few seconds to listen. I washed my hands and face in cold water, then took my time approaching the river, where there was a dock, and a tire swing suspended from a massive oak. There was also a dilapidated boathouse hidden by trees, a single room on stilts over the water. Normally, I would have savored how the air changed, as it always does in the hollow of a river, but I was too tense. There'd been no more stray voices, yet I was sure I'd heard someone talking.

I shielded my eyes to look through the boathouse window. I expected a place for storage but instead saw a bamboo couch and chair, minus the cushions. The cushions were laid out on the floor as if someone had been sleeping there. Aside from a lamp and some fishing gear, that's all there was to see.

I tried the door anyway. It wasn't locked. Floor and pilings swayed beneath my weight when I entered. The space within smelled vaguely of old wood, with a hint of fragrance that had the tang of orange blossoms at first but faded to a vanilla softness. It reminded me of a Chanel perfume I like although rarely wear.

The fragrance vanished when the wind caught the door and slammed it behind me. I jumped, and sputtered a phrase I seldom use even when alone. Then was startled again when laughter floated up through the floor. A man's voice said, "You caught me, I surrender. But you mind if I ask what you're doing here?"

I could have sworn the voice came from inside that little room, but there wasn't a closet, just a cabinet and some shelves. A sliding glass door looked out over the river.

I said, "Who . . . where are you?"

"Not where I want, considering the circumstances. I'm going to have to ask you to turn your back, miss."

"Turn my . . . ? I'm not doing anything 'til you show yourself."

"I guarantee you don't mean that."

"I do."

"You really don't. I'd rather not warn you again."

"This is ridiculous." I pushed aside a curtain of beads and saw that the sliding door was open wide enough to slip through onto a walk-around deck. I stepped out, thinking I'd surprised a trespasser in a canoe, but there was no canoe, nothing, until I looked down and saw a man smiling up at me from tannin-clear water. He was naked, as I couldn't help but notice. He was also aware of the good visibility, which was obvious by the way he tried to hide himself by clinging to a piling.

"Good Lord," I said, spinning away, "get some clothes on. Where's your boat? Get moving before I tell the gentleman who owns the place."

It was a bluff, of course, and only caused the man to laugh again. "I'll tell him myself," he replied. "How about you step inside, young lady, and pull that curtain so I can get my britches on."

There was a wisp of accent in his words and vocal rhythm—from out west in cowboy country, maybe. Only then did I notice Levi's and a blue plaid shirt folded neatly over the railing, Wellington boots and socks aligned below. I asked, "Do you have permission to be here?"

"Far as I know, I'm the only one who does. I manage the groves for Mr. Chatham."

I thought, *Uh-oh,* as he continued, "The water's a bit chilly, it being winter and all. You mind hurrying a bit?"

"I am so sorry," I said, and banged the glass door with my shoulder when I hurried inside. What was I going to do? The cabin wasn't visible from the boathouse. I had no idea if Reggie was still paying his respects to his dead employer or waiting for me at the car. The temptation was to run, but that would have attracted the worst sort of suspicion when Mr. Chatham's body was found.

I heard sloshing water; the little house vibrated with weight and the sure movements of a man. "Dang it. You see a towel in there?"

An orange beach towel was folded on a cushion I had nudged aside after entering. I poked it through the curtain with my back turned but got a glimpse of him in the side window's reflection. He was fit-looking, older than expected, with matted gray chest hair and a wide rack of shoulders. Admittedly, I would have allowed myself to see more, but the beaded curtain clattered closed.

"My name's Hannah Smith," I said, then apologized again, desperate to buy time. This required small talk. "That's a shame about your citrus grove. I noticed the trees when we drove in. Anything you can do to get rid of that awful disease? Our trees have it, too."

"How big's your grove?"

"Well, I'm unsure of the exact acreage, but big enough for me to be interested. My great-grandfather planted some of those trees a hundred years ago."

"That old, huh?" He sounded dubious. "Tell me your name again."

I did. "Citrus greening," I continued. "I'd never even heard of it 'til a year ago."

"Most call it *H-L-B,* and it's been coming for a lot longer than that," the man said. "HLB stands for a Chinese word that means 'Yellow Dragon.' A long word, hard to pronounce. I'm making some headway on techniques to slow it down. That's why Mr. Chatham hired me. Say, is he up at the cabin? Yesterday, he mentioned he was going into town this afternoon. Otherwise, I would've checked before taking a swim."

"Yes," I said, "in the cabin. He's been there most of the day, I'm told."

"All day? Are you sure?"

"Far as I know. Reggie said he uses that old truck in the carport sometimes."

"I'll be darned. I'm surprised he didn't come out and say hello. Not that I know him that well. I've only been here three months—a little less." After he said it, the floor vibrated like a drum. I pictured him hopping on one foot, getting his boots on. Then he came through the curtains smiling, with an outstretched hand. "I've gone and upset you. I can tell because . . . well, I just can, that's all. Sorry about that. Your next visit, I promise, you don't have to worry about this happening again. Only time I swim the river is my afternoons off when I'm sure no one's around." He held the front door open for me in a gentlemanly way. "Do you mind if we don't mention it to Mr. Chatham? He's a stickler when it comes to rude behavior, as you probably know."

All I knew for certain was, we couldn't return to the cabin until Reggie was ready.

"I'm the one at fault," I said. "I came down here because I thought I heard people talking. Reggie asked me to check."

"He brought you? In the limo? That's quite an honor."

"Yes," I said. "Reggie did the driving, of course."

The remark was so stupid, I wasn't surprised by his puzzled reaction. I had no hope of weaving sense out of the nest of lies I was creating, but Kermit Bigalow was polite enough not to press. "Voices, huh? I didn't see anybody."

"Could've been birds, I suppose. Mockingbirds, they can sound like people. Let's take a look; check the trees along the river."

"Hmm." The man stood there, the door wide, waiting for me to exit, but then showed smile lines from jaw to cheeks and snapped his fingers. "I'm a dope—it was me. A few minutes ago, I was on the phone with my daughter. Doesn't matter where I am, or the time of day, I wouldn't miss a call from her. She has her own ring, so I bellied up on the deck like a seal and put her on *Speaker*. Forgot all about it 'til now."

I smiled, too, but was sweating on the inside. "That's so sweet. A daughter."

"Nothing in the world like it. Most men want a boy first time around. Not me. You have kids, Miss Smith? Or is it Mrs.?"

"How old is she?" I asked rather than answer the question.

"Ten going on eighteen. You'd have to meet her to understand. Some of the things she says—

my gosh, you can't help laughing. Here, have a look."

Normally, it is a joy to meet an adoring father, but it took some work to keep my smile frozen while he produced a phone and swept through a dozen photos of a pretty little girl. Her nam was Sarah, a tomboy with braids and a missing front tooth. The child, or her mother, was fond of bib overalls and red ribbons, but there were also shots of her in a dainty party dress with shiny black flats that buckled, white socks flush at her ankles. A great big smile on the face of a girl who enjoyed dressing up.

"I spoil her rotten," Bigalow grinned. "Can't help myself. All the teachers say she should be in advanced classes, but my wife thinks public school's best for now. We've gone 'round and 'round about that."

"I just bet you do spoil her," I said. "That's a good thing, not bad."

"You really believe that?"

His interest in my opinion was sincere, which was unexpected. "You can't spoil a child with too much attention and love. That never made sense to me, people who claim you can." I started to add something about the girl, and the sun rising on her daddy's head, but stopped when a woman on horseback came riding out of the trees at the edge of the river.

"Uh-oh," Bigalow said. "She's not gonna like

it, finding us here. That's Lonnie Chatham. Lonnie doesn't like anyone being on what she considers her property. Including me—but especially other women when her husband's around."

"Never met her," I said. "She's jealous of a man that age?"

"She's that mean," the grove manager replied. "Or nice, depending on who she's talking to, or what she wants." Which is why he was taken aback when I charged out the door and waved to get the woman's attention. Meeting Mrs. Chatham might be unpleasant, but it was better than her surprising Reggie inside the cabin. Blessedly, she saw me and kicked the horse into a trot.

"It was wrong of me to speak that way about his wife," the man said, joining me outside. Not nervous about his remarks, just regretful. "I'm forty-two years old, Miss Smith, and I still haven't learned to stop my mouth from saying what's running through my mind. Tell Mr. Chatham what you want, but I felt the need to admit that to you."

"Call me Hannah," I replied, "and stop worrying. I've spent half my life apologizing for things I've said, even though I meant most of them—at the time anyway."

He showed his smile lines again; cinnamon hair thinning, freckles showing through his tan, a man who was an inch shorter than me, and ten years older. "Call me Kermit. And when Lonnie gets here? It might be best if you just sort of follow my lead."

I am a better judge of women than men—a trait that has plagued the women in my family for generations. Particularly my aunts, three of them named Hannah. For two of my namesakes, their flawed judgment resulted in violence and an untimely death. This sad fact, which I seldom share, has kept me awake at night, particularly if there is a moon and wind. It has also caused me to be wary in my dealings with men.

Loretta describes my behavior as prudish and cold, often adding, "No wonder you're childless and live alone."

My mother, of course, could not resist taunting fate, and her oversized infant, by saddling me with the name Hannah and the weight of my family's unfortunate history. She has always had a sharp, judgmental tongue, but I blame the brain aneurysm for her decline into downright meanness. Perhaps it is my excuse to forgive the woman who bore me, and whose own life has not been easy.

Either way, it is true, I suppose. I have side-stepped the attentions of more men than I have embraced—not that large numbers can be assigned to either column.

When it comes to reading women, however, I believe my instincts are better than most. That's why when Lonnie Chatham appeared, I had to caution myself because I disliked her immediately. It wasn't her appearance so much as her attitude. She was closer in age to Kermit than to her late husband yet spoke with the veiled enmity of a queen interacting with the hired help. She sat atop a horse of glistening maple, so we had to look up. She seldom bothered to look down.

"Your days off are called days off for a reason, Kermit. I don't see your truck"—the woman's sculpted face became a cameo silhouette—"but I don't care how you got here, just that you're here. You know I exercise Axel on Friday afternoons. Swimming in the nude again, were you? Or just snooping?"

This was asked with a saucy edge that was laced with accusation.

Axel was the stunning Thoroughbred, who stood fifteen hands tall, with withers so muscled they strained beneath the tiny caramel saddle that matched the woman's caramel riding boots. The animal snorted and backed against the reins, too wild-eyed to be a gelding.

The grove manager kept a watchful eye. "My truck was due for an oil change, ma'am. It's parked behind the maintenance barn, and this young lady—" The horse sidestepped, came close to rearing, so he stepped forward. "How about I hold his halter, Mrs. Chatham?"

"Only if you want to lose a hand. I'm still waiting for an explanation."

"This is Hannah Smith. Reggie was kind enough to bring her out for a tour. She owns a citrus grove that—"

"And you pick the only afternoon in the whole damn week I actually look forward to? Axel is easily upset. Strangers upset him, and his nose picks up on all that damn organic crap you've been spraying on the citrus. Now it'll be hell wearing him down until he's civil enough to ride."

Kermit attempted to explain but was interrupted again. "Is Harney up there?" The woman's head swung toward the cabin, which was screened by trees and moss. "I don't see the limo, and no way in hell Reggie would drive that damn old truck."

"The Lincoln's there, ma'am," Kermit responded, because that's what I had told him was true.

"It's not supposed to be. Harney claimed he had meetings in town this afternoon. I wouldn't be surprised if he came here today just to spite me."

"Mr. Chatham's been in the cabin most of the day," Kermit replied. "Must'a finished early. I can't say for sure. We haven't spoke, but I know he's up there."

I was relieved by how smoothly the man parroted my lies, but also felt a stab of guilt.

Lonnie Chatham looked down. For the first time, her eyes, dark beneath a coil of blond hair, focused on me. "Let me guess why you're here, sweetie. Harney always did have a soft spot for the earthy types. From your clothes, I'd say you like to fish and hunt; probably right at home with the boys. I saw a similar blouse in an ad for Bass Pro Shops. I admire women who prefer comfort to style."

I felt my face warming. The stallion's antics gave me time to think before replying, "I love your boots, Miz Chatham. Bass Pro might be just the place to find an outfit that's not quite so stiff and gaudy."

It was the worst I could manage. I couldn't risk an insult so rash it would cause the woman to order me off the property or go charging up to the cabin.

Kermit mistook my remark for a compliment, or timidity. His face began to color, and his tone changed. "Mrs. Chatham, please. You can speak to me any way you like, but this young lady's my guest. She's in the citrus business. That's the only reason she's here, and Reggie was kind enough to arrange a meeting. She's interested in the new techniques I've developed to—"

The woman, still focusing on me, ignored him. "Bass Pro, huh?" she said. "I'll make a mental note if I ever have cause to stop at Walmart. Did you happen to notice how well Kermit's 'new techniques' are working on this year's orange crop? Or were you too dazzled by his cowboy looks and aw-shucks manner? My husband was certainly taken in fast enough."

I ignored her tone. "Citrus greening disease is complicated," I replied as if the term was familiar. "From what I've heard, a lot of people are impressed by Mr. Bigalow's new ideas."

Kermit gave me a sideways glance and managed not to smile.

Axel, the stallion, did another spin. The woman grabbed his ear and twisted it to calm the animal —a rancher's trick I'd seen before, so was mildly impressed—yet her eyes never left me. "What's the name of your company? I don't remember seeing you at the party the governor hosted for the Grove Owners Association. Were you there? His annual party at the mansion in Tallahassee?"

I sensed a trap. For the first time in a while, I chose the truth as a haven. "If there was a party, I didn't get an invitation."

Beside me, Kermit released a slow breath.

The woman glared at us both, but her mind was on me. I sensed it: a look of assessment that gauged my beauty—the lack of it, more likely— my gawky tallness, the proportions of my hips and breasts, although she would have to guess at both. I wore a baggy, collared turquoise shirt—

draped, unbuttoned, over a white camisole—and pleated fishing shorts. My legs, at least, might give her pause.

No . . . her eyes dismissed me as no threat.

That's when Reggie, thank god, made his presence known. Dwarfed by oaks, he stumbled toward us in a hobbled-old-man way, yelling, "Oh lord, oh lord, you folks come quick. I believe something bad's happened to the governor!"

Four

A short while later, Kermit exited the cabin, shaken by the brief hysterics of the newly widowed Lonnie Chatham, then her ensuing rage. Because I was outside, standing at a respectful distance, I had heard the peaks and valleys of both emotions but could seldom decipher the actual words.

"He was a good man," Kermit said, joining me in a patch of sunlight. It was late afternoon, and the wind had turned. He studied the cabin while we listened. "Do you think she was acting when she first realized he was dead? Her crying seemed real. Guess I didn't expect that."

"They were man and wife," I said. "No one knows what goes on in another person's heart."

He shook his head. "I haven't been here long, but long enough to know they avoided each other. But you're right—I'm a poor choice to judge who a man marries. There was more than thirty years' difference in their age, but that wasn't the problem, from what I saw."

I was thrown by his odd admission about marriage, but asked, "Then why did he?"

"Marry her?"

"Or her him? She's an attractive woman."

"If you like beauty queen types, I suppose."

"A lot of men do. It's not uncommon for younger women to find older men attractive."

The look Kermit gave me inquired *Are you serious?* meaning money, not love, had been her objective. "You'd have to ask Reggie. He'd know —if he's willing to talk, which I doubt. Loyalty is a rare quality. Lonnie is finding that out right now."

This was punctuated by the woman's muffled profanities coming from inside.

The grove manager winced. "God knows what'll happen now that he's dead. It's Reggie I worry about. She's giving him hell with both barrels, blaming him for leaving Mr. Chatham alone for so long. Can't blame her, in a way. A man in his eighties, with a history of heart trouble? It's not like Reggie. Never seen a more devoted man in my life, yet he allows something like this to happen."

The guilt that welled within me was deserved. I knew it, felt sick about my role in the matter, but it was too late to go to the chauffeur's defense, nor could I confide the truth to anyone. So I had to stand there and say nothing while more yelling reached us from inside the cabin, "Stupid, worth-less bastard" loud enough to hear.

This was too much. I started back toward the river, saying, "Hope you don't mind, but her horse was getting spooky, so I walked him a ways and found those empty stalls by the maintenance barn."

"Just now?"

"While you were inside. He's bolted in, good and tight—don't worry about that—and I gave him a bucket of water. I should probably check on him."

"You've got more nerve than me. Axel is a biter."

"Not once we got going," I said, relieved to be putting some distance between us and the cabin. "It was either that or he'd have busted his tether. She's upset enough as it is."

Kermit looked back and stuffed his hands in his pockets. "The EMTs are on their way, so I should probably have those gates open. Want to come along? There's no reason you should have to stay here and witness the rest."

"Can't," I said. "Not and leave Reggie alone when she's so mad. I'll hang around and keep an eye on the horse. I'll be fine."

"Loyal, too," he mused in a pleasant way. "But Reggie might be embarrassed when he comes out and realizes you heard the way she spoke to him. A man his age, with his job, pride's about all he has left. If that."

"What do you mean?"

"My guess is, he's lost his job already. Lonnie has always been jealous of how close he was to Mr. Chatham. She knows they've shared a lot of secrets over the years, so that makes Reggie a threat. She might try to fire me, too, but I've got a year's contract—depending on how things go."

I shook my head, unsure of what to do.

"Hannah, can I ask you something? I won't repeat a word. Could you smell liquor on Reggie's breath? That's what she's accusing him of. Being drunk on duty."

The whiskey Reggie had spilled on his dead employer.

"Absolutely not," I said. "The only thing I can think of is that when he found Mr. Chatham's body, he took a drink. Who could blame him?"

"That's the confusing part. I was the first one through the door, Lonnie behind me. There was a glass laying in Chatham's lap, which made sense. It explained the alcohol smell, but there were two extra glasses next to him. Both had some scotch left in the bottom. That's what she's trying to make Reggie admit—that he and her husband were in there, having a private party with a third person, when he died. Now he's trying to cover up what really happened."

I stopped, faced the grove manager. "A party with me, I suppose."

"She's a jealous one. I believe I mentioned that."

"I wasn't asking about her. What do you think?"

"I'm paid to grow citrus, not think, but I took

your side. Or tried to. That's when she told me to get the hell out." After a pause, he added, "Hope I'm right."

I pulled the tail of my shirt up just enough to expose my jeans. "Does a woman who wears fishing pliers on her belt strike you as the party girl type?"

"I'll be darned," he said. "Are those stainless?"

"Let's have this out right now," I said. "That's what I do. I'm a fishing guide. I do have a few orange trees, but I'm not in the citrus business."

"I knew you weren't in citrus," he said, "and I'm not accusing you—"

"She is, apparently. A third glass of whiskey, who else could it be?"

His soft brown eyes did not waver when they locked onto mine. "Could have been me who drank from that glass. Ever think about that? Me and someone who ran off when you and Reggie showed up in the limo. I'm surprised that wasn't your first suspicion."

Overhead, an osprey was whistling a wild circle above the trees. It was an excuse to look away when I asked, "Why in the world would I suspect you?"

"Because of what you told me earlier. Mr. Chatham was here most the day, you said. You and Reggie didn't show up until later. That's the way it happened, right?"

From the gentle way he said it, I feared he'd

known all along I'd been lying but was giving me another chance.

For some reason, Kermit's daughter popped into my head, a girl with an adoring father whose job might be on the line if I dragged him any further into this mess. I couldn't let that happen . . . nor could I allow myself to ruminate on the consequences. If I did, I would lose my nerve.

I did an about-face and started toward the cabin. "Go on and tend to the gates. I've got something I need to clear up."

"Hold on," he called. "That's not what I was after. Don't poke a hornet's nest unless there's a darn good reason."

I walked faster, aware he was hurrying to catch up.

"Whoa, there. This isn't going to accomplish anything. And it won't get Reggie off the hook."

"My reputation might have something to do with me telling her to her face," I replied, and kept going.

"Hannah, listen. I'll back your story. Whatever you say, I'll go along with it. And what's it matter now? Chatham's already dead—unless he was murdered."

This was the last thing I expected to hear.

I stopped, and fumed, until he was close enough to speak in confidence. "Now what are you accusing me of?"

The man made a calming gesture with his

hands. "I'm not, but *she's* capable of anything. You've got no reason to trust me, Hannah, but I wish you would. Someone needs to guard you from how she might react." He looked toward the cabin in a meaningful way.

I replied, "I don't need guarding. If I did, I'd buy a dog."

"You don't know Lonnie Chatham."

"You don't know me. She knows even less," I answered. "Whatever the coroner finds, it'll show Mr. Chatham died of natural causes. That much I'll guarantee. I'm doing you a favor, Kermit, by not saying more. Go on, now"—I swept a hand toward the maintenance barn— "go open those gates, and, from here on out, just tell the truth. It's advice I should've learned to follow myself."

Worry lines creased the man's forehead while he studied me. "I don't know why I'm doing this, but . . . Okay, here goes. I'm going to tell you something I shouldn't. It'll make you see the situation differently."

"If you shouldn't, then don't."

"I'll risk it. You stood up for Reggie. That's all I needed to find out. You could have snuck off, could have let him take all the blame, but that's not the kind of person you are. I just proved that for myself."

"Suggesting I'm a murderer is your idea of a test?"

He took a quick step to place himself between me and the cabin. "Look, I don't always do things the smartest way, I admit, but—"

"Smart? Rude and unfair, is more like it. Cruel, too. I thought the world of Mr. Chatham."

"That's exactly why you need to hear what I have to say." He reached to place a confiding hand on my shoulder, then abandoned this small liberty when he saw my reaction. "Walk with me a bit. I want to show you something."

I didn't budge. "I'm picturing an ambulance and police cars at the gate, waiting to help a grieving widow. Maybe you deserve to be fired."

"You've got a temper."

"A *conscience*," I said. "That's the way I choose to think of it, but you're entitled to your opinion."

The grove manager sighed in an exaggerated way. "Every cop and fire station in this county has the combination to those gates. Mr. Chatham was lieutenant governor, remember? Plus, they haven't had time enough to get here. Come on, Hannah. Please?"

Along this branch of the Peace River, oaks traced a shady ridge, a canopy of elevated turns and mossy switchbacks. When we were near the water, the grove manager said, "There's not much of a current, but I always swim upstream.

Fifteen minutes, close to a half mile. The swim back, I more or less just drift and enjoy the sights. Real quiet, you know?"

"What about gators?" I had to ask.

The man chuckled in a self-deprecating way. "I'd rather you think I'm brave than admit what I don't want the wildlife cops to know. But I'm no braver than the next guy. Mr. Chatham wouldn't tolerate any gator big enough to bother his livestock, or his grandkids. Truth is, I'd already put a couple down before he told me to do it. I bring Sarah here sometimes and let her splash around. Can you imagine risking a child to save a gator?"

Thinking about his daughter, again.

"Here's what I wanted to tell you." My eyes followed when he pointed to the boathouse. "I caught Lonnie inside there with another man, their horses tied outside. Actually, I heard them before I saw them—understand what I'm saying? She didn't see me, but I think she suspects."

"Good Lord," I said. "This happened today?"

"Not more than five minutes before you showed up. You would've caught them yourself if I hadn't stopped for a swim."

Stumbling onto Mrs. Chatham—with her husband dead in the back of the limo—was a scenario I didn't want to contemplate.

"Friday afternoons," he continued, "there's usually no one around. Lonnie and the guy she was with, they didn't see my truck, or my stuff on the railing, so they were . . . well, let's say not afraid to make all the noise they wanted. I didn't want to surprise them—hell, I didn't know what to do, but I needed my clothes. So I did a breaststroke upriver for a hundred yards or so to give them time, then made all the racket I could coming back. Even then, I cut it too close. I got a glimpse of those two hightailing it toward their horses but pretended not to notice."

"I suppose it took them a while to get their clothes on," I said, "when they heard you coming."

"Nope. Both of them were bare-ass naked, elbows and feet flying. The man, he damn near fell on his face when he dropped a sock, but that Lonnie, she never looked back. She's kept herself in shape, by god, I'll give her that." Kermit grinned, picturing it. His grin faded. "Trouble is, she suspects I saw them. I could tell by some of her comments, and the way she treated you. Why else would she ride back here to check?"

Under the circumstances, it was wrong to laugh, yet my nerves were on overload. Tears threatened. Then it dawned on me. "She knows."

"I just said that."

"No, that's not what I mean. I'm talking about the third glass of whiskey. She would've checked the cabin before bringing a man into that boathouse, don't you think?"

"Of course she did." There was a pause, while he stared at me. "I did, too."

It took a moment for the meaning to dawn on me.

"Don't worry," he said. "I'm not going to say anything."

Now I was confused. Had he or hadn't he seen us unload the body? I said, "If there's something you want to ask me, ask. Let's clear the air right here and now."

"It's none of my business. Besides, it doesn't matter. Who's Lonnie gonna tell? Or the guy she was with? They can't say a word without giving themselves away. That's what I meant, you'd see the situation differently."

I did but was still unsure. "Because she was having an affair on the day her husband died. I understand that much, but I suppose it depends on how much she cares about her reputation. Hers and the man's. Is he local?"

"I recognized him, but it's safer you don't know. Lonnie has a mean streak. Worse than mean."

"You think she'd actually do one of us harm if she knew what you just told me?"

"She's a woman who finds ways to get what she wants," he said. "I wouldn't want to put you in her crosshairs."

The grove manager did it then—put his hand on my shoulder to move me along. "We need to get going. I always meet Sarah at the bus stop at four."

Intuition told me the man was trustworthy, yet I knew better than to count on such thin reasoning. My aunts were strong, tough-minded, independent women, but as Loretta has said too often, "They all tarried in the Lust Line when God was handing out brains."

It wasn't lust I felt when we bounced down the lane in his truck. Instead, I felt oddly comfortable . . . and safe.

Five

In February, sunset comes early, so it was dark by the time Reggie took me home, but, once again, I was at the wheel of the Lincoln Town Car. The little man had hardly said a word since I'd shushed his protests about riding in the passenger seat. When I continued west rather than take the south ramp onto I-75, however, he stirred. "I hate them damn interstates, too," he said. "One day, the whole state of Florida's gonna be nothin' but asphalt, assholes, and graveyards." He'd been huddled inside himself, sniffing, trying to hide his bouts of despair, so it was good to have an opportunity to converse. There were questions I wanted to ask, and I might never have another chance. If nothing else, today I had learned that sad truth.

"Not all change is bad," I said gently. "You'll feel better after a while. Why don't you stay the night with Loretta and me? You can sleep on my boat. I've got a charter in the morning, but you could fish off the dock. The snook hang there thick in a little drop-off. I'll show you."

"I'd rather have a mess of mullet," he replied. "Soapfish, that's what we used to call them snook. That hussy the governor married, she'd probably love to tie into one and have her picture took for a magazine wearing a bikini. Not me. Lonnie and the tourists, they can have them snook."

Snewk—he pronounced the word in a way typical of folks from Carolina who, long ago, had ventured south and settled on the Florida peninsula.

"You never approved of Mrs. Chatham, did you?" I said. "I got the impression Kermit Bigalow doesn't care for her, either. He showed me around a section of citrus he's trying to save. Experimenting with different chemicals and techniques—that disease is near impossible to kill. But I think he was just trying to spare me from dealing with her."

All that got was a snort of derision. I couldn't be sure regarding whom.

I didn't press. We'd turned south on U.S. 41, the Tamiami Trail, where traffic wasn't too bad near Punta Gorda, before Reggie stirred again.

"That woman's not smart as she thinks, but she'll see. You just wait 'til the governor's lawyer tells her what's what."

"Are you talking about his will?"

"Some folks are in for a surprise, Miz Hannah. That's all I'm at liberty to say. Did you hear the way she spoke to me?"

I dodged the truth by mentioning Axel, the Thoroughbred horse, and reminding Reggie I'd toured the groves. "Figured you both had a lot to discuss," I said. "You were Mr. Chatham's closest friend, after all, then you had the police to deal with. They didn't ask me much, Reggie. All I did was confirm what you'd told them. I hope that's what you wanted."

It was a veiled question that failed to produce results.

"Spoke to me like I was trash," he continued. "She said even worse with the *po*-lice around. Me, having to stand there and listen with poor ol' Harney on a gurney with a sheet over his face, barely dead and not yet in the ground."

When I tried to soothe the little man, he only got madder. "Excuse my language, Miz Hannah, but that woman is a bitch. That's the word for her, and she is riding for a fall. She has kicked the wrong stump this time, by god. Know what she did? The lil' tramp fired me in front of everyone there."

"Them listening?"

"Oh yes, she did."

"I don't know what to say. That was cruel, Reggie. When she calms down, maybe she'll see it was wrong."

"Hell she will! And after near forty years of service, too. Yelled at me in front of the *po*-lice; told me to get my shit out of my own house— her exact words—and be gone within the week. Well, we will see whose shit gets packed first." He sat back, chortling, "Tee-hee-hee," but in a broken way, then buried his face in his hands.

I didn't know Reggie well, wasn't even sure of his last name until a detective had referred to him as "Mr. Hutley." But we had shared rides with Mr. Chatham together, and private moments when Chatham had stopped to visit Loretta. Never had I heard him issue an impolite word, let alone speak with such bitterness. I didn't fault the man, was furious on his behalf, but needed more information before I could decide what to do. I hadn't asked Kermit if I could share the boathouse story with Reggie, but he hadn't told me not to, either.

I asked, "Do you want some water? There's a Burger King up ahead. Their sweet tea's not too bad."

The former chauffeur had to gather himself; he sat up, rubbed his eyes, and adjusted his cap. "No, ma'am, thanks just the same. But another scotch would hit the spot. I just stocked up for the governor; got a bottle of eighteen-year-old Dewar's in the cabinet. Mind if I crawl in the back and have me a taste?"

"As long as you buckle up," I said.

"I'll pour a short one for you, too, if you like."

"Don't you dare," I said. "Stay put until I find a place to stop so you can get out."

Reggie preferred to climb over the seat. This put his knees near my face momentarily, then his size-eight shoes, which I helped along with a push. I heard the laminated door open, the clink of glass on glass, followed by a long, savoring silence. Half a mile, I drove, before I spoke.

"Firing you like that in front of strangers—no matter how upset she was, it was just downright mean."

"Two *po*-lice-men and an ambulance woman standing right there. Then Lonnie much as accused you of being a paid sporting girl 'cause of the extra scotch I poured to settle your nerves. Glad you didn't touch that glass now?"

"You told them it was for me?"

"I know how to keep my mouth shut. Just as we discussed, I stuck to the story we agreed on. That's something else Lonnie doesn't know. You're the smart one, Miz Hannah. Not her. I'm feeling better and better about hiring you to straighten things out."

The compliment, and my concerns about fingerprint experts, were superseded by what I'd just heard. "She hinted I'm a prostitute?"

"No, it was an uglier word she used."

"How much uglier?"

"A sight uglier, but it's not a word I feel comfortable saying in front of a lady. That woman has a mouth on her."

"She called me a whore? Actually said it?"

"Yes, ma'am; more in a general way, regarding your looks and the way you dress. Maybe 'cause of them three scotch glasses I was dumb enough to leave behind, I don't know. But she wanted in the worst way for them *po*-lice to believe the governor died while having sport with you. My opinion on that matter, I'm not at liberty to share."

"That blond bitch," I whispered, and tightened my hands on the steering wheel.

"Pardon me, ma'am?"

"That *witch*," I said, loud enough for him to hear. After another quarter mile, I again heard the clink of glass on glass. "I want to ask you something, Reggie. It's been on my mind. Why did a man like Mr. Chatham marry a woman like her? She's pretty enough, I suppose, in a fake, beauty queen sort of way, but, my lord, she's mean. Even Kermit, who seems as nice as he can be, said as much."

Since I had modified the grove manager's opinion of the woman, it seemed only fair to reference him as a source.

After a long silence, Reggie replied, "Are you asking for yourself? Or your mama?"

It was true, my motives were mixed, but I said, "I'm asking you as my client. I won't repeat a word without your consent."

"Can't, Miz Hannah. Sorry. That's another one of those confidential matters I'm not at liberty to speak about. As to your mama, this much I can tell you: her and the governor, I've never seen two people in my life cursed by such strong love and bad timing."

This was a revelation. "That's hard to believe, Reggie. Not the timing part, but, if he really loved her, then—"

"Honey, that's what I'm getting to. Why those two never married. Mostly, it was because the governor couldn't bring himself to leave his wife and children. His first wife; the only one he ever had, far as I'm concerned. Now, there was a lady. A fine mother, too, but Miz Lilly—that was her name, Lilly—she had female issues. I don't know the terms for such things, but, truth is, I doubt those two ever had the same feelings as the governor had for Loretta."

"He didn't love his wife?"

"Very much. But it weren't the fever kind of love. You know the difference? That kind of love, there ain't no understanding even when it happens."

"I'm not sure," I said, but, in my heart, I did understand, and the admission was painful.

Reggie took me at my word. "That's 'cause you never experienced it. Don't take offense. Few men and women do. Lord knows, I never had such luck." The man sniffed, already a little drunk, and there was more liquor waiting in his belly.

I said, "Why don't you pass me a bottle of water, and grab one for yourself? Drink it down.

They say if you wait until you're thirsty, it's too late."

A bottle of Evian appeared near my ear. "You don't mind, I'll set my thirst aside for later. Where was I? Oh—talkin' about fever love."

"No, you were explaining why he married a woman who's got a mean streak and half his age."

"That's what I'm getting to, but there's more you've got to understand. The governor was all man when it come to women, but he was faithful . . . mostly. Particularly when he was a young man. Then Miz Lilly's female issues come along and temptation got the best of him. Other-wise, I truly don't believe he'd have ever strayed. You know your own self, he was a deacon at Foursquare Gospel. Never missed a Sunday, unless he had duties in Tallahassee."

Strange, how tense I suddenly felt, no longer concerned with Lonnie Chatham's petty insults.

I said, "We were members for as long as I can remember."

"Yes, you were churchgoing people. All you Smiths—the good ones anyway."

"I appreciate that," I said, giving him a look in the mirror. "Then Loretta switched to the Church of God on Pine Island. I liked the preacher but preferred Chapel-By-The-Sea. By then, I had my own boat."

"Foursquare Gospel," Reggie mused, "them

folks could make a joyful noise. Many a time, I sat there in the heat of a summer morning, always a back pew, watching ol' Harney sneaking looks at your mamma—I didn't call him governor in those days 'cause he weren't. Called him captain, 'cause he was. He'd hired me to work one of his shrimp boats, back when we was makin' visits to the Yucatán. You sure was pretty, the way your mama dressed you in bows and ribbons."

I spoke to keep myself from getting emotional. "I hated those starchy dresses."

"And let everyone know, too! The way you tugged at your sleeves and couldn't get comfortable. Many's the time you caused me a smile. The governor, too. He was a man for noticing details."

In my mind, I pictured Harney Chatham striding down the aisle with the collection plate, a confident man with shoulders and a smile, always in a suit with a bolo tie and boots.

"I was just a girl," I said, "so it didn't strike me as odd the way he'd sneak an envelope into the plate when he got to Loretta. They'd always just nod and smile, then he'd move along as if the money was from her."

"She was poor, your mama, with no husband, and a child to support," Reggie said as if I was unaware.

Rather than mention my mother's disinterest in

working, or her inability to hold a job, I let the remark pass. "Mr. Chatham was being charitable," I said. "I realize that now. But, in all those years, I never once suspected the two of them were, well, *close* . . . And in church, of all places. Reggie, you're the only one who knows how I finally found out. I'm not bitter—really, I'm not—but I don't appreciate being treated like a fool."

"This sure is some fine scotch," he responded. "Why not have a taste instead of being so hard on how life is?"

"I'm not. I blame myself for being naïve."

"Blame? When it comes to fever love, there's blame enough to go around. But none of that makes a lick of sense when you're old enough to look back. Harney said as much just a few days ago. Where's the wrongness of falling in love?"

"Marriage vows address that issue," I responded, but not in a sharp way. "If they don't, I'm pretty sure the Bible does. But we're off the subject. What's this have to do with him marrying who he did?"

"I'm tryin' to be gentle toward your feelings, honey."

"There's no need. If you don't want to discuss it, that's fine, too."

"Strong love and bad timing," Reggie said again, and let it hang there before getting to the point. "Did you know Miz Lilly went to Hope

Hospice a week after your mama had her stroke?"

This was a shocking piece of information. I felt my stomach knot. "I had no idea."

"That there's your reason for why they didn't marry. Four, going on five years ago, it was. He lost both his women 'bout the same time—your mama in a different way, of course. Part of her was missing after that thing in her brain broke. And them operations only made it worse. No offense; she comes and goes, your mama, and she's still a fine woman. But it was never the same for those two."

"That's so sad," I whispered.

"I've yet to hear the preacher who can explain such shitty-awful goings-on," Reggie agreed. "The governor was a strong man, but the year that followed just about broke him. I know. Seven days a week, I hauled him back and forth 'tween hospital beds—Miz Lilly's and your mama's. The two of us was always on guard against a slipup of some kind so you children wouldn't suffer more hurt by learning the truth."

"You must have come after hours," I said. "I never saw you. Not once. And I visited Loretta every day."

Reggie's *Tee-hee-hee* chortle sounded almost normal. "That shows we was good at what we did. Many's the time we sat parked in some shady spot, waiting for you to leave the hospital so as not to cause you more upset. The governor was kind that way when it came to young'uns and people he cared for."

I didn't trust myself to respond.

Reggie's voice softened. "Lonnie Dupree—that's her maiden name. She showed up about the same time, which is the thing I'm not at liberty to speak of. But I can tell you something the governor said the day after their wedding. He says, 'Reggie, I might've been better off using my pistol than making the mistake I just made.' "

"After only one night?"

"Could be, he knew from the start. Lonnie is the type who gets her way, and she's got a beautiful body on her, I'll give her that. The governor was a fool in that regard and she knew it. They had history together, those two. They went way back."

"My god, how many affairs did he have?"

"That's not what I'm saying," Reggie replied. "She was just a local girl back then, a cheerleader at Florida State. The only dealings the governor might've had with a cheerleader, other than parades and such, would be to try and help her out of trouble, not trick her into bed. You ever hear that saying, Miz Hannah, about no good deed going unpunished?"

With his tone, the chauffeur was relaying a guarded message. I attempted eye contact in the mirror. "She had something on him. Forced him into marriage for his money. Is that what you're telling me?"

"I never said no such thing," he replied, but in a way that confirmed it was true.

"That's hard to believe. Mr. Chatham was a powerful man. Why would someone with his connections allow himself to be buffaloed?"

"You ain't been listening, girl. The last few years whittled the governor down somethin' terrible. His spirit, I'm saying. Miz Lilly died, which was rough enough, then there was your mama's brain surgeries that didn't bring her back —not as he'd hoped. When that witch Lonnie showed up, the governor didn't have much fight left in him."

"He gave up," I said. "Gave up on Loretta. That's terrible, but I guess I can understand. She was never the same after that first surgery. That poor, dear man."

"Gave up on himself, more like it. It about kilt poor ol' Harney to know his chance to marry your mama had passed him by."

I fumbled with the window switch and let the winter air chill me. It didn't help. Ahead was a Taco Bell and a Shell station. I chose the Shell station because the restrooms were outside.

The door marked *Women* was locked, so I used the men's room. Otherwise, someone might have seen the tears streaming down my face.

Six

My emotions were under control as we waited for traffic at the intersection for U.S. 41 and Burnt Store Road. "Lonnie was blackmailing him," I said.

Reggie got as far as "Didn't say that" before I interrupted, "Even if she wasn't, just hear me out. Something happened today I didn't tell you. It concerns her; something bad she did. I don't know if it makes a difference, but I'm willing to trade information."

"I'm not at liberty to trade anything," Reggie replied, "How bad we talkin' about?"

He was still in the backseat, where the lacquered tray was open, the bottle of scotch within reach.

"Depends on your morals," I said, "but it's probably too late. She was in the boathouse this afternoon with another man, just before we pulled up. They were naked, in there alone. Kermit saw them run off. All her crying, those accusations she made about the three whiskey glasses—the way she yelled at you—it was all an act. She knew darn well Mr. Chatham didn't die in the cabin."

"Say what?"

He slurred his words, so I repeated the details.

"Kermit was in the river, swimming," I said, "and he doesn't strike me as the type of man to lie. He thinks Lonnie knows he saw them, but he's not sure. Either way, she had to go along with our lie."

"The new grove manager. Why would he trust you with a story that could mean his job?"

I said, "I'm still wondering about that myself. He doesn't like Lonnie, so maybe he sees you or me as an ally after she inherits the property. The important thing is, Lonnie knew her husband's body wasn't in the cabin until after we arrived. She couldn't admit that, of course, so she went to the police with her accusations, hoping they'd figure it out, or we'd confess. That's the part I don't understand. Why risk the police taking a closer look if she was having an affair the afternoon her husband died?"

Reggie sobered. "That there's a street that travels both ways."

"I'm aware of the irony," I said. "Neither side can throw stones."

"Oh, that Lonnie would throw any stone she gets her hands on. You got a name for the man she was with?"

From his tone, I could tell the chauffeur had some names in mind.

"Someone local. Kermit said it was better I didn't know. He said something else. He told me Lonnie is dangerous."

"A conniving, lying tramp, is what she is," the chauffeur responded, yet with a fresh optimism that didn't make sense. "She got caught screwin' another man before the governor was dead—as far as she knows anyway. Ain't that great! By god, that whore has met her equal in you, Miz Hannah."

I flashed a warning look in the mirror. "Excuse me?"

"Sorry, ma'am. That didn't come out the way it sounded."

"I hope not. Watch your language or I'll put you in a cab. Now, tell me what she did to make Mr. Chatham marry her."

Traffic had thinned; I started my turn, but Reggie leaned over the seat and urged, "Go straight, go straight!" meaning Burnt Store Road, which angled southwest along the coast toward Cape Coral.

I applied the brakes. "That's not the shortest route."

"Are you working for me or aren't you?"

"What's that supposed to mean?"

"Means I just made up my mind about something. I want to hire you properly, with a contract and all so you'll keep what I'm about to show you a secret. If you're working for me, I know it'll stay confidential."

"I already told you that, so let me do the driving, if you don't mind."

"No. Bigalow's got a point. That woman's dangerous, so it's best more than one of us knows why the governor did what he did." He leaned over the seat and pointed again. "Go straight—it ain't far."

As I asked, "Where?" my cell phone rang.

No caller ID, but I recognized a number I'd recently entered.

It was Kermit Bigalow.

The grove manager said, "Lonnie wants to terminate my contract. But that's not why I called. Do you have a minute?"

"I'm in the car with Reggie."

"Are you on speakerphone?"

I found the question unsettling until he pushed ahead, saying, "Doesn't matter. With all that was going on, I just remembered something you said earlier. About your citrus grove, that some of the trees are more than a hundred years old. Is that true? I'd be surprised if it is."

"I can understand the confusion," I said, "but why would I lie about the age of a tree?"

"Not lie," he said, "just mistaken. I should have worded it differently." When he chuckled an apology, I pictured freckles on a tanned face. "Thing is, after Hurricane Charley, the Florida Ag Department mandated that every citrus tree in this part of the state be destroyed. It had to do with the spread of a fungus disease. They didn't notify you?"

I didn't answer immediately. On both sides of the dark road, mobile homes slid by in grids, some still decorated with Christmas lights. Behind me, I sensed Reggie scoot closer, listening.

"That was fifteen years ago," I said. "Are you asking me as a person or as a member of the citrus industry?"

"As a friend," he said. "Nothing official, but it could be important. You can trust me, Hannah."

I wasn't so sure. I muffled the mouthpiece and whispered over my shoulder, "Are you following this?"

Reggie's whiskey breath replied, "We gotta turn right in about three miles. There's no signs, so use your brights."

I returned to the phone. "My mother owns those trees. It's not up to me who I trust or don't. I don't mean to be rude, but what's your interest?"

"Staying employed and paying my bills," Kermit chuckled. "My personal opinion is, ordering those old groves cut was the single biggest biological mistake this state has ever made. Stupidity or hubris, it's hard to say, but I wish people would've had the nerve to tell those Ag Department cops to go to hell."

Loretta had said worse than that when men in government trucks had showed up, handing out notices and giving orders.

I told him as much, and relaxed a bit. "My great-grandfather planted grapefruit and oranges, and a big tamarind on a parcel behind the house —this was back in the early nineteen hundreds. Some of them are still standing. The honeybell oranges came later, but I wouldn't call it a grove. Over the years, my mother's had to sell off acreage to pay the bills, mostly pasture, but not the citrus."

"My folks had to do the same in California because of taxes. Are they sour oranges? That old rootstock is darn near impossible to find. About thirty years ago, everyone switched to Swingle or Carrizo because of virus."

Those names were foreign to me.

"Aren't all citrus trees from that period sour?" I asked. "We have sour tangerines, too, the last I checked. Mostly, I just pick the honeybells and Duncan grapefruit and ignore the others. Not even those lately, because of the citrus greening—"

"Yes, HLB," Kermit said. "It won't be long before we're all out of business if we don't find a fix. That tour I gave you this afternoon barely scratched the surface of techniques I'm experimenting with. The reason I'm interested—" He stopped, interrupted by voices in the background; a woman's muffled words, then a child saying, "Daddy . . . you promised."

"Gotta run," Kermit said after a short exchange with his daughter. "Just one more thing. Those old trees, are they still producing? I don't doubt the disease has damaged the leaves, but how's it affected the fruit?"

I said, "I've got a friend, a marine biologist, who asked me something similar this morning. I didn't have an answer for him, either."

"A special friend?"

The grove manager had his family nearby, so I didn't mind the playful insinuation.

"No one would call a man like him romantic, but he is smart. His idea was to single out trees that aren't diseased and backtrack to the reason. A different soil type, or elevation, or a different variety—anything. That's assuming we still have trees that're healthy. Saltwater's his specialty, not citrus farming, so maybe he's way off."

"Thinking out of the box," Kermit mused. "That's what I'm trying to do, too, but your friend doesn't understand how complex the disease is. I'm afraid there aren't any simple solutions. On the other hand . . . yeah, I've got to ask myself why hundred-year-old trees are still alive?"

"If they aren't," I said, "I can point you to some backcountry islands where key limes and other citrus grows wild. You'd need a boat and a machete."

"You're not talking about original Spanish seed stock?"

I replied, "I have no idea," and left it there because Reggie was pointing again, urging me, "Slow down . . . hit them brights. We gotta take a right up ahead."

"How about I check the grove tomorrow?" I said to Kermit. "I'll call you after my charter."

"I'd appreciate that. Better yet, if you're free in the afternoon, I wouldn't mind seeing those trees for myself. It sounds nice, the little fishing village where you live. Sulfur Wells— is that the name?"

We had talked about that earlier, the man interested because he was new to the area via a job south of Anaheim, then a research position at the Lake Alfred Station in central Florida.

Even so, I was reluctant to agree until he said, "I'll bring Sarah along, if it'll help change your mind."

I liked the idea of leading his little tomboy daughter around our property; I told him so, and hung up.

"You forgot to ask about the man Lonnie was with," Reggie scolded as I turned west onto a narrow road, with potholes, where weeds had sprouted knee-high, no houses around in all this darkness and open sky.

"Tomorrow," I told him.

Something else was on my mind. There is no explaining why an empty road and weeds in the headlights suddenly changed my mood and my reasoning, but it did. It caused me to rethink my quick decision to meet with Kermit, a married man, albeit a devoted father. We wouldn't be alone if he brought Sarah along—yet, I didn't want to give him the wrong impression.

I pulled over and sent a text that read:

Bring your wife, too. I'll invite my biologist friend.

Seconds later, his response pinged my phone:

Great. Just googled Sulfur Wells.

"Do you trust the new grove manager?" I asked Reggie, pulling back onto the road.

He was still hanging over the seat, searching for the next turn. "Why would I? Only knowed the man a few months. The governor thought highly of him, though. He's supposedly an expert in his field, but that's no reason to trust a person. I couldn't count the number of experts I've met through the years. Why you ask?"

In the middle of my answer, Reggie lunged again. "Look'a them eyes glowing—you see that? Up ahead, something scrambled across the road. Had some size to it."

I didn't see anything, just potholes and weeds, so returned to the subject. "Kermit seems like a nice enough man. It sounds like Lonnie is going to fire him. That'd be a shame. He's got a family to take care of, and his daughter's a doll."

"A dog, maybe, or coyotes," Reggie said. "Coyotes are thick, these days. Wished I'd've brought a gun. You bring a gun?"

I felt my jaw muscles tighten. "Silly me," I said. "I've been so busy moving dead bodies around, firearms totally slipped my mind. Reggie—why not just tell me what happened instead of dragging me all the way out here?"

"There'll be a gate on your left," he said. "When I open it, pull through. Make it fast, then wait until it's closed. We don't want any company."

We were on foot, hiking across a section of raw land Mr. Chatham had bought years ago on spec, back when the city of Cape Coral was still a hundred square miles of swamp and mosquitoes. To create buildable ground, developers had dug four hundred miles of canals, and piled the fill higher than the hopes of fast-talking salesmen who pitched the lots as "Waterfront Homesites." They did it mostly by phone, when the weather up north had turned frosty. Many of the canals dead-ended far from navigable water, but that detail wasn't mentioned in the low-down-payment contracts. Other details were omitted, too, as was the truth about a serious miscalculation, or the developer's lack of scruples. Dredging more canal frontage than any city in the world had damaged the region's aquifers and forever changed Florida's water table.

A flurry of legal suits had ensued.

This all happened twenty years before I was born, but there are still so many empty lots and dead-end streets that, seen from the air, Cape Coral's outskirts resemble a jigsaw puzzle that was abandoned due to lack of interest. What the city doesn't lack is friendliness, and an interesting mix of people, which is why the community has grown and thrived despite its shaky beginnings.

Not out here, though, north of the city limits. It was just Reggie, with me following along, beneath stars on acreage as flat as Kansas wheat. When we came to a line of cattails, he stopped. Ahead, I could hear water spilling over what appeared to be a cement weir.

Flowing water was a rarity in a canal this far inland.

"This is one investment the governor didn't get his money back," Reggie said. "But that's okay, considering what I'm about to show you." He patted his pants, then the pockets of his jacket. "You happen to bring a flashlight?"

"I left it with my gun," I replied. "Next time you ask for my help, I'll pack for an expedition. If there's something you want me to see, maybe you should come back alone when the sun's up and take pictures. I've got a charter in the morning."

"You're getting irritable, Miz Hannah."

"Nope, I'm getting mad. Instead of walking a hundred yards, why didn't we park the car here? For all we know, we could be standing in fire ants."

"A Lincoln Town Car ain't an off-road vehicle, ma'am. The governor was fussy about them tires and so am I. Hang on . . . Could be I got some matches from the Over Easy. They got good pie there."

"Don't bother," I told him, and jogged back to the limo. When I started the engine, the poor little man looked frazzled and wobbly in the head-lights, so I babied the vehicle across a field of wire grass—until I noticed several pairs of glowing red eyes in the cattails along the canal where Reggie stood. When I sped up, the animals—whatever they were—crashed into the water. They had some weight to them. I could tell because the windows were down and I heard the splash.

"My lord, my lord, they's giant lizards," said Reggie. He was still backing away as I pulled up. "Never in my life has there been a day like this day here. Ten, twelve feet long, one of those bastards. I might be drunk, but I ain't imagining things. My lord . . . they could'a grabbed either one of us."

"Get in the car, let's see."

I assumed he was right but had exaggerated the size. The canals of Cape Coral were prime habitat for Nile monitor lizards that had escaped or been released as pets. The population in the area had flourished, thanks to an abundance of house cats and family dogs.

"They have no predators and plenty of food," I explained as we crept along in the limo. When there was a break in the foliage, I angled the headlights onto a long stretch of water.

"We're both wrong," I said.

"Don't think so. Those ain't gators, with those pointy heads and red eyes. Giant lizards, I'd swear."

"Nope," I said. "Lizards wouldn't last long here. They're saltwater crocs. I've seen them in Florida Bay, and Turkey Point—there's warm water there because of the nuclear power plant. Every now and again, one will show up on Sanibel, but what in the world are they doing this far inland?"

"Water in this here canal is warm as the dickens, if that makes a difference. Does it?"

"Reggie," I said, "you didn't bring me here to talk about crocodiles."

"That there's your answer," he replied as if he hadn't heard me. "They hit a hot-water spring when they dug this canal and it flooded the place. So the governor bought the land cheap and put in that little dam. You think those crocs will bother us if we climb up there and take a quick look? That's what I want you to see."

"A weir with a spillway?"

No, the aging chauffeur wanted me to see something else.

I left the limo running and followed him to a welded barrier that was easy enough to slip around. The retaining wall between the flowing spring and the canal was a slab of concrete capped with cement. It was a cool night. As I neared the spillway, the water's heat radiated a sulfuric warmth.

"Have a look," Reggie said, and stepped away from the slab.

"Graffiti. So what?"

"Look closer."

I did. Twenty years ago, Lonnie Dupree had written her name on the capstone in wet cement. She had added a date and her palm print.

"January first." I was shielding my eyes from the limo's headlights. "Why is this important?"

"She didn't sign her name 'cause she wanted to, believe you me. It was after the governor threw a big New Year's Eve party—then he did that young woman one hell of a bigger favor. Her name and handprint, he made her do it as insurance—a sort of confession if she ever talked about what happened that night."

I couldn't see Reggie's face, just his cloaked silhouette, because he stood between me and the car. "She must've killed someone," I said. "Or hid something she wasn't supposed to have. Why else would they come the next day and pour cement?"

"Mixed it the same night," he corrected, "but the work stretched into the small hours. That's all I'm at liberty to say as of now. I wanted someone else to know, Miz Hannah. Oh"—he indicated a nearby corner—"you'll see a spot there I sanded away twenty years ago, but not fast enough."

"What are you talking about?"

"Evidence," he said. "Evidence the governor left behind out of sloppiness. I thought it was taken care of, but, nope, I was a day or two late with that sander. Can you imagine? After doing what she did, Lonnie snuck back the next morning with a camera and brought along two witnesses willing to party their way to a notary and get papers signed. A cheerleader bein' that smart, it was unexpected."

"Pictures of what? Mr. Chatham's fingerprints? I doubt if a court would accept that as evidence. Or was it something else?"

Reggie watched me inspect the area he had sanded but didn't respond.

I asked, "While she was at it, why didn't she

get rid of her name and palm print? I don't expect she told you, but you've got to wonder."

"And risk making a powerful man angry? I dunno . . . she was just a girl, at the time, who done what she did, then came to him begging for help. Those was the drug days. No telling what she was on. *L-S-D,* I forget most the names. Cocaine? There was one come up from South America, it was the worst. Devil's Breath, they called it. Kids walked around like dead folk."

I said, "If she was on drugs, why would she care what anyone thought? She would have destroyed all this."

"A dumb girl her age might've risked it. But not that Lonnie. She waited until Miz Lilly was dead, and the governor was old and weak, to play her trump card. She'd been holding that card back for twenty years. By then, her own life had 'bout run out of blue chips."

"I was right, she must have murdered someone," I said.

The chauffeur shrugged.

"If there weren't crocs here back then, there had to be gators. Why bury a body, if that's what it was, under concrete? Gators would've taken care of any evidence. You told me this much; tell me the rest."

Reggie, turning toward the car, said, "I like riding in back. You mind driving while I enjoy myself another scotch?"

Seven

That night, after I'd gotten Loretta to bed and walked the nurse safely to her car, I researched Florida's unsolved murders for the time period I'd seen etched in cement. I discovered nothing of interest until I narrowed the search to include people who'd gone missing in January of that year.

What I found reminded me not to judge others in haste, including Lonnie Dupree.

A *Tallahassee Democrat* story about Raymond Caldwell, age twenty-two, jumped out at me. He was the big-city son of a man who owned car dealerships in Jacksonville and Atlanta. Despite his advantages, Raymond had taken a dangerous turn. He'd been in trouble numerous times for DUI, and drug possession, including a pound of cocaine. It was a felony charge that ended his career as a college linebacker and, some believed, a shot at the NFL.

I'm not a football fan. To me, the stunner was that he had been charged with sexual assault three times while a student yet his football scholarship hadn't been revoked until the cocaine incident. One of the assault cases was still pending when his family reported him missing on January fifth. The local sheriff's department had issued a BOLO, a "be on the lookout," but took a different view of the disappearance. They also issued an arrest warrant, citing parole violations and Raymond's failure to appear at a preliminary hearing scheduled for January fourth. His family was forced to forfeit a $100,000 bond.

"We're watching airports, and agencies in all border states have been alerted," a spokesman was quoted as saying.

For a year, the media hyped the story, but interest faded. The last follow-up piece was ten years ago. In it, a former roommate remembered Raymond Caldwell talking about how much he loved South America. He had spent summers there as a teen, working on a cattle ranch owned by a friend of his father's.

The implications were obvious, but Caldwell was never extradited because he was never found.

I had no proof that Lonnie Dupree had known Raymond Caldwell. I had no proof she was one of his assault victims, yet the timing was too eerily similar to believe otherwise. I was on overload when I pushed away from the computer and carried a mug of tea to the stern of my boat for some air.

If Lonnie, or Harney Chatham, had murdered the young man, they had chosen the perfect victim and the ideal time. Yet, I felt no remorse.

As I am aware, a presumption of innocence is a cornerstone of law. I am also aware I have a bias that borders on fury when it comes to sexual assault—particularly if the suspect has been charged multiple times. If people, not just men, would give the subject serious thought, they would understand why only a small percentage of women are willing to report such a crime. The courage it requires! Not only must the victims share the humiliating details, they must then endure the sneering insinuations of attorneys paid to paint the truth as a lie.

From what I have experienced, and from secrets shared by women, the only difference between sexual assault and cold-blooded murder is this: rape victims are destined to relive their subjugation nightly, yet without the redeeming hope that the monster in their dreams will be banished by the electric chair.

I admit my bias, just as I admit I believe rape should be punished as a capital crime. It's not a conviction I discuss in church, nor with any-one but my closest friends. I'm a hypocrite—another personal flaw of which I am aware.

Just researching the subject caused my stomach to knot, so I switched topics and looked up the drug Reggie had mentioned. Devil's Breath. I'd never heard of it, didn't expect to find much. But there it was, although better known as scopolamine, a pharmaceutical made from the seeds of a plant that grows in the Amazon Valley. Huge, drooping white blossoms; a striking perennial that, in the wrong hands, also produced what some articles called "the world's most dangerous drug." The seeds, ground into powder, can be slipped into a victim's drink, or even blown into the face to inhale. The effects were horrific. Victims remained conscious, but lost all short-term memory, as well as their free will. They could be led around like zombies and submitted to whatever they were ordered to do. Surprisingly, it was prostitutes who most often employed the drug, to separate clients from their billfolds, their debit card numbers, sometimes even the title to their homes. Streetwalkers were known to make a paste, rub it on their breasts, then invite potential clients to kiss their nipples. That's all it took.

Men used it, too, of course. Once again, I was back on the subject of date rape. This was enough for one night.

The dock my Uncle Jake built zigs and zags through the mangroves, then two hundred feet out into the bay. I walked to the end, where there is a cleaning table and a power switch for the goose-neck lamps spaced along the way. They were off. I flicked a separate switch, and the water beneath my feet was illuminated by a floodlight. Mullet exploded around me in a chain reaction while night herons squawked from the trees. A school of ladyfish, with golden tubes for eyes, scattered into darker water. I stood watching a slow flow of life—shrimp and dollar-sized crabs, and a couple of sea horses—riding toward whatever destination tonight's mindless tide might determine.

Melancholy is an emotion I occasionally suffer and its weight blossomed within me. The chill of Mr. Chatham's dead lips on mine when I did CPR; Reggie's stories of lost love, tragedy, possibly even rape and murder—all kited through my head, then taunted my heart.

It was a Friday night. To the west, across miles of black water, a halo glow reminded me that people were having fun on the islands of Sanibel and Captiva, yet I was alone.

The only person to blame, I decided, was me.

It was still early, just a little after eight. Thanks to my uncle, I grew up fishing the backcountry waters of Southwest Florida, so running a boat at night was safer than risking drunks on the highway. I stepped aboard my fishing skiff and confirmed it was set to go. Unlike the 37-foot Marlow that is my home, it is a fast little boat, built flat as an iron to run shallow yet is as stable as high ground.

After I'd transferred some safety gear from the Marlow to my skiff, I returned to the house to check on Loretta. She had moved from her bed and appeared to be asleep in a recliner, but the lingering sweetness of marijuana proved this was a ruse to shoo me away.

"I know you're awake," I said, gently. "Smoke what you want, I don't care, but open flames are a danger in a house this old. It's your safety I worry about."

She pretended to be startled by the sight of me standing in the doorway but soon dropped the act. "It's your snooping that worries me. Your holier-than-thou attitude, too. First, I can't attend bingo; now you accuse me of doing god-knows-what." Her eyes followed mine to a nearby ashtray, where there was half a joint and a lighter. "Where'd that come from?" she asked. Said it with a theatrical innocence that would've fooled anyone else.

"I'm going out for some dinner," I responded, "but not until you're in bed and the doors are locked. Keep the phone close. Just hit the *Redial* button if you need me. Come on . . . back in bed, and stay put this time."

It took some mild bantering; the typical back-and-forth, during which I was seldom sure if her mind actually wandered or if her rambling oddities were said for dramatic effect. Insults aimed at me were typical subject matter, as were her tangents that embraced the supernatural. My mother has always had a witchy side. There is a reason. Our old house sits on the remains of a shell mound that, according to archaeologists, dates back two thousand years. The previous inhabitants were a favorite topic of Loretta's, particularly their king. She claimed the king often spoke to her; that they had long conversations, and he sometimes even slipped into her bed at night—uninvited, of course.

Thankfully, my mother's stories always ended there. As she is aware, there is a fine line regarding details of the king's visits not to be crossed or I might believe she truly is crazy, which would mean I can no longer leave her alone.

Loretta hates having a nurse in the house after sunset. As a result, she proves her sanity on a daily basis by editing her ramblings with care.

Tonight, she chose the ghosts of Indian maidens as a topic. "They were singing to me earlier; prettiest wood flutes I've heard—beautiful flutes, carved from bamboo—while the men danced around a fire. Naked as jaybirds, they were. God only knows what might've happened next—if you hadn't barged in."

I listened patiently. She was in bed, sitting up, a sheet and blanket over her legs, while I fluffed pillows.

"I wish you'd respect my privacy. Just because you don't date, or can't keep a man in your life, doesn't mean there aren't normal women who enjoy good singing and a fire. There's nothing in the world wrong with socializing with friends, even if they are members of the opposite sex."

"Was the king dancing, too?" I asked.

"What king?"

"The Indian chief. You know who I mean."

"The hell I do. I got no idea who you're talking about—and keep your paws off that man, whoever he is. Where's the channel changer?"

On the dresser was a small TV with cable reception. I found the History Channel and placed the remote within reach. "I think I'll run my skiff across to Sanibel and get some dinner. Loretta . . . Loretta"—I had to say her name twice—"pay attention in case I have motor trouble. I won't, but you never know. The tide's flooding, so I'll cut behind Chino, then cross from York Island to Dinkin's Bay. Can you remember that? If I need a tow, you'll need to send someone."

"If I knew where the damn channel changer was, maybe I could think straight. Do you listen to a word I say?"

I placed the remote on her tummy. While I was neatening up and checking windows, she spun through a dozen channels until she found a Cary Grant movie, black-and-white, with Katharine Hepburn in a sequined gown.

"That's the way a woman is supposed to dress. I met her many'a time—Miz Hepburn lived on Boca Grande, you know. Your uncle would bring her by in the boat after they'd shucked a mess of oysters. She was a true lady, that one, but Miz Hepburn loved her a mess of raw oysters as good as any man."

"I remember her," I said, which was true. "If you need me, all you have to do is call or walk down to the dock. Bang on my boat's cabin, so you don't scare the fire out of me. I should be back before midnight. You got all that?"

"When I was dating," Loretta replied, "gentlemen would pick me up in a car. A decent girl wouldn't be caught dead buzzin' around in a boat at night alone, especially dressed in those Boy Scout clothes of yours. Often, the gentleman would come in a limousine—the most beautiful black Lincoln you've ever seen. I have dated a king or two, now that you bring the subject up."

I stopped messing with the curtains. Until then, she hadn't said a word about Harney Chatham's death, nor referenced what had happened today.

"How is the king getting along?" I asked in a gentler way.

My mother's sharp blue eyes blazed, then dulled as she blinked and thought back. "He's dead," she said. "The king's dead as he can be."

"Is that right?"

"You known damn well he is."

"That's too bad," I said, still unsure. "When did he die?"

110

She blinked and stared. "Don't matter. We all die before our time. It came to me in a dream—this was before them beautiful wood flutes and singing. I don't want to talk about it." Her eyes returned to the television, blinking faster. It was a while before she spoke again. "The king went out happy. I can guarantee you that much."

I refused to respond to that.

"Happiness is a rare thing, Hannah. Especially for a man or woman who suffers this life alone. That's another reason I worry about you so."

The woman had a knack for offering the kindest advice in the meanest ways. This told me she was wide awake. I resumed what I was doing. "Suffering is a choice I've yet to make," I countered. "Should I bring an extra bottle of water? I've heard smoking grass makes people thirsty, if they can stay awake long enough."

"It's your smart-aleck ways and prudishness, too, that worries me. Has the law been snooping around?"

"They've got no reason," I lied. "How about that water? Tea would keep you awake."

"Tell me the truth."

I stood to leave. "If you're talking about Mr. Chatham, isn't it a little late for the truth?"

Bleary blue eyes blinked up at me. "Don't be cross about something you can't understand. He loved me, you know."

I replied, "Yes, he did, Mama," and gave her a kiss on the cheek.

Melancholy followed me out the door.

Outside, I glared at the stars while a dark wind stirred the mangroves with the distant hooting of owls. The idea of a trip across the bay, alone, had lost some of its luster, but I wasn't about to give in to self-pity.

Who could I phone to urge me on? My best friend, a woman sheriff's deputy, was visiting her wealthy aunt in Palm Beach—she would have been my first choice. Nathan Pace, a weight lifter, was my second, but he was traveling with his boyfriend. Then Marion Ford came to mind. Never had I met a man who disappeared, then reappeared, without so much as a warning, but he might be at home, working in his lab tonight.

No, I decided. In my current state, I couldn't be trusted. The two of us were like gunpowder, if left alone in a room. One touch of his hand, I would be guaranteed a lengthy search for my underwear and shoes come morning. A safer choice was his friend, Tomlinson, who also lived alone on a boat. On the other hand, unlike me, Tomlinson was seldom alone.

While I stood there battling indecision, the lights of a pickup truck angled around the curve, where a giant mastic tree shields a view of docks and miniature cottages known as Munchkin Land. The truck wasn't local. It was traveling slow like someone lost. When the vehicle stopped in front of the house, I walked toward the road, eager for the distraction of a driver in need of directions.

"Hannah?" a man called out the window. "I thought that was you."

I recognized the voice, and the face.

"Kermit!" I replied.

"This is embarrassing," he said, getting out. "I was restless, and was hoping some of the old orange groves were close to the road. Turns out, I was right, so don't think I'm stalking you."

I laughed at that.

Under the circumstances, I was as pleased as if I'd chanced upon an old friend in a foreign land.

I could lie to myself, as I often do, and pretend I felt no physical attraction for the grove manager until after we were in the cabin of my boat, me elevated in the captain's chair with a glass of white wine, him in the settee booth with a Diet Coke.

This was not true. We had spent an hour hiking around, inspecting citrus trees, both of us with flashlights. By day, there would have been no need for the occasional hand-on-elbow contact that darkness and bad footing require. By day, that small familiarity would have seemed less intimate, and unacceptable.

After dark, though, the briefest contact can

become a secret communication—all deniable, of course, depending on the message and the response.

Among trees my great-grandfather planted a century ago, that's where I first felt a chesty, respiratory tension and an awareness of Kermit Bigalow. It was easy enough to hide, of course, because our conversation remained strictly on a formal, friendly plain.

"See these little bastards?" He was pointing out microscopic bugs that peppered the underside of a tangerine leaf. "They carry the bacteria from tree to tree. Under a microscope, they resemble moths, but they're bizarre-looking. More like they have the head of a catfish."

This struck me as amusing. I should have known then what was happening and sent the man on his way.

"Psyllids, they're called," he said, pronouncing the word *sill*-ids. "There are three types, mostly from Asia, and they've been spreading around the world since at least the late eighteen hundreds. I don't think the connection is accidental. Citrus, the earliest forms, originated in the Orient, too."

"Spray doesn't kill them?"

"Depends on what country you're talking bout. Brazil produces three times the citrus we do because its EPA restrictions aren't nearly as tough. I worked down there for a while with a man who owns more groves than all of Florida combined. At the first sign of these"—he ground the insects to paste with his thumb and dropped the leaf—"they literally nuke every plant and tree for miles. We can't get away with that here."

That brought South America, and the story of Raymond Caldwell into my mind. For an instant, I came to my senses. "How'd you like Brazil?"

"People are great. But with all those chemicals in the lakes and water, in the markets on everything you touch? It's no place to raise a daughter. You'll understand, Hannah, when you have kids."

I found his fatherly concern and caring tone attractive. Kermit was fit, with veins showing in his forearms, but not large enough, it seemed to me, to be a college linebacker.

He took my elbow while our flashlights led us to the oldest citrus trees in the field. They were as squat and gnarled as Halloween, but loaded with fruit, beneath a starry sky with clouds.

That was a high point—the surprise of seeing oranges plump and ripe, not withered with disease.

"I'll be darned," Kermit said. "You might be on to something, young lady. Hang on . . . I've got a knife."

I said, "The leaves don't look so good, but you're the expert." By then, I could recognize the telltale yellowing and see for myself that psyllids were matted like ticks on the undersides of the leaves. There were signs of canker, too.

"It's the fruit that matters. Whoa—lots of juice in these. That's a good sign. Here, have a taste."

He handed me a freshly cut wedge, then pawed around in the limbs, using his light for a closer look. "Once the bacteria enter the tree, they attack the inside layers of the bark. The *phloem*—that's the tree's vascular system; what blood vessels are to us. The trunk can't transport water or nutrients the tree needs. It's like being starved to death and strangled at the same time. After five or six years, they're dead, but the fruit's no good long before that."

I took a taste. The pulp was tart as a lemon and caused me to pucker, but good. "They're called sour oranges for a reason, I guess. My mother used them for marinade on the rare occasions she cooked, and I've had chefs ask permission to pick a bushel. Do you really think this older rootstock might help in what you're doing?"

"Dunno." He stepped clear of the branches. "This one has the disease. No doubt about that, but it seems to be holding up a lot better than our modern trees. Did you say some original Spanish seed stock grows on an island around here? From now on, I need to listen when you have something to say."

That pleased me. So did the intensity of his

interest, but he had misunderstood. "Not if you're talking about trees planted by Ponce de León, explorers like him, who brought the first citrus to Florida. That was four hundred years ago, for heaven's sake."

"Longer," he said. "It's not the age, it's the purity of the genetic stock that matters."

"I'm not sure what that means. The places I know, they're islands that used to be farmed, but they're deserted now. Always where there are Indian mounds. There has to be high ground. I look for gumbo-limbo trees; that's the first sign citrus might grow wild in the backcountry. I've found sour oranges, and key limes, and there's at least one place where there are good white grapefruit."

"Indian mounds?"

We started back, and talked about history for a while, before returning to the subject of citrus planted in the 1500s. The Spaniards had done it to provision returning ships in a land where they'd hoped to find gold.

Kermit said, "I was picturing some remote spot where trees reproduced without being grafted, or cross-pollinated, or genetically altered in some way. Even those back there"—the old trees, he meant—"are varietals and hybrids. They're old, don't get me wrong, but they're at least four hundred years removed from the original stock. It's a silly idea, probably. The idea of seed banks came way too late—why save something you've made better? Now there's no going back . . . unless you believe in time machines."

"I don't," I replied, "but there are a couple of spots on this coast that might be just as good. My uncle used to load up the boat, and we'd go camping for a week at a time. Machete islands, he called them, because we had to cut our way in." I thought for a moment. "Years ago, he brought back seeds—a sour orange, and some guavas, too—from a place that was pure hell getting into. I know they sprouted; a couple were doing pretty well, but I haven't bothered to check in a while. My mother sold that piece of land a while back."

"Wow, that would be something to see." He sounded enthusiastic. "Tomorrow, when I bring Sarah, would you mind pointing those trees out?"

We were near the house by then, and I could see his face in the porch light. Not a handsome man in the Cary Grant way, but solid-looking and healthy, a man who was at the peak of his confidence after forty years of earning it.

In hindsight, I would like to believe it was the threat of melancholy on a Friday night that caused me to do something I normally wouldn't.

"It's not even nine o'clock yet," I said to the married man. "How about something to drink while we talk? I can show you around my boat."

Eight

In the morning, my charter got off to a rocky start—which is only fitting, I suppose. My clients, a husband and wife, were staying at Jensen's Twin Palms on Captiva Island, and it wasn't until I arrived that I realized I'd gone off and left the lunch I'd packed and my landing net behind.

"You seem distracted," the man, whose name was Gentry, observed. "Is everything hunky-dory in your world?" He and his wife said things like this; old-fashioned and humorous, always in a caring way.

My world wasn't hunky-dory, but I wasn't being paid to discuss personal affairs.

"I'll buy you lunch at the Collier Inn," I said, which was on nearby Useppa Island, one of the most beautiful places in the world. I borrowed a net, and shoved off, for I was eager to leave my self-recriminations behind.

I had fished with this couple before. They were both competent with fly rods in their hands—not always the case in the charter business—and I wasn't going to waste the opportunity. It was one of those rare days when a fishing guide wants to be at a dozen different spots at the same time, which is exciting. The air was cool but warming beneath a high blue sky. After a week of wind, it had flattened, and the bay was slick as glass, and as clear.

An hour later, my internal distractions were knocked flat, too. I was standing on a platform above the motor, poling the skiff along, when a massive shadow appeared in a sandy basin ahead; the shadow black, four feet long, the sand beneath golden in the morning light.

It was a log—had to be. This wasn't the season for tarpon, and a shark would be on the move, not lying stationary in this low, falling tide.

"Quiet," I whispered, and crouched low.

The shadow seemed to drift backwards, as buoyant as light. The shadow turned a degree with the slow flick of a yellow-glazed tail.

It wasn't a log.

Mr. Gentry saw the shadow, too. "Whoa, look at the size of that thing. What is it?"

"Snook," I said. "Twelve o'clock," meaning directly in front of the boat.

"Can't be."

"Twelve o'clock," I repeated, "but too far to cast. I'll tell you when. Who's up?"

Casting a fly rod requires room, so anglers take turns when a fish is spotted. Mrs. Gentry had already missed a shot at a redfish, yet I asked anyway out of politeness.

"Darn thing's as long as my leg," the man whispered. "Are you sure that's a snook? Never seen one so big in my . . . Oh my god"—he turned to his wife—"she's right, Hannah's right, it's a snook. See there, Dolly?"

He liked to call her "Dolly," or "Dollface," although his wife's name was Sherry.

The push pole I use is eighteen feet long. It's so hollow and light, the pole vibrates like a reed when I auger its tip into hard sand. I skated the boat forward, saying, "I'll swing the bow around when we're in range. Go ahead, start stripping out line. Mrs. Gentry, watch for knots when your husband casts; then, if you don't mind, come sit back here by the wheel."

They were a nice couple, the Gentrys. Retirement age, or close, vacationing from Tennessee, where they'd just sold their business that had something to do with science—the biotech industry, they'd said. They had money and their health, and treated each other with an easygoing deference that was fun and showed their relationship still enjoyed some spice. The pair had fished all over the world—rainbows in Argentina, bonefish in the Yucatán—but never again would they get a shot at a trophy fish like this.

Reggie's Old Florida snobbery regarding the species had been unfair and misleading. A snook is among the most beautiful, powerful fish in the world: long, sleek, silver gray with yellow highlights, and a black racing stripe on its sides. As table fare, it is excellent, but the season was closed this time of year, and I am strictly catch-and-release anyway when it comes to game fish.

What little bit of breeze there was came from Mr. Gentry's right. I babied the skiff around until he had an ideal left-hand wind. When we were eighty feet away, I wedged the pole as an anchor. "Don't worry about the distance, we can always sneak closer. Take your time . . . If you're not happy with the cast, just strip in and give her another shot."

"Her?"

I said, "Loosen your drag a notch, too."

"How can you tell it's a female?"

"Male snook, at a certain age, become females. I'm judging by the size. I could be wrong—hurry up, move."

Mr. Gentry, instead of hustling to the bow where he belonged, was grinning at his wife. "In that case, you're up, Dolly. I'll take video while you set a world's record. Go on . . . my knees are clacking, I don't think I can cast." He pushed the fly rod at her.

It was a sweet gesture, yet I felt a sinking feeling. The husband was a better caster; a snook of any size requires strength to land, and this was no time for a polite debate.

Mrs. Gentry, thank god, wasn't demure. Instead, she grabbed the rod and slipped up onto the casting deck with the aggressiveness of a falcon, then eyed her prey.

"Holy shitski," she murmured, and began arranging line at her feet and doing all the other little things anglers do before launching their first cast.

I felt better after that.

The fish lay broadside of my skiff. In the quiet pool of gold, a glazed tailfin maneuvered a slow pirouette; the fish resembled a cannon swinging into position.

"She's not going anywhere," I whispered. "No rush . . . nice and smooth, take your time," but, in my head, I was thinking, For heaven's sake, cast the darn thing.

Mrs. Gentry did. I had rigged four rods, all top-of-the-line Sage gear, but each with a different fly, or lure. The lures were feathered streamers, some with hackles, that I had tied myself. It's something I like to do at night on my boat—when not engaged in dangerous behavior with married men. Her red-on-white streamer whistled past my ear on the first false cast, her tailing loop was so bad, but the woman regained her composure. She double-hauled . . . waited for the rod to load, hauled again, and then shot eighty feet of line with a loop that could've pierced armor.

The feathered lure, deployed by fifteen feet of invisible fluorocarbon thread, plopped softly on the surface. It landed beyond the fish and to the right.

Mr. Gentry, watching through his camera, said, "Hell of a cast, Dolly!" while I urged the woman, "Strip! . . . Strip! . . . Strip! . . ."

The rhythm was important. Slow, at first, like a funeral dirge. After that, it all depended on how a fish behaved.

My focus narrowed into a tunnel of turquoise and shadows. From my elevated perch, I could see the lure's red hackles breathing clear water. I could see the fish's dark mass pivot to find the disturbance in its golden pool, then move in slow pursuit.

"She's on it," I said. "She's following . . . If she hits, let the rod do the work. Mr. Gentry, you be ready to clear knots, and make sure your wife's not stepping on line . . . A little faster, ma'am."

Strip! . . . Strip! . . . Strip! . . . Strip! . . . Mrs. Gentry's right hand moved with the rhythm of a wounded bait, her technique perfect: knees bent, rod tip almost in the water.

The snook exited the pool. It was gaining speed when it slipped over the sandy rim and vanished into a field of shallow turtle grass.

"Where'd it go?"

"Oh, shitski . . . Did she spook?"

"Keep stripping . . . Strip faster," I ordered, for the fish had reappeared not as a shadow but as a submarine wake only a few feet behind the feathery streamer.

Strip!Strip!Strip!—red hackles breathed a desperate rhythm as if trying to escape.

"Slower . . . Slower," I said. "Okay . . . stop. Let your streamer sink . . . Now strip fast."

That's when the great fish hit. In the shallows, on a small boat, events happen simultaneously when thirty pounds of instinct and muscle react to the strictures of a fly line. The glassy surface boiled a whirlpool of sand; Mrs. Gentry's rod melted into a question mark, bent by an inexplicable weight. The glassy surface exploded; salt droplets showered us. The massive fish shot skyward, levitated a slow-motion arc; then water imploded when it fell from the sky. My boat rocked; a stunning calm ensued. But only for a microsecond. A series of cannonball explosions added more waves and confusion, then the fish ran. It ripped off a hundred yards of line with such speed that, in Mrs. Gentry's hands, the reel screamed of metal tolerances better endured by a machine gun.

"Let him run, keep the rod high," I yelled. The push pole was free of the sand. I turned the skiff in pursuit. "Mr. Gentry, grab your wife's belt. She almost went over on the first run, and I'd rather lose you than her right now."

Laughter was a form of nervous release.

"My god, what a cast. Perfect, Dolly; perfect

location. Hannah, you ever seen a better cast in your life? That fish has to weigh forty pounds."

Nice, the proud way he spoke of his wife.

"More like thirty," I said, yet wanted to believe he was right about the weight. He'd been right about something else: the fish might be big enough to set a new world record. Not in terms of weight overall, but in length, and possibly weight, too, for I'd tied a fairly light 1× tippet into the leader. Even with Bimini knots at both ends, the tippet would test out at less than fifteen pounds of breaking strength.

"We've got to get some line back. You ready, Mrs. Gentry?"

"Tell me what to do, but hurry. I'm shaking like a terrier," she answered, then told her husband, "Doug, darling, do me a favor—please stop chattering and sit your butt down. I need to concentrate. Isn't that right, Hannah?"

I smiled. In the first minutes of hooking a big fish, emotions ebb and flow. The exhilaration of a hookup is fast displaced by dramas that guarantee the uncertainty of landing a big fish.

Using the push pole, I got the boat moving in a straight line. It was the product of selecting small variations in fulcrum angles, then bowing the pole with my weight like a gondola driver. I poled and Mrs. Gentry reeled, or surrendered line, in a seesaw battle, depending on the course of the snook. Her husband provided encouragement. He often changed camera angles but did a good job of staying out of the way.

Ten minutes later, the fish hadn't lost any speed or strength. Worse, it was dragging us steadily toward a bank of mangroves on the east side of Patricia Key. Mangrove roots are loaded with barnacles and coon oysters, all razor-sharp, so we had to turn the fish or lose him there. I was explaining what we had to do when the husband interrupted, saying, "What the heck is that boat doing? They see us, don't they?"

I'd been aware of an approaching outboard but had paid no attention. I took a quick look off the stern. Speeding toward us was a wide, flat skiff, with a black catamaran hull, and engines powerful enough to plow a rooster tail. The driver steered from a tower built over the counsel. A couple of passengers sat below, the boat half a mile away but closing fast.

"He sees us just fine," I said, and resumed what I was doing until the escalating roar demanded another look. When I turned, the boat was still on a collision course and close enough I could see the driver. He was a big-chested man with a handlebar mustache, and he wore a green golf visor backwards. He seemed to be looking directly at me, grinning, while his stereo boomed out music loud enough to hear the vibrating bass.

Mr. Gentry lowered the camera and began waving his arms. "What the hell's wrong with that idiot? Hey . . . Hey, we've got a fish on!" he shouted as if that might do some good.

It did not, so I hefted the push pole to get his attention. The driver watched me, still grinning. I used the pole to point at the fish we were fighting; the fish fifty yards out, and enough blades of grass fouled on the fly line to make that visible, too.

I shook the pole in an aggressive way, then pointed again. Only then did the driver alter his course a few degrees, but not enough to miss our fly line unless I did something fast. I jumped down onto the deck, yelling, "Grab your wife's belt. Hold on, Mrs. Gentry, we've got to move."

In a rush, I fired the engine before the propeller was submerged and slammed it into gear. My skiff shot forward. This provided a shield for our line, and the fish attached to it, but also put us directly in the path of the boat. The grin vanished from the driver's face; he spun the wheel so violently, he nearly flew off the tower, but held on and glared through his bizarre mustache. This wasn't punishment enough, so he swung the wheel in retaliation and swamped a wall of water over my skiff as he flew past, the roar of his twin outboard engines and stereo deafening.

An instant later, Mrs. Gentry's voice pierced the din. "The boat . . . it snagged my line . . . He's got my line! What should I do?" She was fighting to hang on to the rod as line peeled away while her husband clung to her belt, all attached to the stern of the speeding boat and its wake of mud and turtle grass.

The drama didn't last. The line snapped—or so we believed until my skiff settled in the bucking waves. Only then was I calm enough to suggest that Mrs. Gentry reel in.

"I'm snagged on something else," she said.

I had busied myself drying seats to hide the fact that I was furious. "Maybe it got tangled around a branch of something. Want me to try?"

"Deadweight, it feels like." She lifted the rod, applied pressure, and gained a few feet of line. Over and over she did this until the object was too close to lift. It was Mr. Gentry, the taller of the two, who saw it first from the casting deck. "My god . . . they ran over your fish, Sher. It's your snook! It is . . . but I think it's dead."

No, the fish was still alive. Barely. I went over the side into the water, scooped it up, and removed the hook. A single silver gash behind the eye told us the snook had been hit by the propeller. The color of the gills was good. They were still pumping water, yet the fish lay immobile in my arms, a great, dense weight.

"Any chance it'll come around?" the husband asked.

"We can't count this as a catch," I replied.

"Wish we could, but we can't. That's a shame. You did a great job, Mrs. Gentry. I can see from here it's over forty inches long."

I floated the fish closer to the IGFA measuring sticker on the gunnel of my skiff. "Forty-two inches, looks like, but I don't want to lift her out—"

"I don't give a tiddly bit about records," the woman said. "Can you revive the poor thing?"

Unlikely, but I had to choose my words with care. I was still furious, and aware that anger is contagious. A successful charter has less to do with landing fish than keeping clients happy. Admitting the fish would die might ruin the rest of the trip. "I'm willing to try, but wouldn't you rather move to another spot? Either way, we have to leave the fish here no matter what. Snook are out of season, and it's over the slot, size-wise, anyway. Take all the pictures you want, of course."

"Isn't there someone you can call?"

I assumed she meant the police, so shook my head and lied to keep the day cheerful. "The guy driving didn't mean us any harm. Particularly on weekends, it's the sort of thing you have to just shrug and smile. Or"—I realized I'd misunderstood—"did you mean to help us revive this fish?"

"Yosemite Sam, and people like him," she said, referring to the driver's cartoon mustache, "find ways to punish themselves. Isn't there a wildlife rescue organization of some kind?"

I smiled for the first time in a while. "Not for fish, but I like the way you think. Sure, we can keep trying. Why not give it shot?"

A nice couple, the Gentrys. An hour later, they were wading along beside me, taking turns babying water through the great fish's gills. By then, my drifting skiff had led us to the back side of Patricia Key, an island that had once been farmed by early homesteaders.

"Are those grapefruit?" the woman asked.

I had failed to notice, or even think about, the wild citrus trees I had described to Kermit Bigalow last night. Near shore, where pilings had outlasted a dock, was a cluster of heavy yellow fruit amid a wall of green.

"They're not as sweet as modern Duncan grapefruit," I replied, "but they're pretty good. I can pick some, if you like. The chef on Useppa might fix them in a salad—don't forget, lunch is on me."

"So typically thoughtful of you, Hannah. Can we stay with the boat while you forage ashore?"

Her tentative manner told me Mrs. Gentry didn't want to give up on the fish. The snook's gills were still working, the color good, but otherwise the fish behaved as if it was in a coma.

I didn't have much hope, so grabbed a bag and

slogged to the island. As I returned, my mood brightened. In a slick area near the couple, water rippled with a splashing swirl. A huge gold-tinged tail breached the surface. The tail lashed, then vanished beneath a tunneling wake. Husband and wife hooted and embraced.

"My world record just swam off!" Mrs. Gentry hollered to me. She was dancing around, both fists raised.

This was a phrase she repeated several times while we celebrated over lunch, then drinks by the pool on Useppa Island.

No alcohol for me, not on a charter. Even so, we had fun, and, as it turned out, more than that. We got to talking about the orange trees, and their biotech background sparked a lot of questions and comments from them—so many that, by the time we were done, I'd filled up a napkin with scribbled thoughts.

My thoughts of the previous evening were again displaced until I could no longer ignore the time. It was nearly three. I was still obligated to meet Kermit and his daughter at four despite what had happened last night aboard my boat.

"Like this never happened," the grove manager had said to me before leaving. His exact words.

It was almost true.

Nine

Aboard the boat that is my home, alone with the married man, what happened wasn't much, at first, but enough to cause me to say, "I'd like you to leave before we both do something stupid."

It was too late for that. I'd already made the error of inviting him into the cozy privacy of my cabin, where stars sparkled outside the windows and the lighting inside was dim.

"Us being here is my fault, Kermit. Let's call it a night and start over tomorrow. Usually, I'm more careful about, uh . . . getting into situations like this."

At first, he feigned confusion. Finally, though, he proved he was an honest man by saying, "Okay, okay . . . I like you too much to lie. I know exactly what you mean. And you're right, I should leave."

This was after I'd moved from the captain's chair to the little booth, which, truth be told, I seldom use because I prefer to eat, or read, outside, and I almost always dine alone. I sat across from him. We discussed citrus, and his life in California, and Lonnie Chatham, then more trivial matters. Mostly, we laughed. I enjoyed our laughter, particularly after the day we'd shared. I liked the sun lines in his face when he smiled. The recollections we exchanged about how we'd met—him in the river, me at the rail where he'd hung his clothes—added a scent of bawdi-ness to the air.

My wineglass was empty by then. This freed my hands for the occasional subtext of an accidental touch. Nothing so obvious I could not pretend it was innocent. Beneath the table, however, our feet were bolder. Soon, I felt perfectly at ease resting an ankle against his— this under the guise of his leg being part of the table. But when his shoes came off and he reinitiated contact, skin on skin, it was too much to ignore. That's when I called a halt to the evening.

The grove manager had apologized his way up the steps to the stern deck outside. I'd made sure the dock lights were out, of course—another sneaky decision—which only softened the man's soft brown eyes when he turned to me to say good night.

"I don't know what got into me, Hannah. Wait . . . that's not true, either. I haven't laughed so hard in a long, long time, or felt so at ease. If things were going better at home, maybe . . . And then there's my job—hell . . . if I still have a job. Mostly, though"—he had placed his hands on my wrists to say this—"it's the feeling I got when I first saw you. You are so damn beautiful, and not in the typical hair spray, lipstick sort of way. Believe me, I've never done anything like this before."

If he had only said "attractive," I might have allowed him to kiss me, for I knew that was coming. I wanted to be kissed; I wanted to be held. The word *striking* might have worked, too, for I'd like to think I am striking in the right dress and soft lighting, but no man has ever called me beautiful—not with honest motives or without irony.

The exaggeration brought me to my senses yet did not slow my breathing. I had to step free of his touch to find air. "That's sweet of you, Kermit, but you can't say such things if we're to be friends. Follow the dock; I'll switch on the lights. I think you can find the way to your own truck."

I didn't expect him to leave without another attempt. He didn't disappoint me.

"Are friends allowed to give each other a hug good night?"

"Of course," I said, well aware of the ledge I had just stepped off.

Time is sometimes difficult to gauge, but it wasn't much later when he whispered in my ear, "Pretend like this never happened. Both of us. We've got no choice and we both know why. But, Hannah? I can't pretend I don't want this to happen again."

Only then did the married man return to his truck.

All this replayed in my head after I dropped off the Gentrys and pointed my skiff home. It was nearly four; I was in a rush and distracted or would have been quicker to notice a boat trailing too close in my wake.

I looked back and did a double take. It was the black catamaran hull. Yes . . . the same boat, but only the driver aboard, with his green visor and wild, red handlebar mustache. His shirt was open, flapping in the wind.

I swung around and pretended I hadn't seen him. We were on the east side of the Intracoastal Waterway. It was busy on this winter afternoon. Lots of cruiser traffic, yachts that plowed a wake, so I couldn't be certain of the man's intentions. Not yet anyway. I increased speed, sledded down a series of waves, then banked into shallow water. Ahead lay three miles of shoals separating me from the dock my Uncle Jake had built and home.

The tide was flooding. Oyster bars and limestone jetties and snags caused by hurricanes would be masked by water, but that was okay. I'd been skidding boats through that maze since childhood.

Behind me, the man with the mustache turned, too.

No doubt now. He was following me, coming fast, and way too close.

• • •

In the 1980s, when Florida banned traditional mullet nets, fishermen forced out of business were offered water leases and the chance to raise clams commercially.

It was a high-risk, low-profit "opportunity." What else could they do?

As a result, west of Demere Key is a vast acreage of Styrofoam buoys and stakes that mark the clam leases and the bags of seed clams that grow beneath. It's an area I avoid out of respect for people whom the government has seldom treated fairly. They didn't deserve the added burden of property damaged by propellers, but that's where I headed . . . until my conscience got the best of me.

Why not stop and have it out with the guy right now?

I tried, but, when I slowed, Yosemite Sam—that's what Mrs. Gentry had called him—nearly rammed his boat over the corner of my transom. He would've if I hadn't jammed the throttle forward. When I glanced aft, he towered above me at the controls and wore the same idiotic grin, his hair and shirttails flapping like flags. To acknowledge eye contact, he flashed the peace sign, then used the same two fingers to throw me a kiss.

The man was crazy.

I had no choice but to run. My skiff is a

21-foot Maverick, built for thin water and over-powered with a 225-horse Mercury OptiMax. Seldom did I invite the eye-watering discomfort by exceeding 40 mph, but the speedometer climbed to 50 as I raced away.

Behind me, the black catamaran had no trouble keeping up; in fact, it could have passed me, which cartoon Sam threatened several times by nosing close to my stern, then jumping my wake, before dropping back.

A mile of water lay between us and the clam beds.

Beneath the console was a VHF radio I seldom use, and also my cell phone. I chose the radio. I contacted the Coast Guard at Fort Myers Beach. After the duty officer had me switch to Channel 22-Alpha, I told her what was going on. Because of the noise, I had to shout, and repeat my location several times.

"Do you feel your life is in danger?" she asked.

Yes, I did, which is why I phoned my sheriff's deputy friend next. Birdy Tupplemeyer is a high-octane woman—a three-year veteran of the force who does not share my reluctance to use profanity or hop into bed with married men. The time would come when I could confide to her about Kermit, but that could wait. I gave her the same information—still shouting, and forced to repeat details, but in a less formal way.

"The crazy fool's gonna get us both killed," I yelled.

"Are you packing?" Her tone was judgmental. I could picture her in a two-piece, pacing by her aunt's Palm Beach swimming pool.

"Packing a gun?"

"Hell yes, you ninny. This dude—you ever seen him before? Doesn't matter. If you're packing, stop your damn boat and threaten to put a couple rounds up his ass. Warn him first—all the standard bullshit. Then do it! Go ahead. Put your phone on *Speaker* so I can testify the scumbag had it coming."

"Only fishing gear," I hollered. "Isn't there someone you can call? It's Saturday. The marine division—there has to be a police boat out here somewhere."

"Jesus Christ, Hannah. Carry; always, always carry. How many times have I told you! And it's not like you haven't already rung that bell."

Shot a man, she meant.

This was true; an incident I rarely discuss.

"Call somebody, for heaven's sake," I said, and stowed the phone.

Racing toward me was a blur of buoys and floating bamboo poles, a few with rags attached to make them visible. They were tied to nylon ropes from which bags of clams were suspended, each buoy anchored to the bottom. The incoming tide held the buoys taut. Ripples showed me the direction the ropes lay and created hundreds of narrow channels to choose from. Stray even a foot, it meant trouble: a mile of nylon rope would snag the propeller and strangle an engine dead.

I waited until the last possible instant to make my turn, then cleaved an angling course. Rows of white buoys scattered to make room. Until then, Yosemite Sam had been taunting me from both sides of the boat, but he realized the danger and fell in line, so close that the nose of his boat shadowed my transom.

Crazy or not, the man was no stranger to water. I began to doubt my plan to lose him here in the lonely backcountry. Maybe it was wiser to return to the main channel, where a hundred witnesses might dissuade him from whatever violence he had in mind.

Road rage on the bay. It is rare among fishermen, but it happens.

I snuck another glance back. Standing high above me, he responded with the peace sign and blew me another kiss. He appeared to be enjoying himself. Scared as I was, that made me mad. On my throttle is a trim switch that can tilt the engine clear of the water. I used it and held tight. The chines of the Maverick threatened to break free when the engine lifted. Soon my propeller was shooting water like a fire hose into Sam's boat.

I didn't see what happened, but the finesse

worked. When I looked again, the catamaran was dolphining wildly off course, kicking a wake of Styrofoam and mud. It gave me some breathing room. I kept watch while exiting the clam lease and got my boat trimmed, the whole time expecting cartoon Sam's engine to stall in a tangle of nylon.

It didn't happen. Somehow he'd dodged enough lines to keep going and was circling back. No idiotic grin on his face now. He reached for something and came up with a short-handled gaff—a stainless hook attached to a pole. It was a threat; he wanted me to see it. I acknowledged the threat with a middle finger, not the peace sign. His gravelly voice was oddly high-pitched for whatever it was he hollered. Then he buried the throttle and came at me full speed.

I was already moving, but not in the direction of my dock. Enraged people lose their ability to reason. I was counting on that; wanted him too mad to think or see clearly. At the wheel with my back to him, I used a middle finger again as if I, too, were having fun—and, truth is, I did feel a wild moment of abandonment.

There was no time to gauge what effect my taunting had. Ahead was a jumble of islands, all uninhabited. Between lay a mile of thin water, the bottom pocked with potholes and oyster bars, some visible, some not. I knew those bars well. So did my Uncle Jake back in the days when he'd taken Katharine Hepburn oystering. The winter months are best, always on a spring low tide. Jake would equip me with boots and gloves so I could wade those jagged shoals without getting cut to ribbons.

As I knew, the biggest oysters lay in troughs between the bars on the bottom that was never exposed. One of those troughs was half the width of my skiff. That was wide enough.

I steered toward it and ignored Sam, who was angling to cut off my escape. I triangulated the distance by instinct. Unless he actually intended to ram me, he would have to reduce speed, then turn sharply, to stay on my tail.

That's what happened. I flew past him, flipped another bird, and let my wake mask a trough through an oyster ridge that was also masked by water. Sam swung too wide. I didn't see what transpired, but I heard it. The howl of an outboard slamming aground is as distinctive as a braying donkey. The staccato *Hee-haw-haw* is similar, minus the metallic edge if a propeller is sheered.

When I heard metal, I knew I was safe yet didn't slow until I found a pothole deep enough to drop off plane.

I looked back.

The black catamaran, with its tower and twin Yamahas, sat exposed in a foot of water. It looked like a trophy on a pedestal. At least one of its propellers had been bent. Yosemite Sam had managed to stay aboard, but that would be hard to prove because he was wet and mud-splattered from the soaking my engine had given him.

"If you stopped to gather oysters," I yelled, "it's better when the tide goes out. By then, you'll need a boat with wheels."

I expected profanity, untethered rage. Instead, the man shrugged in a sheepish way and replied, "You ever have one of those days? Some of the dumb things I do, I swear, there're times I don't think I got a brain in my head. Especially when I'm trying to impress a pretty woman." He commented on his bent propeller, then asked, "You ain't mad, are you?"

My lord . . . the guy was deranged. Or was he acting? There was some nasal Cracker in his voice, but the accent had a guttural tinge. German, Pennsylvania Dutch . . . no telling. Maybe this was satire, his parody of Southerners and other hicks.

The possibility implied a slyness—and an intellect—that scared me, as did his size—a huge head, chest, and hands. Yet I did my best to show a brave front.

I switched off my engine. "What's wrong with you? This morning, you saw we had a fish on and intentionally cut us off. Then you pull a stunt like this? If I wanted to press charges, I've got my clients as witnesses."

"Uh-oh, I knew it. You're mad. Serves me right, I guess." This was said in the glum way of a child who'd been scolded. He swung down to the deck with surprising agility. The catamaran hull tilted beneath his weight. "All I wanted was to get a closer look."

"At a fish? We lost a big snook because of you. Then you nearly swamped us."

"Sure am sorry," he said, "but you're wrong about my reasons. My clients catch plenty of fish. What I wanted was a closer look at you."

Good God. Now he was hitting on me?

I said, "How many beers have you had today? If you're not drunk, you've lost your mind."

"Hell, I'll admit it. Probably a little of both. Here, I'll prove it"—he began pawing through a console drawer—"I got a fishing magazine someplace with your picture on the front. A real pretty one. I was bragging to my clients about it. Then there you were, stealing one of my best snook holes. Not that I minded, 'cause of who you are. Like fate, you know?"

Snewk, he pronounced the word, but with difficulty. Maybe I was right. It was an act.

"You claim to be a guide? You should buy a bus and stick to bridge fishing. I've never seen you or your boat in my life."

"Starstruck, I guess some call it," he replied. "Then I go and make a damn fool out of myself after you gave me the finger back there. Flirting

—you knew what you was doing. How you expect a man to act?" He gave up on the drawer and opened a cabinet. "That dang magazine's here someplace."

I said, "You stay away from me, understand? I reported this to the Coast Guard. Next time, I'll swear out a warrant."

"Ain't there some way to make this right? I'll buy you dinner. Champagne, the whole works. Or do you like to dance? I've been taking lessons. Big as I am"—he did a waltzing two-step across the deck to illustrate—"tango is a specialty, but I prefer swing dancing." He spun an invisible partner, then was done with it and peered over the side, seeing scuttling crabs and a mountain range of oysters. "I don't suppose you have a shovel I can borrow?" After a beat, he added, "Or a bottle of Tabasco?"

No twang when he said this, which confirmed it was all a charade. Same with his slow, sinister smile, teeth bared, beneath a mustache the size of a boomerang. "Know what might be fun? Sit here with a case of beer and eat oysters, just the two of us, until we're both so damn horny that, later, down the road, you won't mind when I tell you to stay out of my goddamn snook spots."

I said, *"What?"*

"You heard me. Chartering's just like any other business, honey. Sex and marketing." He glared for a moment, then slammed a hatch open, done with me, too.

Eerie, the feeling I got, the two of us out here alone, separated only by a few yards of water and walls no higher than the gunnel of my boat. What if he had a gun inside that hatch? What if he came after me on foot or bulled his boat off the bar faster than anticipated?

I started my engine, snuck a few photos of him, and the boat's registration numbers, then sped away.

It was half past four. I was late.

Ten

Kermit's daughter, Sarah, appeared on the dock as I was tying up. She had an orange in her hand. "Daddy said I'm supposed to give you this. He seems in a hurry to leave, but he's always like that. And to thank you for letting us take samples from your trees."

Through the mangroves, I could see a white pickup truck parked, or waiting at the side of the road, with a tarp tied over the bed. The mix of relief and disappointment I felt was blurred by the adrenaline still pumping through me.

"Sorry I'm late," I said. "You can tell your daddy that for me. Did you have fun?" I was positioning bumpers so my skiff wouldn't bang against the dock.

"Guess so. I like your hair. I wish Mama would let me cut mine like that. It's hard enough just to talk her into letting me wear jeans. Short hair's better, don't you think?"

I smiled. "Not if I had braids as pretty as yours. How about a cold bottle of water? Or do your parents let you drink pop?"

The girl, a skinny little thing in coveralls and a T-shirt, showed her missing front tooth. "What's that?"

"Soda drinks. *Pop*'s the sound the bottle makes

when you open it. That's the way it was explained to me anyway." I stepped down into my skiff and opened the cooler. "I might have some juice in here somewhere, too."

"As long as it's not orange juice. I'm sick of it. My whole life, everything's smelled of oranges. Even my room, because we've always lived in citrus groves. Oh—and I'm supposed to call you Miss Smith or Captain."

I told her that using my first name was perfectly okay, and traded her a bottle of water for the orange in her hand. "I like the tanginess," I said, holding it to my nose. "But I understand. I didn't grow up in the citrus business like you. Did you get this off one of the old trees out back?"

The girl shook her head no, but her attention was on my boat. "I'd love to go for a ride sometime. I bet it's fast."

To the south, distant islands shielded the black catamaran and its driver from view. I said, "Opinions about that might vary . . . but I guess it's fast enough. I've always liked boats, too." I pointed to the 37-foot Marlow that sat prettily, with its dark blue hull and white trim, moored on the opposite side of the dock. "I live on that one."

"Really? I've never met anybody who lived on a boat before. I bet it's nice. Can I see inside?"

"Not if your daddy's in a rush. Come back, though, and I'll take you for a ride. Maybe we could even fish a little—as long as it's okay with your mother. Better yet, invite her along."

The instant the words were out of my mouth, I regretted the offer. I had no right to intrude on another woman's family, even in this mild way.

"Mama hates the water," the girl said. "She hates Florida, too, because of the bugs. Not me. I love the water. I'd live in the water, if I could. Daddy says I swim like a fish." She studied me a moment in the wise way some children possess. "Did I say something wrong?"

She had correctly gauged the wistful change in my expression. I forced a plastic smile. "A lot of people don't like Florida. There's nothing wrong with that. Your mama's right. Sometimes the bugs and heat are hard to live with."

"If you don't like it," the girl said, "why do you live here?"

"I wasn't talking about myself."

"I sure would love to go for a ride in your boat. Are you afraid of sharks? I'm not. Daddy took me to the beach once, and I swam way out past the waves. When I'm old enough, I'm going to learn to scuba dive. Do you scuba dive?"

"I'm like you," I said. "I could live in the water."

As we talked, I finished with the bumpers, then stepped up onto the dock. I had to stop myself from doing what seemed natural—offering the girl my hand. Instead, we walked single file to shore.

• • •

Kermit swung out of his Chevy Silverado when Sarah was safely inside, her seat belt buckled, and closed the door. We exchanged polite greetings and shook hands in a business-like way. "Talk to you for a moment?" he said. "I wanted to ask you about dock rentals."

It was an excuse to move away from the truck, which was running, with its windows up. As we walked, he spoke in a low, confidential voice. "I know I should apologize for last night, but I can't. I don't regret a thing, Hannah. I've been thinking about you all day."

"Not another word," I said. My eyes were on the truck, where Sarah was fiddling with the radio. "It never happened. We both agreed, remember? That's the way it's going to stay."

"Come on, Hannah. Talk to me. Please?"

"I am talking to you. You're not listening."

"Admit what happened and I will. You can't pretend—"

"I'm not pretending. We're done with this. I don't blame you, I blame myself, and that's all I have to say."

I started toward my boat. He took a step and blocked my way. "Okay, okay. I keep telling myself it was just a one-night thing, but . . . why do you think I was in a rush to leave before you got here? I knew if I saw you, I would—"

I said, "Bring the subject up again, Kermit, we're done even as friends. I mean it."

"You're serious."

"Yes, I am." With my chin, I indicated the truck. "That girl's more important than any six of us, and I won't play a role in hurting your child. I'm sorry about what went on between us, I truly am. Don't make it any worse."

His face flexed with sun lines. "Worse? I can't imagine it getting any better—but I'm coachable."

The humorous way he said it was so unexpected, I softened a bit.

"Finally," he said. "A smile."

"You're a mess, Kermit."

"Don't pretend you haven't been thinking about me, too."

"You don't want hear what I've been thinking about," I said, and shooed him toward the truck. "Go on, now, and behave yourself. It was just a kiss, for heaven's sake."

That was nearly true. One polite kiss had led to a much longer kiss that spanned long, foggy minutes of consent, then a few woozy seconds of exploration, before I had finally said, "Enough," and sent him away.

Kermit, serious now, said, "It meant a lot more than that and you know it. Can I call you tonight?"

I looked at the ground, then into his eyes. "I won't answer if you do."

"Even if it's to talk about that?" He meant the orange I was holding.

"Kermit, I'm all wrung out—you wouldn't believe the day I've had. Please don't push. Why can't you let things go?"

"Tonight, around seven," he said. "You can tell me about your day, and a thousand other things I want to know about you."

"I'm not going to warn you again," I said. "Don't stop here again, and don't call me. Give us both a month to realize how stupid it was, what we almost did."

"Almost?"

"You heard me!"

He said, "A month's not going to change anything. We'll discuss it tonight. After that, if you don't change your mind . . . But you will." He looked toward the truck, Sarah inside. "She likes you, I can tell. You're both beautiful tomboys."

This infuriated me.

"Don't you dare play that card," I said, and strode away.

Loretta was on the porch, watching. I didn't have to see my mother to know. Even from the dock, I could feel the tension created by her presence, and the critical workings of her mind.

A phone call to Birdy spared me for half an hour. After telling her about the run-in with

152

Yosemite Sam, my deputy friend said, "Text me the photo of the guy and I'll run the numbers on his boat. Legally, I can't share what I find out, but who knows what I'll do after a bottle of wine?"

"There's something else that happened," I said. I gave her an edited version of my evening with Kermit and the conversation we'd just had. I answered a dozen questions before asking her to promise to intercede if I weakened.

"Why would I?" Birdy said. "Pick the right married man, it's like owning a puppy you don't have to babysit or muzzle on Saturday nights. Let him talk oranges all he wants; the whole time, you can use him like a sex toy. That's advice from the only friend you have who knows how badly you need to get laid. Besides, you wouldn't ask for help if you weren't already a lost cause."

"We sure are different, the way our minds work," I responded, yet conceded the truth of every word she'd said.

Loretta wasn't so easily dealt with. She was still on the porch when I entered and had spent the delay fuming. "You might warn me in advance before inviting strange men onto the property," she said. "If it'd been night, I might've shot him for stealin' our citrus."

"Or invited him in to share a joint," I replied, picking up an ashtray. "Did Mrs. Terwilliger give you your afternoon pills?"

"The moon-eyed look on that man's face when he got in his truck—my lord. Who is he? I bet he didn't mention he was married, did he? Of course not. They never do."

"Loretta," I said, "maybe you would've found an exception if you'd bothered asking the married men you dated. His name's Kermit. His daughter and wife are both as nice as they can be." I glared for a moment. "Kermit was hired by Mr. Chatham. Remember Mr. Chatham?"

"What's her name?" my mother responded, which was unexpected. It threw me for a moment.

"Sarah," I answered. "She's starting to lose her baby teeth . . . They're so grown-up, at that age. I might take her for a boat ride."

"Not the daughter's name. She brung me a bag of sour oranges, god knows why. What's his wife's name? You said you met her."

I had made no such claim. It was another attempt to rattle me. "I'll introduce you when she brings Sarah back for that boat ride," I countered, which came off smoothly enough to attempt a change of subject. "How about a nice glass of sweet tea?"

When I returned from the kitchen, however, I was reminded why I'd moved out of the house while still a senior in high school. Loretta wouldn't let the matter go.

"Kermit, huh? Wasn't that the name of a frog?"

"A wealthy one, as I recollect," I said, removing

a wad of bills from my shirt pocket. "That reminds me. My clients gave me a hundred-dollar tip today and booked me again for Monday. You should've seen the snook they landed. I'll stick your half in the jar."

That's what I paid Loretta, half of my tips, for the use of "her" dock.

"More rich Yankees. If taxes get any higher, they'll own the whole damn state."

"They're from Nashville, and you've never met a finer couple. If you don't want their money, just say so."

"Are they rich as Kermit? I bet he told you he was rich, too. Don't believe it. No one with money would stoop to stealing citrus." Using both hands, she took a sip of her tea. "What'd you put in this? It ain't sugar. We too broke to buy real cane sugar now? Bet if you made tea for him, it'd be sweet enough."

Ignoring the woman only made her meaner, but I ignored her anyway. I went through the kitchen to the mantel over the fireplace, where, beside the clock, was a vase with a lid. I made sure the lid clanged good and loud after I deposited a fifty. But easy profit wasn't enough to derail an interrogation.

"Are you sleeping with him?"

"Hard to keep track," I said, spooning more sugar into her tea. "I average about seven men a week. Which one you talking about?"

"Might as well said seven hundred. You'd be walking different if that nonsense was true. I mean, the married man just now! He looked at you like something served with gravy on a plate. Don't tell me you two ain't having carnal relations. Lie all you want, but I know the signs."

"You've had plenty of experience," I said agreeably.

"None of your sass. I know, because I watched your face when he got out of the truck. And the way your body acted—that's something a woman can't hide. Hannah, the way you perked up, pilots could've seen your nipples from an airplane. It ain't that cold out, sweetie. You think the frog-named man didn't notice?"

I straightened my collar to allow a quick glance down. My shirt was frost gray with buttons and vented sleeves from L.L.Bean; a size too large, for that's what I prefer. Beneath was an Athleta sports bra, designed for modesty and comfort. Fishing can be wet work, so I'm careful about such things.

"I believe I'll speak with Tomlinson about the weed he brings you," I said. "You've either got the eyes of an eagle or you're hallucinating. Loretta"—I held up a warning hand—"I don't mind insults in private, but if you ever speak like that in front of others, I'll . . . I'll—" I couldn't think of a threat I hadn't made, nor one that offered the hope of working.

"In front of Kermit, you mean?" she chimed in. "You're a fool if you think he came here just to steal a box of oranges and a citrus tree. You know how I hate a person who nags, but—"

"Mr. Chatham trusted him," I interrupted. "He hired Kermit to save his groves from disease. I'm helping out of respect for a man who was good to us—" Midsentence, I stopped and backed up. "What do you mean, 'stole a tree'?"

"Because he did. I saw him do it. Well . . . saw it in his truck. This was just before your skiff pulled up."

"It would take a backhoe and a trailer to cart off one those trees," I said, and studied my mother's face. Was this an exaggeration intended to badger me or did she believe it had actually happened?

Loretta sensed my seriousness. Always careful not to cross the line—it would have meant a night nurse—she decided to retreat. "Guess you're right," she said in a careful, uneasy way. "But Hannah? Personally? I wouldn't trust the bastard—even if he didn't steal a tree small enough to hide in that Silverado he drives."

Now I didn't know what to believe.

I heated up the dinner Mrs. Terwilliger had prepared and left wrapped in foil, then returned to my boat to shower and change.

Sunset was around six-thirty. It would be dark by seven, which is when Kermit said he would

157

call. If he called . . . if I answered—or even if I didn't—I needed the truth about Loretta's claim. As tired as I was, I changed into boots and hiked back to the citrus orchard. Sarah had left a book there on a towel, which I collected, but there was no sign of a missing tree, including seedlings I hadn't noticed.

I felt better . . . but then remembered the wild orange seeds my Uncle Jake had planted on land that was no longer ours. Kermit had seemed keenly interested. I hadn't revealed where the tree was (only one had survived), but he might have assumed it grew on an adjoining property, which it did.

The sky was a swirl of saffron and arctic blue, but there was still some light. I skirted the remains of a canal dug by the same ancient people who had built mounds in the area, then slipped through a fence. It had been five years since my uncle had died, or since I'd tried to find that young tree, but I knew the acreage well. Childhood memories of building secret huts or dreaming away in secret places are slow to fade. Even so, I found a dozen spots that looked familiar, but not what I was looking for. Possibly, the new owners had cleared the land for building or pasture.

It was nearly dark. There was comfort in the fact that a five-year-old citrus tree would be too big for one man to handle, so I headed home.

At seven sharp, Kermit called. I was alone, sitting in my cabin's settee booth by then. I don't know why the ring startled me so—perhaps because I'd thought about little else while the minutes dragged past. Sarah's book—which, in fact, was a sketchbook—was an acceptable excuse to answer. The drawings inside, however, provided a dozen reasons why I should not. Her stick-figure people showed angry women, but only smiling, oversized men. Trees exhibited anger, too, with canopies that boiled like smoke. Sometimes, beneath Sarah's pencil, the paper had torn. When a girl with stick-figure braids was the subject, she was always by herself, and dwarfed by trees or a smiling man. Only when the girl was swimming, or paddling a canoe, did the artist grant her a beaming, stick-figure smile.

I didn't answer the phone. I chose to sit immobile and stare as it buzzed on the same table where I had shared the married man's touch last night. When the buzzing ceased, I waited through several more slow seconds, hoping for the ping of a voice message.

There was none, but I grabbed up the phone and checked anyway.

It was Saturday night. On every island where lights blossomed, people weren't alone and lonely. They were living their lives, having fun.

I began to pace . . . until I realized I could call Kermit back. That was perfectly acceptable—

as long as I didn't wait too long. There were many believable excuses: I'd been in the shower, the phone was buried in my purse, I'd switched it off and forgotten the darn thing. If it was business he wanted to discuss, then returning a missed call was the polite thing to do. Oh—by the way, had he stolen the young tree my uncle had planted?

My finger hovered above the *Redial* button . . .

I couldn't do it. The drawings of a lonely child prohibited the risk of confusing her more. No one understood that better than I.

He'll call back, I thought, then scolded myself for entertaining such a thought as hopeful. Worse, how would I react if, tonight, he surprised me yet again by truck?

No more tests for me. A wiser choice was to reactivate my plan for the previous evening. This time, I made it to my skiff, and my skiff carried me safely to Dinkin's Bay on Sanibel, where I found the biologist playing chess with his friend Tomlinson. With me, I brought a sour orange for discussion, along with questions about the drug my mother had been smoking.

Fearing that Yosemite Sam and his boat might still be stranded in the backcountry, I stuck to well-traveled channels both ways.

That story was something else I shared with my friends.

Eleven

Monday afternoon, after another enjoyable charter with the Gentrys, I drove inland to the Agricultural Research Station in Immokalee and presented a box of tree leaves and fruit to citrus pathologist Roberta Daniels. We'd gone to high school together—one of those pleasant coincidences that wasn't so coincidental. We'd also been in the same 4-H club.

"I was a little surprised to get your call," she said, greeting me in her office. "Farming never struck me as an interest of yours."

My interest in citrus had blossomed during the last two days but was still secretly fueled by suspicion. Profit, however unlikely, was another motive, thanks to my fishing clients. The Gentrys knew a great deal about genetics and biotech patents.

I accepted a chair, saying, "I raised leghorns my first year in 4-H, then rabbits, but switched to clams. It's what the state wanted us island kids to do, but, fact is, I got so attached to those rabbits, I couldn't bear to sell them to a butcher. Eat a clam, though, it's almost like you're doing them a favor. Can you imagine the monotony of hanging underwater in a bag?"

Roberta had turned into an attractive, confident

woman, yet still had her easygoing manner and farm-girl laugh. "That's why I quit showing Holsteins and took up that—" On the wall, a photo showed her as a teen in the cockpit of a crop-dusting airplane. "We got free lessons, and flying got me interested in Ag science. You know, ways to protect crops without using poisons. There are days, I don't know whether to thank the program or cuss it."

"Four-H, you mean."

"Head, heart, hands, health," she nodded. "I bet you still remember the oath."

We both did; the hand gestures, too. We were still laughing when Roberta pulled an orange from the box I'd brought, then inspected a couple of leaves. "What do we have here?"

"That's sour stock my grandfather planted way back. There're a couple of grapefruits in there, too, I picked on one of the islands. They grow wild, some places."

"Feral citrus," she said, correcting me, while she viewed the leaves under a light. "Well . . . these have a few canker lesions, and some leaf-miner activity—see the wormy-looking tracks? There's psyllid damage, too, but not bad . . . not bad at all. The yellow dragon blotches jump out, if you've toured as many dying groves as I have." She consulted her phone. "That's why I don't have much time. There's a grove near Arcadia I have to inspect. The owner's battling

his butt off to save his crop. He knows this will probably be his last year in business if we don't come up with an answer fast."

Her attention returned to the box while she brought out a paper plate and a knife. "Are you asking if this fruit's okay to eat? Looks okay . . . but there's only one way to find out. Or is there something else on your mind?"

The hall wasn't busy, but the occasional person strolled by. "Can we speak privately?" I asked.

We weren't close friends in school, but Roberta winced as if it pained her to say no. When she began to explain the rules of a state-funded facility, I apologized and moved on. I told her about Kermit's interest in historic Spanish rootstock, and shared the theory about fruit that originated in Asia perhaps being more resistant to insects that also came from Asia.

"I've heard the name before," she said. "He's respected in the industry, but the scientific types, the true brainiacs, tend to dismiss him as a private-sector cowboy. Typical. You wouldn't believe some of the egos in this business. Hilarious, really, how vicious it can get. So I wait, ignore most of what's said, and form my own opinion. You and Kermit must be pretty close, huh?" Roberta, who wore a wedding diamond, had noticed I did not.

"We just met," I said. "Something I didn't make clear is, this isn't Kermit's idea. A friend of mine, a marine biologist, he's the one who came up with it. I just happened to pass it along. Maybe that was a mistake."

Roberta took the possibility more seriously than I expected. "Really? Maybe it was. If there was a list of discoveries made by people out-side their field, it would cover this room." She gave it more thought while halving the orange. "I don't know . . . it seems so simple—too simple, really. Beat an incurable disease by literally returning to the roots of the original tree. Here . . . let's have a look."

She slid the plate toward me, and used a pencil to point. "Aborted seeds are the first thing I look for. These little guys are plump and healthy as can be. This is the calyx button—it's where the stem connects to the center column of the orange. Looks good; no yellow stain, which is typical of HLB. But the leaves have been infected. You saw for yourself. That tells me the disease hasn't had time to affect the fruit—eighteen months is all it takes, which isn't long. You said your great-grandpa planted the tree?"

"Almost a hundred years ago," I said, "but that could be an exaggeration."

"Hmm," she said. "It's possible. Either that or the fruit's more resistant, for some reason. Which is very, very unlikely, Hannah. Still"—she sat back to clean her hands—"it's an interesting angle."

164

"I have some other friends, a retired couple. They felt the idea had probably already been tried and failed. But since you and I have known each other so long, they said why not wrangle a meeting and ask you personally?"

"Nope, this is the first I've heard of going back to the original rootstock," the woman said, and rolled her eyes in a humorous way. "It's a little too obvious for us highly trained experts. The more complex, the better—that's academia for you. In Texas, a lab is trying to splice spinach DNA with citrus genomes . . . I'm serious, by the way . . . Others are infecting periwinkle flowers with HLB to see what happens, then experimenting with penicillin, and some cryptic biocide —I can't pronounce the darn name. Here, we're plodding along with a three-pronged approach: insecticides, supplements, and the equivalent of a dose of aspirin. It's a technique developed by Maury Boyd, a guy literally fighting for his life. It's not perfect. The combination helps, but everyone knows the industry is doomed if we don't find a cure within the next few years." She sighed, then shrugged and got to her feet. "I don't think Spanish rootstock is the answer, but what the heck? I can ask around. Who are these friends of yours again?"

"Actually, they're my clients—I'm a fishing guide now."

"I remember that about you: you liked to

fish. How's it going, you in a business that's traditionally all men?"

"I stay busy; do light tackle, mostly. My clients, the ones who said I should talk to you, they just retired from a company they started. One's an attorney, the other's a scientist, so I figure they know what they're talking about." I paused before adding, "They founded a company called Biotech International."

Roberta's eyes widened at the name—or the word *Biotech*. I'd done a Google search on the Gentrys. They had pioneered the field of bio-technology, so the name and the word were practically synonymous.

I liked her slow smile. It brought a devilish light to her eyes. "Look at you, Hannah Smith. I remember you as the quiet one in the back of the room; a varsity swimmer who played clarinet. What I should have remembered is, you got straight A's. Biotech International— that's as big as it gets."

"One of the things I like about guiding," I said, "is you never know who you'll meet."

"When they got on your boat, did you have any idea who they were?"

"Not until I picked a few wild grapefruits for them and then we started talking about citrus at lunch. The way their faces lit up, I could tell they're already bored with retirement."

"You're serious about this."

"I don't know enough about it to be serious, but they seem serious enough. They're paying a full day's charter fee for every day I spend working on a project they're considering."

"My goodness . . ." She began packing her laptop. "Say—why don't you ride with me to this grove near Arcadia? We can talk more on the way."

The girl who'd once led Holstein cows into a show ring waited until we were in her pickup to say, "Anything we discuss in the office is proprietary, but we can talk freely now—this is my truck. Hannah, let me tell you something. If you get a patent on a bio technique that's even close to something that works—even years from now—you could make millions. Trouble is"— she smiled, still wrestling with the concept—"it won't."

Even so, at a stoplight she asked, "Do you think there's a chance I could actually meet Dr. Gentry and her husband?"

All my life I've lived in Florida, but had never seen oranges processed from start to finish. The owner of the grove was too busy to show me around, and Roberta was too busy doing her job, so I was assigned a guide—when he wasn't busy. Fine with me. It gave me room to piece together things on my own—and also phone Mrs. Gentry to tell her the progress I was making.

The northwest section of the grove—because it was the windward corner, I suspected—had been withered by disease. This left twenty acres of fruit to pick, and several crews were going at it as if they were in a race. In a way, they were. Oranges don't continue to ripen when they hit the ground, they rot. February is peak season. It was profit now . . . or never.

Two-man teams, with red canvas bags over their shoulders or strapped to their belts, hustled a ladder from tree to tree. One man climbed and picked; the other picked, too, while steadying the ladder. When their bags were full, it was a race to semitruck-sized containers at the end of a row. Amid the catcalls and laughter was the combustion hum of open-cab vehicles called goats. (My guide didn't know why.) These were equipped with a large hydraulic scoop that operated like a mechanical arm. The scoops transferred fruit from the containers into waiting open-bed trucks, and off the trucks roared to a nearby processing plant.

As I watched, strolling among the fragrant rows, I noted that each laden tree was connected near the roots to various tubes and sensor wires, not unlike a patient in a hospital's intensive care unit. The grove owner was, indeed, fighting for his economic life.

Citrus trees, at peak sweetness, are also in full bloom. The color contrast of heavy-hanging oranges among blossoms of orchid white was pleasant. The tangy scent first reminded me of orange blossom honey . . . then of the perfume Shalimar. Automatically, I thought of the boathouse, and Kermit. His friendly face and brown eyes floated around in my mind until I saw Roberta striding toward me. It was not the first time since we'd arrived. About every fifteen minutes she had reappeared to continue a back-and-forth argument going on in her head.

I didn't understand what she was talking about but had listened with a feigned intensity as if I did.

Spanish rootstock couldn't possibly make a difference for one simple reason: it no longer existed. On the other hand . . . many citrus varieties were *nucellar*. This meant they might produce clone seedlings. Clone seedlings might be virtually identical to trees first sprouted five hundred years ago.

In the space of one conversation, the woman had gone full circle, first dashing my hopes, then fanning them to life. Now here she was again, determined to impeach her previous conclusion.

"Okay, okay, here's another problem. Not all citrus varieties are nucellar. Some are *zygotic*—two entirely different things. Their seedlings are produced sexually through pollination, so they inherit genetic material from both parent trees. With me so far?"

"I'm not sure," I said, though I was sure—I had no idea what she was getting at.

"But here's what really throws a wrench into the mix: zygotic and nucellar citrus embryos can occur in the very same seed. Isn't that crazy?"

I conceded, "Which is bad news, I guess. Okay, that much I understand."

"No! What I'm saying is, your biologist friend might be right. If—and this is one heck of a big if—if seedlings from the original Spanish stock still exist, they could only be found in a spot so remote that there is zero chance of cross-pollination."

"Now we're getting somewhere," I said. "You're telling me what you call feral citrus— oranges or grapefruit I find on islands that were once farmed—they are definitely not the same as the original Spanish citrus. Is that right?"

"Zero chance," she said. "That doesn't mean older rootstock isn't heartier. It's worth checking into. But, aside from a few feral trees, face it, Florida's too populated for a genetically pure ancestor of those trees to survive."

"Maybe not," I said. "I might know just the place. My uncle and I picked oranges there years ago—if I can find the spot again. It won't be easy. He never used a GPS, or even a chart."

"Not so fast," Roberta countered. "One"— she held up a finger to keep count—"I don't think it's possible the original stock hasn't been genetically altered in some way no matter how remote. Two, aside from the samples you brought, there's no reason to believe older sour rootstock is more resistant to the disease. We've got nothing to compare the samples to. That's the tragedy. Know why? Because after the last big hurricane, some idiots in Tallahassee decided all the old citrus had to be destroyed—including our oldest pioneer trees."

"Roberta, hold on," I said. "I feel like I'm in a Ping-Pong match here. The Gentrys want me to see this thing through, and I will—unless you tell me it's pointless."

"Oh, but I didn't! What gave you that impression?"

I had to smile at the look of innocence on her face. How in the world could I possibly be so confused?

I said, "When the weather improves, I plan on trailering my skiff to Marco Island and do some exploring from there."

"In the Keys or Florida Bay?"

"At the edge of the Everglades," I said, intentionally evasive.

"I understand why you can't be too specific—and I'm not asking—but you need to watch yourself, Hannah. You wouldn't go alone, would you?"

"It's a rare day I don't spend time on the water

on my boat alone," I replied. "Are you offering to go with me?"

"That's not what I mean. I'm talking about the Everglades. I know a couple of rangers and they say the snake population down there has gone insane. They've seen pythons, even some anacondas, that could swallow a man whole."

The imagery she used, and the question I was about to pose, required me to maintain a brave front. "The place I have in mind isn't a saw grass area," I said. "It's more to the west; a back-country, brackish area where mangroves begin at the edge of the Gulf. Or—I'm thinking out loud here—we could tow my skiff and use my bigger boat as a sort of base camp. I live on a thirty-seven-foot Marlow I restored myself. It's really nice inside; plenty of room to sleep two. We could take our time; do an overnight, and anchor off somewhere where the bugs wouldn't be too bad."

It took the woman a moment. "We?"

"I hope so."

"You're inviting me? I don't know what to say."

"I'd invite your husband, too," I said, "but my boat doesn't have that kind of privacy. We need someone who understands citrus, and I'm convinced I don't qualify. I spoke to the Gentrys a few minutes ago. They're all for it. I doubt if we'll make a cent, but you and I would split whatever—"

"Wait . . . you told Dr. Gentry about me? She said it was okay?" Roberta was flattered, this woman who worked in a small government office with a view of tomato fields on the outskirts of tiny Immokalee.

"I call her Mrs. Gentry. She's already read a couple of your research papers."

"You're kidding."

"Nope. What do you think?"

"I'd love to. Of course I would. It's not about the money, although, lord knows, we could use it. But I only get weekends off. How many days would we be gone?"

"Depends on my memory," I replied. "It could take a while. The area I have in mind, there're more mangroves than water, so it might be slow-going in a boat. We can work around your schedule, but it would be nice to have at least three days. Otherwise, there'd be a lot of driving back and forth."

"I've already used up my vacation time," Roberta said, and sounded genuinely disappointed. A little later, she added a couple of more reasons she couldn't go, including lessons of some sort she taught on Sundays.

This seemed to settle the matter.

We went to a nearby processing plant. A foreman equipped us with hard hats, safety glasses, and ID badges. Inside was a noisy assembly line of stainless steel rollers, pumps, and pasteurizing vats, from which exited a robotic battalion of juice cartons, all streaming toward destinations around the world. The building was gymnasium-sized and smelled of Christmas cookies and orange cake.

We left hungry. A short drive away was Mary Margaret's Tea and Biscuit in the old downtown area of Arcadia. The nineteenth-century name matched the décor. I ordered an orange scone, and was sipping hot lemon-lavender tea, when I happened to mention the biologist Marion Ford, who owned a seaplane.

"A plane like his would be ideal for narrowing down the search area," I said, "but the timing's bad. He left on a trip yesterday. No idea when he'll be back. You've never met such a man, when it comes to disappearing."

The long silence that followed caused me to look across the table at Roberta. She was staring at me in mild disbelief. "You said there wasn't much water where you're going."

"There's not. But if the tide's right, there would be enough to land, I suppose."

"Could you afford it?"

"To what, buy a plane?"

"No, rent one for a day. Planes aren't cheap, but I'd be willing to split the fuel just to keep my hours up. As it is, it's a struggle to log enough time to keep my instructor's license. That's what I teach Sundays—flying—to kids in 4-H."

I remembered the photo in her office. "That's nice, giving back to an organization that helped us both, but I don't mean a crop duster. We'd need a plane with floats."

In reply to the woman's matter-of-fact nod, I asked, "Are you telling me you can fly a seaplane?"

We left three days later, a Friday morning; packed everything we could possibly need into a Cessna with pontoons—except one simple item.

That item might have helped save Roberta's life.

Twelve

From a small plane, Marco Island is a mosaic of green fairways and ivory condos that line the beach until the Gulf of Mexico floods inland, making the land uninhabitable. A thousand square hectares of wilderness lie beyond—a vast delta of saw grass and mangroves that separates Miami, on the east coast, from Naples, one hundred miles to the west.

After we had been flying low over swamp for ten minutes, a dappled orange blur grabbed my attention. Roberta circled back. The area seemed about right, so we landed. What appeared to be wild citrus trees might have been dead mangrove leaves. Sacrificial leaves, the yellow ones are called, for it is the tree's way of venting salt—or so some believe.

I was sitting on a pontoon, my feet in the water, and explaining this when Roberta, my new partner, said, "Dang it. I went off and left my machete. You didn't happen to bring an extra, did you?" She was standing next to me, pawing through her bag, which was in the rear of the plane.

"You won't need it as long as you have gloves," I assured her. This was said with the unruffled optimism that is typical of children, and the dangerously naïve. It had been years since I'd been to this isolated spot—if it was the right spot—so I could not fathom how the area had changed, nor what awaited us. We were alone, miles from the nearest boat channel or road, denied even the comfort of a horizon. Here, the sky was choked to darkness by a screen of foliage that, aside from a strip of water, tolerated no swift escape.

"I'll go first," I said, and slipped off the pontoon into the water. I expected to sink into muck. I didn't, for Roberta had found an ideal spot to beach the plane: a shell ramp that angled up to a shell ridge, where the burnished trunks of gumbo-limbo trees promised high ground. Within a few minutes of hiking around, I knew it was the wrong island, but that was okay. I'd been here before as a girl. There were some interesting things to see.

"Let's have a look," I called. "This isn't the place, but we're close. I've got my bearings now."

"Do we need water?"

"We won't be that long, but you might want bug spray."

Already, the silence of lapping water thrummed with the drone of mosquitoes. I wore sleeves, gloves, and long pants. From a Ziploc bag I removed a jacket made of DEET-impregnated netting and pulled it on. Roberta appeared. She was using one hand to swat and carrying a can of Deep Woods OFF! in the other.

"How in the world did people survive in places like this?"

I replied, "A lot didn't. The name isn't on most charts, but I think this is Faka Union Island. People used to farm here."

"Any citrus?" She swatted, and stomped her feet. "Hey—do you mind spraying my back? But don't get any on my skin—that's important. I'll tell you why later."

I took the can and used it carefully. I didn't remember seeing orange trees here, but I had remembered something else. "I'm glad you kept your maiden name—it would have been harder to find you. But I'm curious. The Daniels side of your family—where are they from?"

When she replied "Pennsylvania," I was disappointed, at first, then mildly relieved. I hacked through the brush and found a narrow path, which was a rarity on these backcountry islands. "It crossed my mind this might be upsetting," I said when I'd found what I was looking for. "The Daniels family has been on these islands forever."

Before us, a cluster of tombstones peeked out from an intrusion of cactus and vines. Not stones, really, but thin tablets of cement that had been inscribed with a stick, or a knife, when the cement was fresh. After a few swipes of the machete, I stepped back.

Roberta was drawn to a tiny yellow charm—a canary—embedded in the smallest stone.

James P. Daniels JR
1911–1913
R. I. P.

"He was only two years old," she said. "How sad for a child to die in a place like this." She touched a meditative finger to the canary charm, then stood and looked around, puzzled by something. "Hannah . . . what is that noise?"

The wind moving through bushes, I'd assumed. I tilted my head and focused. Drag the weight of a fire hose slowly, slowly over an expanse of dead leaves, and the sound would be similar. More disconcerting, the activity originated from two . . . possibly, three directions.

"Whatever it is, it's close," I said.

"This isn't where you expected to find oranges, is it?"

I continued trying to ferret out what the noise might be until Roberta pulled my arm to turn me. "Come on. Let's get out of here—I don't like the vibe of this place."

When we were safely buckled into the plane, wearing headphones and voice-activated microphones, we laughed about how spooked we were.

"Like a couple of kids! I was damn near running by the time I saw the water—and me, in my condition."

"Probably raccoons," I said. "The sick ones, they can be weird; slow, like zombies—" I stopped. "What do you mean, 'my condition'?"

"Tell you later." Roberta was using the throttle to taxi us away while she perused the gauges.

I remembered her saying *No bug spray on my skin* and knew what her condition was. It all fit with her concerns about saving money. "Let's head back to Immokalee," I suggested, for that's where the plane was hangared—a little airport east of town used mostly by the crop dusters that lined the tarmac.

"Not already. We've already paid, and there's a four-hour minimum. I thought you said you had your bearings?"

I did. Even from where I sat, I could look through the windshield and triangulate the landmarks my uncle had used to find that secret place long ago. The markers didn't appear on charts, or in GPS software. It might take a full day to find the exact spot, but I knew I could get us close.

"Are you sure?" I asked. "Some of the details are coming back to me. The bottom there is probably all muck. No telling how deep. Climbing off a boat is one thing; but we can't get that close. We'd have to wade ashore. Who knows how many tries it will take us to find that tree. Or *trees*. I can't remember if there was more than one."

"How far?"

"From here? Four, maybe five miles. But now that I think about it, I'm pretty sure the spot is too narrow to land a plane. Why not just fly around; do a search from the air, then come back later in my boat?"

"We're already here," Roberta said in a determined way. "When we're airborne, tell me which way to turn."

Forking into Buttonwood Bay, miles east of Marco, are three tidal rivers that are navigable by small boat, and a fourth river that is not—unless you travel with a man who loves bushwhacking.

That's what I'd remembered as I hiked around Faka Union Island. In the plane, I confirmed my recollections with a chart. Mangroves had sealed the mouth of the fourth river centuries ago—possibly, eons ago—so the average boater couldn't get in. That's why, as a child, the spot had stuck in memory as a narrow bay.

It was my Uncle Jake's favorite place for catching what he called bronze snook. *Bronze* because a lifetime of feeding in tannin-red water had colored their skin that way.

Jake, like many fishermen, was irrationally

territorial, and devious, when it came to protecting a good spot. I don't know how he discovered the remains of a feeder creek that twisted into the river, but he did. He'd returned with a ripsaw and clippers and pruned his way in, foot by foot, pulling me and a skiff behind. His masterstroke was leaving a curtain of mangroves untouched so no one would notice the tunnel he'd cut nor suspect it led to a pristine stretch of water.

"I bet God hasn't been here in a thousand years," Jake had said when we finally broke free into sunlight.

That's the way I remembered the place: no human spoor; palm hammocks and black mangroves a hundred feet high that shaded basins of clear water; rivulets that dropped off, black and deep, near the bank.

"See that tall stretch of trees?" I said into the microphone. "Head for that."

We flew low over the water and turned back. When we did, I spotted a twisting scar in the mangroves. The passage my uncle had cut still existed but was visible only from the air.

"This is it," I said. "See those pods of gumbo-limbo trees? That means high ground, probably shell mounds."

"Which one?"

There were several pods of gumbos along a series of watery switchbacks.

"I don't know, but we picked oranges on one of those mounds. All I remember is how thick the brush was hiking in—you couldn't see the sky for all the thorns and vines. And the birdlife—birds everywhere. There seemed to be egret or ibis nests in every tree. I would've never found this by boat. Even if I had, we'd have had to cut our way in. A canoe is what you'd need."

Roberta replied, "When I'm wrong, I admit it. I didn't think we had a chance in Hades of finding— Hang on . . ." She looked at home wearing earphones, one hand on the yoke while she paused to punch buttons on the GPS. "I'm saving these numbers for when we come back," she explained.

I assumed she meant there wasn't room enough to land, which was a relief. "I told you it was a narrow stretch of water. How much muck, that's the big question. I've heard of places, you sink to the waist. People can't free their legs because of the suction, so they—"

"There's plenty of room to land," she cut in, her focus back on flying the plane. "What I meant was, you were right. There's nothing around here but swamp and saltwater for miles in every direction. If the Spaniards planted citrus, there might be clones—and there's not much chance they've cross-pollinated with modern trees. Wouldn't that be cool?"

We landed.

• • •

The first spot we tried was deceptively easy. Roberta stayed with the plane. I slogged in alone, thinking it was the fastest way to check an area where several shell hillocks dotted the mangroves. Muck was ankle-deep for twenty yards before I hacked my way inland for a quick look.

"This might take a while," I said when I got back. I climbed onto a pontoon and sat for a moment, breathing heavily. "The hardest part isn't getting through the mangroves; it's cutting through to high ground. First there's a wall of catbriers, and there're so many strangler figs—those prop roots they drop? It was like squeezing through bars. And mosquitoes— my lord, they're worse than the last place."

"No signal," Roberta said, looking at her iPhone. "Why am I not surprised?" She placed it on the dash and looked past me through the open door. "I don't see any bird nests. In fact . . . I don't see any birds. You said there were ibis and egret nests everywhere. I wonder what happened?"

Odd . . . I had noticed the same thing, but only as awareness that something—I wasn't sure what—was wrong about this place. No birds. No raccoon scat, or even gopher tortoise holes, had I seen. Their presence would have been dismissed as commonplace. Their absence, however, had registered in my subconscious as shadow knowledge—a potential warning.

A tendril of breeze furrowed the water's surface. The rented plane swung a few degrees in search of air.

"You're okay standing on the pontoon," Roberta said when I was holding on to a strut, then yelled, "Clear!" and she started the engine.

The next low rise was around a serpentine bend. Our prop kicked spray; pontoons flooded a wake ahead of us. Among the flotsam we pushed to the bank was proof that feral citrus grew here. I'm not sure who saw it first, but we both yelled, "There's an orange!" at the exact same instant, so precisely in sync that we were laughing when Roberta killed the engine. All the while, we stared with affection at that solitary piece of fruit. It bobbed along beside us, just out of reach, then disappeared beneath a wall of leafy green.

"Now all we have to do is find the tree," I said.

I set a small anchor while Roberta did another search through her bags, her movements quicker because she was excited. "Wish to heck I'd brought that machete. Oh well, doesn't matter. I'm going in this time. I don't care how thick it is—I can't let you get all the credit when we win the Nobel Prize. What do you think it'll feel like to be rich?"

Here, in this remote place, money didn't matter.

The missing machete did. I had no idea how much—or, perhaps, I sensed the importance, but, again, in the back of my mind. It was a niggling awareness of danger that was signaled not by the presence of wild creatures but by their absence, and by the encroaching gloom of shadows and black water.

I said, "Why don't you stay with the plane—just until I'm sure it's okay."

Roberta's head reappeared above the seat. "What do you mean, 'okay'? Did you see something?"

Not one living thing had I seen. "Could be gators around," I said. "That's all I meant. We don't want to both be halfway to shore if a gator surfaces."

"In saltwater?"

"Sometimes. Or a croc. There's probably nothing to worry about, but why not be extra-careful now that"—I stopped before mentioning her pregnancy—"now that we've found what we're looking for?"

She didn't notice my near slip. "Geez, talk about a nightmare scenario. A gun is what I should have brought. Hey"—the girl who had once led show cows into an arena grinned—"are you actually worried or just trying to scare me?"

The words of my friend Birdy, the deputy sheriff, were replaying in my head: *Always carry. Always, always, always . . .*

Yet, I said, "A gun's the last thing we need, flying around in an airplane."

I slipped off the pontoon and tested the bottom before risking my full weight. It felt as springy as clay. I'd cut a walking stick at the last stop. I speared it ahead of me and took a long, sliding stride, as if skiing. In my fanny pack was a trowel for digging seedlings and a large net bag for storing oranges. In my right hand was a machete I'd taken from my uncle's toolshed. It was old, with a leather wrist thong, the blade as long as my arm and very, very sharp. After another sliding step, I became more confident. I'd feared the springy bottom was a false crust, but it seemed okay.

"I'll bring water and the bug juice," Roberta hollered. "I've got that little camp shovel, too, and some other stuff we might need."

I glanced back and saw that she was already in the water, hip-deep, with the plane floating high on its pontoons behind her. The shoulder pack she was lugging looked heavy. When on foot, I prefer to travel light. Two trips can be faster than one if the terrain is rough, but, outdoors, companions must be allowed to make up their own minds.

I quickened my pace. What I'd said was true: it was unwise for us both to be in the water at the same time. A few steps later, the bottom softened and began to fall away. Rather than resume my sliding technique, I lunged toward shore, which was only a few body lengths ahead. It was a mistake. Beneath my feet, the rubbery crust broke. A step later, I sunk to my knees in a pudding of muck, the first low branches of the mangroves just out of reach.

I turned and called to Roberta, "Go back, there's no bottom here."

Too late. She was already bogged down because of the heavy pack on her shoulder. Nor did she have the advantage of a walking stick. I watched her struggle for balance, then she made a humorous whooping sound and fell forward with a great splash. My friend floundered for a moment—more wild splashing—and righted herself, her hair dripping and both arms black to the elbows with mud. "Next time, I'll learn to listen to you," she laughed.

I called, "Get rid of that pack—we'll find it later. Are you stuck?" As I spoke, I yanked my right boot free. The effort suctioned my left leg deeper.

Roberta was having the same problem. "Geez . . . Dang it all! This is like trying to walk through glue. Do you think it would be better to crawl? You know, distribute the weight . . . Whoops!"

Again, she splashed forward, but was still in good spirits when she was upright again. She started to say, "I wish we had video of this because—" then stopped abruptly, her attention suddenly on something in the water to the right. I watched her expression go slack; her face drained ghostly pale. She attempted to speak through parted lips but couldn't find words until instinct reverted to a child's high-pitched wail. "Oh my god," she screamed, "Hannah, what . . . what the hell is that?"

It was an alligator, I thought at first. No . . . the creature swimming toward her sailed too smoothly atop the water's silver veneer. Gators ride low. This animal swam with its head up, as high and motionless as the prow of a Viking ship, while its body, fifteen feet long and as wide as my thigh, carved a curving, escalator wake.

It was a snake—a giant Burmese python. Ford, my biologist friend, had provided the name. Only twenty yards of water separated Roberta from the snake's insect eyes and vectoring tongue.

"Dump that pack!" I hollered. "Get on your belly and crawl to the plane."

She tried but only sank deeper. "Hannah, what should I . . . ? Shit . . . I'm stuck. Goddamn it—do something. Throw me your machete! Oh Jesus Christ, it sees me—hurry . . ."

Panic helped me bust my left leg clear of the muck. I fell forward. I wrestled my right boot free. I fell forward again on my hands and knees. Survival instinct sent me crawling toward the trees. Then Roberta screamed another sickening plea for help—help from God, this time. Not me. I spun around. The python was there. It had stopped, its eyes at eye level with my friend's face. A flicking tongue scanned her body for heat—two beating mammalian hearts thudded within. Roberta stared back at the snake's massive head. She was panting, frozen, and still holding that damn pack instead of the machete she needed.

A microsecond later, the snake acted. The speed of its strike didn't register. The thunk of fangs hitting bone did. Then the length of the reptile was on her; a writhing, coiled mass that boiled the water, and silenced a squealing plea that possessed no words.

Thirteen

When the python struck, I yelled something, no telling what, it all happened in such a blur. I belly flopped toward Roberta, then scrambled and crawled through mud, slowing only when I was close enough to know there was no turning back.

Rational thought played no role in what I did. My friend's screams and wild thrashing were like an electric prod. The snake was too big to coil its entire length around Roberta yet tried to by swinging its tail section like a bullwhip in search of something more to grab onto. I lunged, got an arm around the animal's girth—and was vaulted high out of the water, then slammed down into mud. I surfaced, fearing I'd lost the machete. But, no . . . the leather thong had kept it on my wrist.

I staggered up, anchored my feet in the muck, and waited, the machete poised above my head . . . waited for the tail section to writhe past me again. My god . . . the thing was huge. As thick as a log, so I used both hands and swung as if chopping wood. The snake's back was a diamond pattern of yellow and black scales. When cleaved by steel, the skin split like a sausage, but the blade snagged for a sickening instant in bone. I pulled the blade free and swung again and again, missing a couple of times, but often the machete bit deep. My frenzy was such that it blinded me to the python's head. Only at the last instant did the snake's open jaws rocket into peripheral vision—not in time to stop the thing from burying its fangs just above my left elbow.

I went down beneath a relentless, seeking weight. The mesh bug jacket I wore became a tourniquet around my wrist. The snake spun; its teeth became a fulcrum. Desperately, I pulled the jacket over my head and wiggled my body free—all but my left arm. The snake's head was tangled in the mesh. No . . . its teeth. The python had released me for some reason but could not free itself. We were locked in a gruesome tug-of-war that I was doomed to lose until Roberta, thank god, reappeared. She grabbed my belt, screaming, "Give it to me . . . give me the machete—I'll kill that son of a bitch."

She would have done it, too, but the mesh snapped at that instant. We both sprawled sideways into the water, then stumbled and staggered, in a panic, helping each other toward safety. We didn't look back until we'd reached the plane.

The python was swimming away but on a confused course. My mind was slow to understand what had happened. The animal's head was tangled in a ball of mesh—a jacket that had been impregnated with mosquito repellant. Chunks of its tail were attached only by skin because of the wounds I'd inflicted.

I pulled anchor; Roberta had to hop back in the water to spin the plane around so we could take off. Not until the doors were closed did we think about injuries. Wheezing, "Oh my god . . . Oh my god," she stripped off her shirt and shorts, but her focus was on her abdomen, which was streaked with mud and yellow leaves. "Do you see any marks . . . teeth marks? Find something I can use as a towel. Oh Jesus, I can't believe this is happening."

I grabbed a bottle of water and an extra shirt from the back. While saying the reassuring things people do, I gently cleaned her belly until we could see there were no visible injuries.

"Scooch around," I said, and checked her back, too. No cuts, or even scrapes, but there was a red, serrated welt across her shoulders as if she'd been slapped with a belt.

"Do you hurt anywhere else? What about your ribs?"

Roberta asked, "How about my lower back, near the kidneys? All I remember is not being able to breathe, that I would drown. My shoulders —it was like being crushed in a vise. But the water, that's what saved me. The snake couldn't seem to find the rest of me because my legs were underwater. I kept kicking."

"No cuts," I said, then asked again about her ribs.

"I don't know, I didn't hear anything crack. That slimy sonuvabitch! It bit you, Hannah, I saw it. Let's have a look at your arm."

A first-aid kit came out while I rolled up my left sleeve, for I was bleeding. We were both in shock. Neither could be sure what had happened. Roberta guessed the snake had struck her shoulder pack when she had lifted it as a shield—the same pack containing the camping shovel I'd ordered her to abandon.

"You should see a doctor anyway," I said. By then, she had her clothes on and had started the plane.

"A psychiatrist, more like it," she replied, "if we ever come back to this fucking place— without shotguns, at the very least. Oh my god, Hannah . . ."

"Now what?"

"Right there! Look at the size of that bastard." She ruddered the plane around to give me a view out the starboard window.

A second python had appeared, swimming in pursuit of the wounded snake. This reptile was longer and heavier, with a head the size of a Doberman. I fumbled with my phone and managed a single, blurry photo while Roberta applied throttle, saying, "Screw it. We're getting the hell out of here."

• • •

Adrenaline can be a stimulant or a depressant. When we were airborne, there was no wild chatter, no nervous laughter. We each settled into ourselves, isolated by residual fear. Through the window, I watched the shadow of our rental plane cross miles of saw grass. It wasn't until we were ten minutes from landing that I said, "You've got to promise me you'll see a doctor."

When wearing headphones, speaking into the stem of a voice-activated microphone, there is always a delay.

"You, too," she said. "There's no telling what kind of germs were in that thing's mouth. At least let me do a better job of dressing it. We'll need sterile gauze and medical antiseptic."

I said, "Most doctors keep that stuff handy, so how about this? Call when you get a signal and I'll drive you straight to the closest clinic. With a story like ours, doctors would wait in line. You can have your pick of obstetricians."

Roberta realized I knew about her condition. "You're a smart one. Was it because I was worried about bug spray?"

"That and your mood swings," I said, hoping to lighten the mood. "Thank god, I was with a pregnant woman. No one else would be crazy enough to charge into that mess and ask for the loan of my machete."

That got a smile, at least. "I just found out—my first trimester. I must've snapped."

"Snapped?" I said. "You went batshit crazy."

Suddenly, we were both laughing as if we really were crazy.

"Damn right I did," Roberta said. "Never, ever squeeze a constipated woman with sore boobs—although, who knows, maybe it helped. I haven't felt a cramp or the need to pee since the damn thing nearly crushed me to death. I'm afraid to check my panties."

I roared at that, while she added, "I have a sonogram on Monday, but, yeah, you're right—we both need to get checked out."

Her smile faded. My friend waited through some air traffic garble, staring straight ahead, serious again. "I froze back there. That's what really happened and I'm embarrassed. The thing wanted to kill me. Crush the life out of me and swallow me—my baby, too. That . . . that filthy sonuvabitch, and it would have if it hadn't been for you. Hannah"—she glanced over—"there's something I want to talk about when we get on the ground."

We were conversing on an intercom system, so privacy wasn't the problem.

"Swear all you want to, I don't care. After what we just went through?"

"It's about my husband." she said. "And the Spanish oranges. I want to be involved, but I can't go back there. Ever, ever, ever. He'd go nuts. Python Island, the place should be called."

"Constrictor Bay," I suggested. "No . . . Choking Creek. That's what it is, a narrow river, because of the way mangroves crowd in, and the mood of the place, that sulfur smell. Didn't you find it hard to breathe?"

The look she gave me replied *No shit.* "You can't go back, either. Not alone, you can't. So let's figure out an alternative. You said you know other places where feral citrus grows?"

"Islands that *used* to be farmed," I said, "all within an easy ride from my dock. But I wouldn't call them remote—not compared to where we just came from."

"Thank god. I'm thinking maybe sour rootstock from the last century would do. All I need are samples, lots of samples, and plenty of good photos, plus some other information. I can teach you how—if you're willing."

"Split up the workload," I said. "Good idea. You shouldn't be bouncing around in a boat anyway."

My pal from high school gave me an appreciative look. Some of her confidence returned. "What we have to do is, we have to find a couple more feral trees that are resistant to the disease. If they're resistant. Maybe they are, maybe they aren't. That's only the first step, because—well, there are a lot of factors. DNA testing might show there's a significant difference between . . . Hang on a sec." She reached, changed radio frequencies, and contacted Immokalee Regional to advise them we were inbound.

"Call your obstetrician," I said when she was done. "We'll talk about it on the way."

Choking Creek. The name settled into my head as we landed.

The waiting room at Immokalee Pediatric Clinic was full, but the receptionist hurried us in when she heard our story. Unfortunately, people sitting near the window heard, too. Roberta's doctor wasn't on call, so a staff M.D. took her to a separate examining room while a male nurse tended to me.

"I've never seen a python bite," he said. "You sure it was a python?"

"Unless you know of another snake that's fifteen feet long and tries to crush you . . ." I reached for my phone. "I might have a picture."

I did. It was a blurry shot framed by the seaplane's window. The nurse, looking over my shoulder, said, "Holy shit. That looks more like the Loch Ness Monster. They swim with their heads up?"

"Those trees in the background," I said, "are black mangroves or buttonwoods. See how thick the trunks are? That gives you some idea of the size. The snake's girth, at least. This isn't the one that bit me. This one's bigger by about half."

"My god. Mind if I see that?" The nurse took the phone and zoomed in, saying, "I weigh a little over two hundred pounds, and this thing could swallow me whole. Did you contact the sheriff's department or the FWC? You should. A snake that targets people needs to be destroyed. Where, exactly, did it happen?"

Until then, I had considered the possibility that, by seeking medical help, I might have to reveal the location of my uncle's secret spot. "East of Marco Island," I said. "All those islands look the same. It would be hard to say for sure."

That seemed to satisfy the nurse. "In the Everglades, yeah," he said. "I've read pythons have killed off just about everything, so I guess we shouldn't be surprised, huh? You know—surprised they're going after hikers. Or were you fishing?"

"Exploring," I said, switching off my phone. "Our mistake was trying to wade ashore."

He changed gloves, lowered a magnifying visor, and focused a lamp on my bicep. "Hmm . . . looks more like a bobcat tried to sink its claws but couldn't get a good hold. You're one lucky girl, know that? I'll numb you up—a debridement brush is no fun, believe me. When's the last time you had a tetanus shot?"

Roberta was still with the doctor when I was done, so I decided to wait in my SUV. A woman who looked too old to need a pediatrician followed me out. Gray-haired, dressed for golf in shorts and a yellow blouse. She was animated and chatty, which seemed okay because she did volunteer work as an advocate for migrants who came annually to pick tomatoes, melons, and citrus. "I couldn't help overhearing what happened," she said. "A python, of all things. My goodness, that had to be terrifying. What I worry about is children who live on the out-skirts. Some parents let them run around wild—or they're both working and can't afford child care. How far from here did it happen?"

The woman was pleasant, articulate in a probing, gossipy way, but she cared about a segment of the population that, for most, remains comfortably invisible. In my eagerness to reassure her, I let my guard down and slipped into an easygoing seesaw of questions and answers. I didn't realize my mistake until she said, "I sure hope Mrs. Daniels is okay. Was she bitten, too?"

"You know Roberta?"

"My husband's family has been in the citrus business since I don't know how long. She wouldn't remember me. My husband—Elmer Lee Ogden is his name—we were both widowed and met only two years ago. Now we split our time between my condo on Marco and his ranch. I have to admit, when he told me Immokalee, I cringed, which only proves how little I knew about Florida. It's some of the most beautiful country you've ever seen. Why don't you come visit some afternoon?"

She produced a card. Abigail was her name. We chatted a while longer, then she returned inside to check on a teenage mother she was helping.

I didn't mention the woman until Roberta was in my SUV and had assured me she was okay. According to the doctor, there was no need for an emergency sonogram, her Monday appointment would do.

"Elmer Ogden has the biggest grove south of the Tamiami Trail," she said. "I wouldn't worry about it. Did you tell her why we were down there?"

"No, just that we were exploring. But her husband might wonder why you were involved. I didn't say exactly where, of course."

"That, I would keep secret—but you don't think we can keep the rest secret, do you? I'm a plant pathologist, not an expert on rootstock. There are at least half a dozen people I'll need to ask questions or for advice. They won't know how to help unless I explain myself. And we need to visit some groves before you start collecting. In fact"—she reached for Abigail's card, which I'd placed on the console—"Mr. Ogden might be a good place to start. He's a gentleman, very countrified in a sweet way, but don't let him fool you. You don't get rich on a thousand acres of cattle and citrus without being smart. He's stubborn, too—stubborn enough to not cut down his pioneer citrus just because some bureaucrats ordered him to do it."

I asked, "Is that true?" I was thinking of another stubborn man, Harney Chatham.

"It's what I'm hoping. Every grove in Florida has some sign of psyllid infestation. If there're pioneer trees on Ogden's property and they show the same resistance as your grandfather's citrus, that means something. Healthy feral citrus on an island doesn't. Not for certain anyway. Could be the insects haven't found those trees yet."

"In central Florida," I said, "there are a lot of stubborn men and women who come from old-time families. Particularly between Arcadia and Sebring. There are big stretches of wild country, so we might have to rent the plane again. I'll make a list of names. Is that what you're thinking?"

"Interesting," she said. "It didn't cross my mind, but I like the idea. Mostly what I'm thinking is, this might be my one chance to make some real money. Enough for a college fund and to pay off the mortgage—maybe even pay off *my* college loans. I took today as a sick day and I've got the weekend off. I want to keep after this thing."

"You still owe money for school?"

She winced in a way that pained me. "Almost a hundred grand to get my Ph.D.—that's double what I make in a year. Now with the baby coming? It's wishful thinking, I know, but how many people claim to have a great idea but don't follow through? We might be on to something, Hannah. I really think there's a chance. So, yeah . . . visit every old-time grove you can find."

In a determined way that was familiar, she added, "We're already here. Why not call your new friend, Abigail Ogden?"

I did, but not before saying, "I'll call everyone I know, but we start tomorrow. First, I need a long shower to get the stink of muck and snakes off me."

Fourteen

It had been fifteen days since I'd heard from Kermit Bigalow, and a week since Roberta had exited her sonogram appointment with a smile on her face. A lot had happened, most of it good, so my guard was down, and it seemed okay when, on a windy Sunday morning, Kermit's name flashed on my phone.

"Don't hang up," he said the instant I answered. "You have no idea how many times I've stopped myself from calling, but this is important. And strictly business, so give me a chance. Okay?"

Rather than start the conversation with a question about him stealing my uncle's orange tree, I asked, "Did Sarah get her sketchbook?" More than a week ago, I had mailed it, and some other things I thought she might like, to Reggie's home, with a separate card asking the little chauffeur to pass the package along.

"She's about worn out that DVD on manatees. Very sweet of you, and she keeps asking when we can visit again. Or live on a boat instead of in a house. Funny, what sticks in a kid's mind, huh?"

Through the windshield of my cabin cruiser, the glass streaked with salt, the bay was a froth of wind and waves. "The weather we've had this week might change her mind," I said. "What sort of business is it you want to discuss, Kermit?"

"So formal—you're still mad." This he said in a gentle way as if hurt.

"You've done what I asked, why would I be? What you're hearing is, I'm a little late for" —it seemed a pious affectation to reveal my destination, which was church, so I said—"an appointment," and blamed the wind, which was true. Chapel-By-The-Sea, on Captiva, was only a few miles by boat but more than an hour's drive by car. It would be another day before the water was calm enough for fishing.

"Then I'll get right to it," he said. "Have you seen Lonnie Chatham yet? I think she's on her way there now. Or she'll call you, I'm not sure. But whatever she does, whatever she says, don't believe her. Can I stop by tonight?"

"What in the world are you talking about?" I said, opening the cabin door. He'd spoken in such a rush, I wasn't convinced I'd heard him correctly but checked anyway for an unfamiliar car outside Loretta's house. In the drive was a white SUV—a Lexus, it looked like—which is something a wealthy woman would buy. I went up the steps to the dock with the phone to my ear.

"Kermit, I can't talk now. If my mother tangles with Lonnie, she might have another stroke."

"Hannah, listen! Her attorneys have locked me out of everything—our house, even my office.

205

My wife's a mess, and Sarah's upset, too. It'll be okay. I've already got another job lined up, but . . . Well, I need to tell you about something in person. I'll see you around sunset, okay? Please. I need your help." After a long silence, he added, "Hannah . . . *Beautiful?* Are you still there?"

That word again.

I couldn't think clearly, so replied, "I can't talk now," and hung up.

Getting out of the Lexus was a man wearing a gray suit, with a gray ponytail that hung between shoulders wide enough to suggest he was a weight lifter or a pro wrestler. Not tall, but thick as a bulldozer. A graying Hemingway beard, and a copper bracelet, added to the effect. He stooped, retrieved a briefcase, and started toward the house. Thank god, Loretta was getting dressed, not lounging on the porch.

"Can I help you?" I called.

"If you're Hannah Smith, the fishing guide, yes you can." He sounded Cuban, which is commonplace in Florida; his voice, a resonate baritone.

"My number's easy enough to find if you're here to talk about a charter," I said. "As it is, I was just leaving for, uh . . . a place I need to be."

His eyes did a slow pan, up and down, taking in my short herringbone jacket, gray blouse, and black skirt. I was barefoot—heels had to wait until I was in my car—but he was polite enough to pretend not to notice. "Myself, I attend early Mass, but twice in one day might do me good—doesn't matter which church. May I drive you? We can talk on the way."

By then, I was close enough to confirm the Lexus did not contain Lonnie Chatham, and took a breath. "I don't know who you are or why you're here," I said. "It's a silly rule I have about getting into cars with strangers."

The Hemingway beard matched the face and his wide, wry smile. "Did Harney give you that lecture, too?"

Harney. Aside from Loretta, I didn't know anyone who'd been on a first-name basis with the late lieutenant governor.

"You were friends?"

"Better. We were confidants." This was said with the inflection used by those who take the word seriously.

"I didn't see you at the funeral last week."

"Nor did I see you—or your mother. I suppose that's because none of us wanted to draw attention. Isn't that right? Sometimes, it's better to blend in."

I couldn't argue with that. Loretta and I had stood among trees, far from Mr. Chatham's casket of mahogany, while a hundred people in suits and black dresses kept their backs to us, listening to the minister read their good-byes.

The man said, "I have a business proposition, Captain—that's what Harney called you, by the way: Captain Hannah. Now I can see why. It's the way you handle yourself, I think, not just because you're tall and . . . by god, attractive, too. I thought he might have been exaggerating about your looks."

A man who used his age to camouflage flirting as harmless fun. With him, maybe it was.

I remained blank-faced while he handed me his card. I was speaking with Sabin Martinez, of Brickell Avenue, Miami, with a second office on Disney Way, Orlando.

I slipped the card into my jacket. "It doesn't say what you do."

"No, it does not," he replied. His voice had an elegance even while slamming doors. "My offer still stands. You don't want to be late to church."

I wasn't getting in the Lexus no matter who he claimed to know. "Are you here because of Mr. Chatham? Or his wife? A friend just called and said she wanted to contact me, for some reason."

"Lonnie? I'll be darned."

He shunned profanity, I noted—or, at least, was careful about it.

"You weren't aware?"

"I've never met the second Mrs. Chatham. It's one of the few mistakes Harney made, I think." He toyed with his copper bracelet, and let me ponder that, before adding, "You'll like what I have to say. It won't take long. Harney trusted me with—how should I put it?—*delicate* matters. Come on . . . You can even drive, if you like."

I looked from the house to the Lexus, then at the dock. "I can spare ten minutes," I said, "but we'll talk here, not in your car. If that's not acceptable, it'll have to wait."

The man followed me to my boat.

I memorized the plate on the Lexus as it pulled away. Only then did I remember church and that I was late—too late for heavy Sunday traffic. Cars would be backed up for a mile on the causeway to Sanibel.

Truth was, I was a little dazed after thirty minutes of listening to Sabin Martinez. Once again, intuition told me I could trust the man—he was a churchgoer, like me, and we had a respected friend in common. But tragedies that had befallen my three namesake aunts urged caution.

On the other hand, the thick leather satchel Martinez had given me was real. So were the contents.

Call me if you need help with anything, he'd said as he left. *Anything. I'm a problem solver from way back.*

What I needed was someone to help organize the thoughts spinning through my head. I also needed to make up my mind about church.

Driving to Captiva was out of the question. If I was to get there in time, I'd have to cross three miles of rough water by boat. Attendance wasn't mandatory, of course, but I am happier if my week is grounded by ceremonies attached to my faith. It is a personal matter. I don't push religion on people, nor do I shy away if derided by the arrogant few who view faith as a childish cliché.

There was another option. Aboard my boat, I jotted down the license number of the Lexus, then carried the satchel across the road, up the hill, to the house. Loretta was getting ready to attend services with her friends at Foursquare Gospel. Every Sunday, she awaited the church bus like a child eager to attend school. When she came out of the bathroom, I said, "How about I call Mrs. Hendry and the girls and drive you, for a change? With this wind, I'd be soaked through by the time I got to Captiva."

"The girls" is how she often referred to her three widow friends.

My mother and I had been at denominational odds for years, so I didn't expect a cheery acceptance. "You might be disappointed," she said, returning to the mirror for a final look. "We don't play guitars and worship crystals— or whatever it is you do at that hippie church. You'd have to actually bow your head in prayer. And sit with common folks, too, not your rich beach-people clients. I wouldn't want to put you out." Her eyes locked onto the leather satchel. "What you got there?"

I wanted to wait until after church. Her friends were all solid and sweet, but, as people age, gossiping becomes a favorite vocation. I tested the water by saying, "Did Mr. Chatham ever mention a man by the name of Sabin Martinez?"

"Why would he introduce me to a Mexican?" she asked. "True, he had a fondness for illegal citizens, and other outlaws, but you know I don't speak Spanish."

I said, "Mr. Martinez is Cuban, I believe, but that's not what I asked. He claimed he was a close friend of Mr. Chatham's. Do you remember hearing the name?"

She remained fixated on the satchel. "Maybe. Depends on what's inside there. If you've got Mexicans bringing you presents, dear, I should know before allowing contraband into my house. If it's a new purse, keep it. You might like masculine things, but it's not pretty enough for me. Now, go wash your hands."

I gave her the satchel. "What's in there is confidential—that's what he told me. You know what that means, Loretta. You can't tell the girls, or anybody else, until Mr. Martinez says it's okay. Are you sure you've never heard of the man?"

"Who? I told you, I don't speak Spanish." She

unzipped the bag, looked in, then looked up at me. Her wild blue eyes took on a glow. "My lord . . . is this all mine?"

I was smiling at her. "Most of it," I said. "There are two envelopes in there with legal documents —but only copies. It's complicated. The will Mr. Chatham left when he died has to go through a probate proceeding, and some other stuff. It all has to be done and read to his heirs within thirty days of his death. That's the law, which means there're less than two weeks left. But his wife got a look at his will somehow. She's already hired an attorney to fight for what she thinks is rightfully hers. Mr. Martinez came to warn us in advance."

My mother's face colored. "That pom-pom cheerleader harlot. She's contesting my inheritance?"

"Loretta, don't tell me you actually expected anything."

"Why wouldn't I? I put in a lot more miles than she ever logged. That woman only wanted one thing from Harney, and it wasn't kept between his legs or his ears, neither. Liked to broke that man's spirit, she did. Is it any wonder he come crawlin' back to me for solace? It was that slut who killed him—not his new thingamabob, which is quite an invention, I'll tell you. Or them blue pills."

The medical examiner had listed the cause of

death as cardiac arrest, perhaps exacerbated by conflicting medications.

"Let's not get into that," I said, and carried the satchel to the kitchen counter. Inside were stacks of hundred-dollar bills, some stiffened by salt-water. This suggested they dated back to the pot-hauling years. "Ten thousand dollars. He wanted us to have this up front. He knew there'd be legal fees—if Mr. Martinez told me the truth."

One by one, Loretta was sliding five stacks her way. "Of course he told the truth. A man like Mr. Martinez wouldn't lie to us. Sometimes, Hannah, I worry about your suspicious nature. It ain't fair to judge others, least ye be judged— that's Scripture, by the way. You'd know that if you attended a real church. As to legal fees, do what you want with your money, but I ain't givin' mine to no damn lawyer."

I clenched my teeth until I had calmed. "You might change your mind when you see this." I opened an envelope. "He left us his hunting cabin and a hundred acres of citrus. You, me, and Reggie; divided equally. Then we get into some complicated areas that an attorney—"

"Salt Creek Gun Club?" she interrupted. She'd spent time there; I could tell by her dreamy expression. "That's the prettiest place there ever was. That river path, where the moss hangs so soft and cool? Many's the time I told Harney we

213

should be . . . we should be buried—" Her voice broke; she grabbed the second envelope and ripped it open and quickly regained control. "This must be for me, too. By god, this is better than Christmas."

The envelope was addressed in masculine pencil to *Darling Lorrie*—Loretta's nickname used only by the former lieutenant governor. In it were dozens of photographs—the oldest, black-and-white prints with scalloped borders. Thirty years of photo technology was in that stack, including faded Polaroids, and color shots so bright, they looked as if they'd been painted. My mother got through a few, saying, "Here's me and Harney at the first moon launch . . . Here we are in Times Square . . . This here was took in a country I can't pronounce—no . . . it was Paris. Yep, by the Arch of Trumpets. I can tell by the pigeons."

"Paris," I said. "In Europe? Where was I while you were jet-setting around?"

"Damned if I know—probably on a camping trip with your Uncle Jake. You expect me to stay housebound while you're out having fun? Thick as thieves, you two—and never did thank me for that tent I patched so you'd have a place to sleep. Neither one, even a word."

My jaw tightened again while her quivering hands chose another photo. "Aw . . . this was Christmas at the Biltmore. You wouldn't know the name—it's a big, expensive hotel in Asheville. Don't Harney look fine in that suit? That's where he . . . that's where Harney . . . where we went after the first time he proposed . . ."

My mother's emotions got the best of her then. She gave a great, shuddering yawn, then broke down, sobbing. I got an arm around her and sat her on the couch. With me, I brought the photo taken years ago at the Biltmore Hotel. While I held her close, I looked into my mother's secret past. Mr. Chatham had been a big, confident man with curly hair and a *Don't cross me* smile. Loretta, who was now a little bird of a thing, had once been a beautiful woman. Proud of it, too, judging from her fashionable jeans and tight snow-bunny sweater. On her face was a sly, territorial smile, her lover's hand cupping the underside of her breast. I might have been looking at the photo of a woman I'd never met.

Strange how the eye is tricked more often by memory than light.

I said, "Go freshen your makeup. The girls will get on the church bus if I don't call them soon. You still want to go to church, don't you?"

She sniffed, and rubbed her eyes. "Every Sunday, I ask the Lord for forgiveness—all the sins Harney and me committed over so many years. I don't know why I bother. I truly don't. The Lord, He knows what's really in my heart, and, truth is, I don't regret one single moment I spent with that man. Not one, Hannah. In fact— you really want the truth?—my only regret is, there were times we could'a been together, but I said no out of conscience. All those lost moments of happiness we could have shared! You don't think God knows? He does. So today, I'll put a hundred-dollar bill in the plate, and buy the girls pizza. You go on, dear. There's no need to drive us."

What Loretta meant was, she didn't want the awkwardness of having her daughter around when she had so much good news—and five thousand dollars—to share with her friends.

I said, "At least let me help you with your makeup. It looks like you've been crying coal dust."

Fifteen

When the door to the church bus hissed shut, I headed for the dock but stopped halfway. The black catamaran skiff was drifting just off the channel, while the driver leered at me over his Yosemite Sam mustache. When he was sure I saw him, he thrust out his arms, as if inviting a tango partner, and yelled something about cold weather, then, "Wanna dance instead?"

His name was Larry Luckheim, according to my deputy friend Birdy, who had shared the information over a glass of wine. He'd moved to the area from Canada via Okeechobee, where the Bass Pro circuit had dumped him for cheating. Quaaludes might have also played a role. Now he was fishing light tackle out of Placida and trying to rebuild his reputation as *Buddy Luck, Native Guide*.

Birdy had told me some other details as well. Twice, women had filed restraining orders against him. There'd been several assault charges related to bar fights, and a court order had mandated two weeks of psychological evaluation. It was three months before Luckheim was released. Bipolar disorder, was the vague diagnosis.

Equally as disturbing, Birdy's background

check turned up zero information prior to the man's twenty-fifth birthday. No driver's license or voter's registration, and no arrests.

On the bright side, it was illegal for Luckheim to buy, own, or possess a firearm.

What Birdy didn't have to tell me was, the man was a bully. I strode toward him, determined to establish the boundaries of my personal world—the dock, my skiff, and the boat that was beginning to feel like home.

"I bet you're more of the clogger type, aren't you?" he hollered. "You've got the look of hillbillies and whiskey in those legs of yours. Oh . . . and catfish. I bet you're death itself on saltwater cats."

I ignored him, while battling to keep my skirt down and my demeanor aloof despite the fact I was barefoot.

"Hey, I found my copy of *Florida Sportsman*. Those pictures don't do you justice, but at least you were wearing shoes. Hell . . . I'll buy you shoes—if you give me your autograph, and let me take you dancing."

He twirled an invisible partner and attempted a sultry look as "they" dipped. The effect was grotesque.

This was not the first man I'd dealt with who was jealous of magazine pieces written about me, a woman guide who taught fly casting and whose clients had won tournaments. Thanks to good photography—and, for all I know, Photoshop—the stories had gotten a lot of attention, most of it pleasant, some not. But this, by far, was the craziest man to take offense.

I went into my cabin, locked the door, drew the curtains, and changed clothes. When I came out, I was wearing khaki shorts and a navy blue sweatshirt. The man was still there, within casting distance of the dock, separated only by the cleaning board and a gooseneck lamp. I took out my phone, let him see me do it. As I dialed Birdy, he grabbed a bait-casting rod and freed a fishing lure that rattled with treble hooks. "Who're you calling? You're not the only one who's got cops as pals. You've been checking on me, girl. That's not right, us being in the same profession and all."

We were close enough now, he didn't have to yell. Instead, he spoke in a cheery, conversational way—then suddenly snapped a sidearm cast. The lure, with its silver gang hooks, came at me like a bullet, threading the space between the lamp and the cleaning board. Before I could flinch, he thumbed the spool and stopped the lure inches from my face. The lure plopped nto the water at my feet while I finally did react in a lurching, clumsy way. Embarrassing—which is what he wanted.

"Why'd that scare you? Hell, I'd choose a Shimano over any sniper rifle in the world.

You've never seen an expert fisherman cast before, have you? Here, honey, watch this."

He did it again. Again, I ducked away from the lure. It was a reflexive reaction I couldn't control, yet I kept the phone to my ear while Birdy's recorded voice said, "You know the drill."

I straightened to my full height and pretended as if she had answered. "Deputy, yes, it's me again. You were right about that restraining order. Yeah . . . same guy, but on my own property this time. Threatening me, he sure is . . . Hang on." I covered the phone. "Your name's Larry Luckheim, right? Or would you prefer to be arrested as Buddy Luck? Give it some thought—your picture might finally make the magazines after all."

The insult took some air out of his swagger. To compensate, he deployed his fake Cracker accent. "You got a mouth on you, girl, but ain't your lips a tad too round for jokes? Here's what's funny—take a guess how many clients you lost to me this week. Two. An old married couple who wanted to pick oranges, not fish. Like I said, it's all about marketing. I told them, 'The only reason you prefer fruit to snook is because you never fished with a real guide.' " He aimed a hairy, bulldog grin at my stunned reaction. "Don't ask their names. Us pros don't give out shit like that."

Underhand, this time, he flicked the lure. Something in me snapped. I threw my arm out and caught the line as treble hooks whistled past my ear. I stepped back and yanked. There is no stretch to Dacron fishing line, and that's what Larry had spooled. The rod flew into the water while steel hooks pierced the back of my wrist. I pretended not to notice. Hand over hand, I towed the rod to the dock, then picked it up, with all the cool I could muster, and began cranking up slack.

"The magnetic spools on these Shimanos," I said, "they're okay for beginners, but don't you lose distance when you cast? I can teach you how to avoid backlash, if that's the problem. You know how to reach me, don't you, Larry? What with stealing my clients, I assume you looked me up."

The man recoiled with benumbed expression. "Goddamn, lady . . . you're nuts, that's what you are. I could've ripped your arm off, if I wanted to—"

I talked over him. "Not out of kindness, you didn't. You could've blinded me, you idiot!"

"Damn right, that too. Next time, maybe I will. Any fool who grabs a MirrOlure bare-handed deserves whatever they get. Don't make me come up there and get my fishing rod. More than just your hand will be bleeding if you cross me."

My wrist, not my hand, was dripping blood, but the hooks weren't barbed, and only one had bit deeply. *Good*—let the man believe I was crazy. Much depended on the question I asked next. "Larry, answer me. Did you look me up on the Internet? If you did, you know I don't tolerate bullying. Not from the likes of you—or anyone else. There were plenty of articles a couple years back that prove it."

He'd seen the news stories. What he'd read was in the nervous pretense of his denials.

"If you ever threaten me again," I said, "I'll do whatever it takes. That's your choice."

He puffed up his ego enough to answer back, "You're saying that story about you shooting some criminal down in the Glades is true? I don't believe it. Never read a newspaper yet I believed. He wasn't much of a man if he stood still for your nonsense."

"If my aim was better," I replied, "he'd be less of a man now. Ask his friends about it your next trip to Raiford prison." I clipped the lure free of the line and stepped aboard the Marlow as if in a hurry to fetch something.

I heard the cat's twin engines fire up, the clank of gears, and felt the rolling wake when Larry sped away. The whole time, I sat shaking in the hollow privacy of my cabin, where I battled the urge to scream, or cry, or telephone for help. But I did neither, save for a few traitorous tears.

No one can save you from a bully but yourself. I'd been through it enough in high school to know.

On the other hand . . . it couldn't hurt to enlist the opinions of a few trusted friends. How would they handle the situation?

On the counter lay Sabin Martinez's business card. I didn't consider him a friend, but the fact he'd been a confidant of a man like Harncy Chatham was impressive.

Call me, he'd said, *if you need help with anything at all. Anything. I'm a problem solver from way back.*

The emphasis he'd given the word suggested that he was, indeed, an experienced *problem solver.*

I studied the card for a moment, then dialed.

When Larry was long gone, I returned to the quiet aft deck of my cruiser, where there are cushioned bench seats and a small teak table. My hands were still shaking. I had to take a moment. I used a first-aid kit and fishing pliers to remove the treble hooks, then called Mr. and Mrs. Gentry's cell phone. They were my only clients who had an interest in citrus. I didn't want to believe they'd go behind my back and hire another guide. Not after the talks we'd had about a partnership in developing a biotech patent.

My faith was well placed. Larry had made up a story or had someone else in mind.

"Are you referring to the crazy man who cut off my snook?" Dr. Gentry asked. "Never in a million years would we hire someone like that, my dear. I can tell you're upset. Do you want to talk about it?"

I shared a few details, minus the threats of violence. "Somehow he knows about you and Mr. Gentry. About what we're doing. And he used it to scare me—either that or he's being chartered by someone else who knows."

"I don't like this, Hannah. It's worth checking into. We might have to hire someone to keep an eye on you."

"You sound worried."

The woman remained serious but mitigated matters with a calming tone. "In the world of biotech patents, there's always something to worry about until the patent is actually awarded. No, I'm misleading you. That's just the start of your worries. During the process, you have data thieves, and leaks of every kind imaginable, and then the international courts to deal with. Science is a noble profession—until money gets involved. Then it's like any other cutthroat business, only worse because . . . well, the stakes are so much higher. It's the foreign companies that fight dirtiest of all. One of India's recent biotech patents changed the entire economy of

Mumbai —more than thirteen billion dollars the first year."

I cleared my throat. "Did you say *billion?*"

My fishing client, the famous scientist, replied, "Get used to it. A million is the numerical starting point in this business. The numbers get bigger fast depending on who, and how many companies, want to license whatever intellectual property you happen to own."

We had never talked money before, just ideas and methods. "Good Lord, Mrs. Gentry, you're not telling me that—"

"No, no, no, it's way too early to predict profits. And there seldom are, by the way. But big egos and the chance for big money—or even a piddly little research grant—can be a dangerous combination. That's what I'm saying, Hannah. The man who threatened you sounds dangerous to begin with. If someone hired him, it can only be to steal whatever it is we're after. Unless he's just crazy. Either way, you need to be very, very careful, dear."

Now I was worried, too. "Someone found out what we're doing, that's obvious."

"They always do. I'll bounce this off Doug when he gets home. We need to have another meeting anyway because of a conversation I just had. I told you that naturally occurring DNA sequences can't be patented? That's true. But I was wrong about my take on a Supreme Court ruling a few years back. There's a loophole when it comes to seed stock. Monsanto has been patenting seeds under what's called a stewardship clause. I knew that, but here's how it applies to us . . ."

She went into greater detail. As hard as I tried, some of the terminology she used was indecipherable. "I don't understand any of this," I said after a while. "I can't believe you and Mr. Gentry have been kind enough to guide me through the process this far."

"Kindness begets kindness, my dear," Dr. Gentry said. "But don't forget, we're businesspeople, too. If you can find that early Spanish seed stock, and if the DNA sequencing is even slightly different, we could really be on to something quite substantial, Hannah. There are a lot more ifs regarding their resistance to disease, but let's save that for later and talk about something serious. How is Roberta, our young mother, getting along?"

There is no excuse for boredom if you live on a boat or own anything that floats bigger than a canoe. Maintenance, if not given daily attention, is guaranteed to become an annual disaster. I spent early Sunday afternoon battling a leak in the Marlow's stuffing box, which was okay because it was mindless work. It gave me time to run through a list of people who might have hired Larry Luckheim to shadow me or to search for wild oranges.

Not a single client could I name.

He was lying, I decided, but I had no doubt he'd been tailing me for a while. Before the weather had turned foul, I'd spent two days gunkholing local islands and collecting samples of feral citrus and their leaves, plus bark scrapings. On an island off the Estero River, I had also found two prime little seedling trees—juveniles, they were called in the trade. These items all had to be bagged, labeled, and logged just so, as Roberta had demonstrated. The procedure required my full attention, so it was possible that Larry had tailed me, or at least gotten a peek at what I was doing. If true, his motives for lying were cloudy at best, but that was to be expected from a forty-some-year-old man who didn't shave, and probably didn't bathe, but who took tango lessons.

I dropped the subject and fixed the leak.

Missing church had left me with a residual feeling of sloth. On Sunday afternoons, the public pool on Pine Island clears two lanes for serious swimmers. Finishing first at high school regionals in the hundred-meter freestyle didn't qualify me as serious, but I do enjoy a hard swim. The wind had swung northwest, the harbinger of a coming cold front. According to NOAA weather, the temperature would plummet into the low forties tonight, and the breeze already had an icy edge. There was also a bandage on my left bicep, and a laceration the nurse had told me not to get wet. I decided to swim anyway. To doubly ensure discipline, I jotted my workout in pencil and pasted the paper it was on on the tile when I was in the pool.

Warm-up laps are the best for letting the mind wander. After six hundred yards, Larry's threats had been replaced by thoughts of Kermit Bigalow; images of his kindly smile and fatherly attention to his daughter, Sarah. Of course I would speak to him if he stopped by my boat at seven. I hadn't actually consented, so maybe he would, maybe he wouldn't. But, if he did, how would I handle it? The news about Mr. Chatham's will could not be shared; I had promised Sabin Martinez. Even if I hadn't, it would be an awkward topic. I would soon inherit a portion of the very citrus operation from which he'd been fired, so how would I respond when the subject came up?

No . . . Kermit hadn't said "fired." He'd said that Lonnie had forced him off the property by padlocking his house. What a terrible thing to do to a man and wife with a ten-year-old daughter. Childhood was tough enough without the added hurt of legalities and changing homes.

On my flip turn, my legs snapped around with

precision. Feet found the wall in sync. I pushed off . . . glided, while my legs imitated the thrusting strokes of a dolphin. When I surfaced, the easy flow of thoughts resumed.

Loretta floated into my mind. With her came a weighty sadness. All those years she had lied to me, her own daughter, yet her only regret was that she had sometimes heeded her moral conscience along with the commandments of her faith.

A part of me was indignant, a part of me understood. I could not deny a secret empathy for two people in love who had dealt as best they could with life's obligations and a tragic run of bad timing.

The longing in my mother's words came back: *I don't regret a single moment I spent with Harney Chatham . . . only the times I said no out of conscience. All those lost hours of happiness we could have shared!*

Inevitably, my situation with Kermit took advantage of what I knew was a sly ingress. I heard his voice saying, . . . *it's the feeling I got when I first saw you . . . I've never done anything like this before . . . If things were different at home, maybe . . .*

Kermit's wife hated Florida. She hated bugs, and boats, and the water. Sarah had told me that.

After another flip turn, and a long dolphining

glide, Kermit was repeating to me, in a whisper, *You are so damn beautiful, and not in the typical . . . way . . .*

This cleared my head for a moment, because I knew better. If I were beautiful, I would not be wearing a black, plus-size Speedo to disguise the extra weight I carried in too many wrong places. Nor would I have spent last night— yet another Saturday—alone on my boat, researching the history of rootstock and the citrus industry.

Why did I even care? I had kissed a married man . . . and had let it go too far. So what! At this instant, all around the world, people were probably kissing like mad, indifferent to silly rules about when to kiss and why, particularly in Europe (or so I'd read), where men and women, married or not, kissed as a matter of common courtesy—even on the streets, where everyone could see. No wonder Loretta and Mr. Chatham had snuck off to Paris to kiss themselves crazy without all the damn guilt they'd suffered here in the prudish boondocks of Florida.

After eight hundred yards, I stopped, adjusted my goggles, and consulted my workout sheet.

"Beautiful day, even if it is getting chilly," a lifeguard said on his way to the office. "I hear a big cold front's coming."

"They might think it's a beautiful day in

France," I replied with a surliness that was undeserved. After that, I began a series of middle-distance reps, but started much too fast. Soon I was plodding along—this time, my mind on Sarah. The ten-year-old who drew sad stick figures was now homeless to boot. Of course, I would discuss whatever business her father had on his mind. The poor man was desperate to care for his family after being locked out of the home that had been provided them by . . .

Locked out.

The term jolted me. It echoed and banged around in my head until the particulars fell into place. Only then did I remember Kermit saying he had been locked out of the house, and his office, too.

I snapped a flip turn and sprinted to the wall as my final lap. I gathered my belongings, pulled a towel around me for warmth, and hurried to the locker room to change. It is rare for me to quit in the middle of a workout, but I suddenly knew—no, I suspected—who had mentioned my name while hiring an unstable fishing guide to search for oranges.

If Lonnie Chatham had locked Kermit out of his office, she now had possession of his files! Quite possibly they included his notes regarding a theory about the original Spanish rootstock.

From my SUV, I called Kermit but got voice

mail. "Give me a call back," I said. "I should be home by seven—if that's still in your plans."

It was a bold stroke that made me bolder. I called Reggie. He was at his cottage, he said, waxing the Lincoln. "Every Sunday afternoon, if I'm not driving, it's what I do. Why you ask?"

"Would you mind some company? I can stop on the way and bring food. Oh—and I need Lonnie's cell number, if you have it. I think she wanted to charter my boat but changed her mind for some reason."

After a silence, he replied, "That woman don't fish for nothing unless it wears pants, and it's too cold to fish anyway. What's wrong, makes you want to speak with her?"

"That's what I need to find out. Do you know a man named Sabin Martinez?"

" 'Course I do, but I ain't seen him in near a month. I can't say why that's a worry to me . . . or maybe Beano paid a visit to you and your ma. Is that what happened? I'd be pleased if he paid you a call."

"You call him Beano?"

"Twenty years or more, that's what the governor called him. Sabe, sometimes, but Bin don't fit the man. As a chauffeur, of course, I've got to be more formal. Call him Captain Martinez, or Mr. sometimes, depends on the formality of the situation. Reckon you'd sound happier, Miz Hannah, if Beano had spoken to you. But wait . . . he must'a, 'cause how else you know his name?"

"Was he supposed to stop by your place? He strikes me as the type who travels a lot." This confused the chauffeur, so I explained, "It worries you, you said, not seeing him for a while. We can talk about it—I'll pick up some barbecue on the way. Or would you prefer I make sandwiches?"

Before we hung up, I reminded him, "How about Lonnie's number?"

"The woman don't speak to me unless she needs something or wants to holler about how useless I am. You could try the house, I suppose."

"Stop by and see her, you mean?" The Chatham ranch was only a mile or two out of the way.

"I wouldn't advise no person to do that—not on a Sunday. You got something to write with? I'll give you the private number to the house."

Sixteen

Double-wing gates were open beneath the wrought iron crest of Chatham's Triple C Ranch. I hadn't planned on turning into the drive, but I did. It was one of those snap decisions that requires a certain stubbornness of mood. Anger helped. Lonnie Chatham had told Kermit she wanted to speak with me. Fine. I'd tried to call —no answer, no message machine—so here I was.

I went through a rehearsal, while the asphalt lane wandered between mossy oaks and pasture where horses grazed, a mahogany-stained barn in the distance. Aloof and professional, I pictured myself, impervious to insults, or snubs, and all other childish behavior. I was here as a professional courtesy, after all. Did she want to charter my boat? I saw myself baiting the woman by offering the names of competent guides, then counseling her, *It's wise to be careful. The fact that a person owns a boat doesn't guarantee a satisfying day on the water.*

No . . . the word *satisfying* was out. There were too many connotations to satisfying that might lead the conversation into awkward areas. For more than thirty years, Loretta and Mr. Chatham had kept their affair secret, but there was no telling what kind of snooping Lonnie had done since the man's death. What if she knew? How would she react when she saw me, Loretta's daughter? How would I handle it?

Calmly. Business-like. The ex-cheerleader could make a fool of herself if she wanted, but I would remain unshakeable.

The fact that the ex-cheerleader might also be guilty of murdering a football player named Raymond Caldwell was something I didn't want to factor in. The thought was in my mind, though, when the drive broadened into a circle. Ahead was a long carport for guest parking, but it was empty. To my right was the barn. It was sided with beveled cypress. The wood glistened like amber beneath a gambrel roof of copper sheathing. Pasture, defined by a mile of painted fence, spread away toward the Peace River, where water sparkled beneath the shade of trees and Spanish moss.

This wasn't just a working ranch. It was an estate built for entertaining millionaires.

My confidence stumbled. I parked anyway and followed a path, lined with scarlet bougainvillea, past a tennis court, to the main house. It was a three-story mansion, built of timbers, with balconies and skylights and high, wooded walkways, so life could be lived inside or out. The mark of Harney Chatham was in all the

Western rodeo detail: branding irons and ornate terra-cotta tiles; the main entrance was a set of massive timber doors; there was a doorbell, and also a heavy horseshoe knocker.

I tried both, which produced only an echoing silence within. Strange. On a place this size, there had to be hired help somewhere, but I'd yet to see a soul. Again, I banged the heavy knocker. Nothing.

Admittedly, I was relieved. I went down the steps faster than needed. When I was on the walkway, shielded by scarlet blossoms, a vehicle started somewhere nearby; tires spun in sand, yelped when they found asphalt, then sped toward the gate.

A truck, it sounded like, but the vehicle was gone by the time I got to the parking area.

Lonnie Chatham, however, was there. She was adjusting the collar of her blouse after exiting the barn, the double doors open wide to the shady space within. Inside was a tractor and other mowing equipment. Plenty of room to hide a car, or a truck. I got the creepy feeling she had been interrupted again and it was her lover's vehicle I'd heard.

I waited by my SUV. She pretended to be unaware of my presence until, finally, she did a perturbed double take. "Excuse me—do you have an appointment?"

I replied, "I was told you were trying to get in

touch with me, Miz Chatham. I called earlier. There was no message machine, and I happened to be in the area anyway, so—"

"Who are you?"

Did she really not remember our meeting on the day Harney Chatham died? Highly unlikely, but I played along and introduced myself. Her three-fingered handshake communicated distaste —until a look of reappraisal registered, as did my name. Everything changed. Suddenly, she was delighted to meet me. "You're the fishing guide! I'm so sorry. My husband was very fond of you, Hannah. And Harney wasn't a man given to compliments. Not in private anyway." There was a wink in her delivery.

I'd expected a confrontation, not a welcoming smile, or a gracious attempt at an embrace, which I fumbled badly. We nearly conked heads.

Laughing, she said, "I wish Harney could see the two of us together. Finally, after all these years. We're going to miss that man, aren't we? All his friends will. Especially us female admirers, huh?" There was another wink, the way this was said.

"I didn't know your husband well, but he was always kind to me."

"Oh, I bet he was! That Harney, he knew how to work a room of adoring women. Would you like some iced tea? Come on"—she directed me toward the barn—"let me give you the nickel tour. If you brought a jacket along, I'd grab it. We have a lot to talk about."

This was all very strange. The woman obviously had a reason for pretending we were new bosom buddies. There must be something she wanted from me . . .

I followed her, saying, "Talk about what, Mrs. Chatham?"

"Call me Lonnie, and don't play coy. You know—and, if you don't, then I'll have the fun of telling you—Harney said you were good at doing that Southern thing. Same with him: his good ol' boy act. He'd pretend not to understand some complex issue when, in fact, he was the smartest guy in the room. Smart enough to listen until he knew damn well where everyone stood."

She spun around. "And I suspect it's the same with you, isn't it, dear? Are you saying you don't know that Harney left you half of our citrus groves in his will?"

That threw me. I couldn't hide the truth. It was in my reaction.

"If we're going to be partners," she said, "there's something you should know up front. I hate being lied to. Save the cat claws for social events, Hannah—what fun would they be without friendly competition, right? But not when it's just you and me. Understood?"

In black riding boots, with her blond hair piled

in a loosely braided updo, the woman was as tall as me. We stood eye to eye. Her focus lingered on the few faint acne scars I no longer obsess about disguising by the careful placement of my hair.

"We don't know each other well enough to make promises," I said. "As to lying, that's not my normal practice. But Lonnie? If we stick to the truth, it'll have to go both ways."

After a ride in a golf cart, Lonnie Chatham led me into an office off the barn. It smelled of leather and hay—a load of freshly baled clover had just been delivered, she said. The walls were covered with ribbons and pictures of livestock, mostly horses, but a few bulls. One was the massive Brangus that Reggie had called Jessie James.

The wall above a walnut desk was Lonnie's personal space. Sun stains from previous photographs told me it had been recently cleared. Hanging there now were memories of her college years; photos and ribbons, glassed and framed. She was the buxom cheerleader in various uniforms. A more elegant Lonnie smiled at me as Miss Florida runner-up, no date on the brass tag below.

"Don't ask the year," she said. "That's one subject where lying is always allowed . . . Cigarette?" She fitted a Virginia Slim between her lips. Didn't light it until after looking me up and down as I took off my jacket. "The only reason I started was, my pageant coach—this was for Miss Tangerine Bowl, way before college—she told me smoking was the best way to stay thin. She was right. I've never needed to diet, or wear baggy shirts to hide a body I was ashamed of." She offered the pack. "Sure you don't want one?"

A pattern had emerged during our ride in the golf cart. Her subtle slights and insults were packaged as kindly observation. Pity was her favorite disguise for criticism. She gazed at me with concern while smoke framed her face. "How's poor little Reggie getting along? I worry about that man. He was never the brightest bulb, but Harney had a soft spot; let him get away with incompetence he would've fired anybody else for. I can't keep him on here—the man's useless at everything but washing that damn car—and, at his age? He's either senile or drunk. Even Walmart wouldn't hire him. Any ideas, Hannah?"

We had toured the estate, from riverfront to the road, and this was the first she'd broached a serious subject or asked my advice.

"I don't know what's in your husband's will except what I've been told. Reggie seems happy doing what he's doing."

Her focus narrowed. "Really? You haven't seen

the will? Who told you that you inherited the gun club acreage?"

Not flustered, I replied, "A man who worked for Mr. Chatham stopped by the house today. He asked me not to discuss the matter or mention his name. I agreed. Hope you understand . . . Lonnie."

"Ah-hah," she said. "The mysterious Sabin Martinez. Am I right?"

I gestured in a noncommittal way.

"Thought so. He's yet to show his face around here, but I've seen him in a hundred of Harney's old scrapbooks. Always somewhere in the background like a shadow, or . . . I don't know, a raven in those movies where you know something bad's going to happen. Early on, I figured Sabin was just a bodyguard, but he was a lot more than that, turns out. Is he still trying hard to look like Ernest Hemingway?"

"I'd have to see the photos, I guess, to understand what you mean," I said.

"Smooth; you're pretty good." She smiled and brushed back a curl. "Last week, I started to organize Harney's personal correspondence. Sabin Martinez, turns out, did what some might call Lysol work. A cleanup man. Men with money and power always need someone like Martinez, but Harney despised the guy. I don't suppose he mentioned that. Harney didn't trust him, Hannah. But why tell you? You're too smart to fall for whatever bullshit scam he's pulling." She reached for an ashtray and took a long, last drag. "Hope I'm right about that."

"I thought you wanted to discuss the citrus groves."

"We are. If you won't level with me about Martinez, let's get back to Reggie. I'm curious. Did he tell you I blackmailed Harney into marriage because of something that happened a long time ago? Wait—" She focused on my handbag, which was on the floor. "Turn your phone off. I want to see you do it."

Something big was coming. Why else would she go to such extremes to be nice instead of ordering me off the property?

"In that case, we both should," I said, then waited to speak until she had complied. "Did your husband mention that I run a small investigation agency? My uncle started it, but now that he's dead—"

She waved me off. "The way this works is, I talk and you listen—for now anyway. I hope that doesn't offend you. I'm about to share something I've never told anyone. Not out of guilt. I want us to trust each other. Understand?"

"I think you're rushing things. We've barely met."

"In a way, but not really. The law firm I pay way too much money has a team of investigators, so I know more about you and your mother than you realize. Don't worry, I'll leave Loretta out of it—for now. This is about us, you and me. There's something we have in common. Something that if a woman hasn't experienced it, she can't understand. Are you with me now?"

I sensed where the conversation was heading. Lonnie Chatham had read about my past. Now she was probing, testing for empathy, before risking details about her past and, possibly, a murder she had committed more than twenty years ago.

Seventeen

Lonnie already suspected Reggie had told me what happened on that New Year's Eve night long ago. Perhaps she also suspected he'd shown me the cement weir where she'd left a hand-print and signed her name. I had neither confirmed nor denied what the chauffeur had confided, but she would know if I appeared too eager to talk.

I said, "Like every woman, I've had experiences I don't feel comfortable sharing. I'm not sure what you're asking."

Her glare accused me of playing dumb. "A traumatizing event. The kind most women don't have to deal with, thank god. What happened to you made the news, for christ's sake. Does that help?"

I let down my guard in a visible way by unfolding my arms. "It's not an easy subject," I said, "but I figured that's what you were getting at. This has to do with the man who attacked me. You read about what happened."

"The man you shot, yeah, but only wounded. Thank god. I was starting to think you're one of those Xanax twits who needs to be coaxed like a child. I want to ask you something, and there's a reason. Did you shoot the guy—I forget his name—did you shoot him after he . . . ? What I mean is, did he get his hands on you first?"

"He tried," I said, aware of what she wanted to know.

"But he didn't . . . ?"

"No," I said. "Never touched me. I didn't give him a chance."

A glossy fingernail tapped another cigarette from the pack. "It must have been close, though, if you're reluctant to talk about it. Consider yourself one of the lucky ones. Rape is a hell of a sad way for a girl to lose her virginity. I'm not talking about you, by the way. From the stories— you were never quoted in the articles—but they gave the impression you were so scared, you might have pulled the trigger accidentally. Is that true or just some bullshit they fed the jury?"

She was seeking an ally regarding her own attacker, I realized—an event that had taken place decades ago. "Every person has a right to defend herself," I said. "Guilt doesn't apply when you have no choice."

"That's all you have to say?"

"I hoped that's what you wanted to hear."

Lonnie Chatham's arrogance vanished, replaced by a surprising sadness and vulnerability. "What I was hoping for was, someone who'd talk openly. We get so few chances, but it's obviously none of my business. I guess I'm as wrong about you as you are about me."

I reconsidered, while she reached to gather her purse and cigarettes. "Hold on a minute," I said. "My attorney told me to never discuss it, but I'll tell you this much: pulling that trigger was no accident."

This earned her attention, and a wilted smile. "Thank you. I know that wasn't easy. I hate to press, but are you willing to tell me a little more?"

I said, "Most of what happened was in the papers. The guy we're talking about had assaulted several women. I'd been hired to track down a girl who was still running from him. He caught me in an open area—my boat had broken down and . . . well, it's a long story. When he came at me, I aimed for his thigh, hoping to knock him down. The pistol was new to me; I've spent a lot of time at the range since then. Anyway, I shot high and the round clipped his pelvis. Afterward, I could've killed him. Maybe I should've."

"Why didn't you?"

"It wasn't a matter of having no choice, although I didn't, I suppose. That's not the way my mind processed it at the time. He came at me; I shucked a round, took aim, and fired. No . . . Truth is, that's not the way it went. First, after I got the gun up and steady, I told him I would count to five if he didn't back off."

"You actually did that? Counted out loud?" She lit the cigarette and sat back, enjoying herself.

"He had to be warned," I said. "Yes, I counted. Well . . . I started at five but skipped to the end because he said something so crude, I won't repeat it. That's when I shot him."

"Skipped some numbers, you mean? Like what? Five, four—*bang?* That's so damn cool."

"I think I made it to three. Then I had to make another decision when he get got up and hobbled off. He was yelling things; threats, mostly. I could've shot him in the back, but . . . I don't know, it didn't seem right. In hindsight, I'm glad. I might be in jail now."

"Jesus, Hannah, that is so very, very ballsy. Five . . . four . . . three, and you did it." Somewhere in the woman's mind, the scene was playing out as if in a theater. "Hold on, tell me the truth—you aimed at his thigh? The chest area, center mass, that's what I was taught. Are you sure you weren't aiming at his crotch? I can see a girl like you doing that. First, make the bastard wait while you count down from five, then *pow*. You shoot his balls off."

"I threatened him," I said, not smiling, "but I didn't do it to be cruel. I was as scared as I was mad. I just wanted him to go away." Before she could ask more questions, I said, "Was it the same for you when you shot Raymond Caldwell?"

The question surprised her, but not as much as I'd hoped.

"Who told you that? Was it Martinez, or that little worm, Reggie? No matter, they weren't there that night. They don't know a damn thing about what really happened. But I am curious about how you came up with Raymond's name."

"I started to tell you," I said. "My uncle opened an investigation agency for his wealthy clients—they had to be careful about hiring part-time help. He was a detective in Tampa before he went into fishing and was good enough at both to open a small office. I worked for him all through school, so it wasn't hard to narrow down what might've happened. You, a college cheerleader; him, a football star who was about to stand trial for sexual assault, but the football star disappeared. The timing seemed about right. Can I ask you something?"

"Fire away."

"Was a drug of some type involved?"

"In those days? Always." Her smirk suggested I was naïve. "You know Harney was in the pot-hauling business. They brought in all sorts of stuff on those boats. Your mother was, too, from what I've heard."

I refused to take the bait. "This is different. The typical date rape drugs didn't come along until later, but I found articles on a dangerous one called Devil's Breath. There are other names. It's a powder; tasteless, and looks like cocaine. If that's what happened, you—no woman, I mean—has a reason to feel guilt for what she might have done to get away."

She gazed at me while her mind worked on how to respond. "You do your homework, I'll give you that. Okay . . . okay. I'll tell you what happened—not all of it, but some. First, we need to come to an understanding about our business matters."

She opened a drawer and brought out an expensive-looking ledger, several notebooks, and some papers bound in a folder. "If I'd actually been blackmailing Harney, I did a piss-poor job of it. Judge for yourself. He left an estate worth close to a hundred million, but all I got was a chunk of his life insurance and the remainder of the citrus grove he didn't give you and your mother. Oh, and Reggie—he's so easy to forget."

"A partnership between just us," I said. "Is that what you're proposing?"

"I've got to find some way to provide for my future. Any idea what a hundred acres of dead orange trees are worth in this part of Florida? Not jack shit, compared to what I have here"—the ranch, she meant—"which all goes to his kids. Me? I'm out in the cold. How old are you, Hannah? Ten, maybe fifteen years younger than me? I know you're single, that you have no children, and you have to hustle to pay bills at the end of the month. Isn't that right?"

She was closer to twenty years older, but I let her talk.

"Almost all women end up alone. That's just the way life is. Sooner or later, we have to look out for ourselves, and I'm not going to end up some sad old woman in a roach-infested nursing home. Think about that while I show you what I have in mind."

She continued talking while I glanced at a plat map, and a couple of other documents. It was difficult to separate the woman's bitterness from her attorney's advice, which was to fight her husband's last will and testament in court. Equally difficult was gauging her sincerity when she said, "If I drag this through the legal system, it'll take years, Hannah. Do you know what that means to you and your mother? You won't see a cent. None of us will—except the attorneys. Do you really want that to happen?"

It was a mild threat, I assumed, to be exchanged for confidentiality regarding the missing football star.

I was wrong.

She opened a folder, saying, "That's why I hired an expert to comb through every asset I can legally claim. My hope was, he'd come up a brilliant idea about how to turn what Harney left me into real money. Maybe he did, maybe he didn't. Either way, you and I are better off working together. Here, I'll show you." She flattened more papers on the desk and waited for me to scoot my chair closer.

"Mind putting out that cigarette?" I asked. "It's hard to get the smell out of my hair."

She complied, but not without saying, in her subtle, superior way, "I remember girls like you in high school—not many, but a few. I bet you played in the band, and dated nice boys. I always wondered what they did for fun."

I was tired of her condescending manner. "The clarinet was more enjoyable than some instruments I can think of. Being a cheerleader, Lonnie, you're probably an expert on the subject."

She glared, then decided, "I guess I deserved that. How about we call a truce until we get things sorted out?"

I agreed, and moved closer to the desk. I was looking at an aerial photo of the citrus groves, the pasture, and Mr. Chatham's cabin hideaway —Salt Creek Gun Club. A yellow highlighter divided the property into hundred-acre parcels.

"Harney wanted to give you the cabin, plus the river frontage and Reggie's little shack. All the highway frontage is mine, except for this narrow little ingress-egress, which we're somehow supposed to share." She ran a finger along the access lane to illustrate, while I noted her careful phrasing. She'd said "wanted to give" instead of "Harney gave you." Already, her mind was made up. She was not going to honor her late husband's wishes.

I played along, and paid attention.

"My expert knows real estate," she continued. "More important, he knows the citrus business. At first, he suggested we package our two hundred acres, get the zoning changed to commercial, and quietly offer it to some big-money developers he knows. Half the trees are dead anyway, so it made sense until he saw this."

The leather-bound office ledger was placed in front of me. Two spiral notebooks were added. "This might be the real game changer," she said. "When I told my guy—this expert—I'd almost thrown these books in the trash, he nearly had a fit. That was two weeks ago. He's had time to do the research, to contact the right people and check everything out. Take a look. I had no idea of the potential value of what's in there—but I'm fairly certain you do." She tapped the notebooks for emphasis.

I opened the ledger instead. Inside, on the cover page, was a man's bold handwriting in ink. I leafed through a few pages, seeing diagrams and notes, all related to citrus greening disease. "This belongs to Kermit Bigalow. His name and phone number, all his personal information, it's right here plain to see."

"So what?"

"I've got no right to be looking at the man's personal papers. You don't either, as far as I'm concerned."

The woman stared with feline intensity. I got the impression she had been waiting for this moment. "Not according to my attorney. Kermit was contracted by Chatham Enterprises, *L-L-C*. Every scrap of work he did was proprietary. In other words, the company owns all his research and everything else he produced on our time. What's the problem, dear?" Her smile lasted through a silence that forced me to make eye contact.

"I don't care what your attorneys say. It doesn't seem fair."

"Fair?" she chuckled. "At your age, if you believe life is fair, you're in for a shock. The law doesn't give a damn about fairness—or justice, for that matter. Are you sure it's not something else?"

I closed the book and pushed it away. "This is between you, your lawyer, and Kermit. It's none of my business."

Her eyes moved to the ledger, then the notebooks. "Open one of those and you'll change your mind. In his notes, you're scattered all through there, including a diagram of your house and citrus grove. What tree is located where, even their approximate ages. He used your initials quite often. Come on, Hannah, do you still think this is none of your business? I know Kermit has the hots for you. That's the real reason you're upset, isn't it?"

I looked away from the notebooks, worried about how much personal detail they contained. "I barely know the man," I said. "We talked about citrus trees, mostly, but—"

"That's not how I know," she interrupted. "It's the way he lit up when your name was mentioned. That Chatty Cathy kid of his couldn't shut up about you and your boat. It was Captain Hannah this, Captain Hannah that, until I finally took him aside. Kermit claimed I was imagining things. But from the look on your face right now, I'd say . . ." The woman nodded as if she'd just confirmed something. "Why, you poor little fool. That was just one of many lies the bastard told Harney and me. God knows how many he told you. I hope you at least had some fun while it lasted."

I got to my feet and collected my purse, saying, "His wife has no reason to be jealous. You don't, either, if that's your problem. This conversation's over."

Truth is, I felt numb and needed air.

"Jealous?" she said, sounding genuinely puzzled. "I don't give a damn about a man like him. He was trying to steal your idea for a biotech patent. That's why I kicked his ass off my property. Well, one of the reasons. Don't you get it? You, your idea, all the research Kermit did—it all belongs to me now."

Yes . . . she had been waiting to say those words. It was in the controlling way she motioned for me to sit down.

I remained standing. "Lonnie, what do you want? Just tell me, so I can be on my way."

"Be sensible," she said. "We have too much in common to be enemies. That's all I'm asking. Kermit was in the process of filing a provisional patent. Do you know what that is? Of course you don't. It's a bunch of complicated forms neither one of us would understand." She reached for another folder, then decided the evidence could wait. "He would've done it, too, if I hadn't locked him out of his office. Be thankful for that, at least. If you don't believe me, I can arrange a meeting with my attorney."

"I'm still waiting to hear what it is you really want." This I said calmly despite the tension I felt.

"If your patent idea works out," she said, "we'll split the profits, minus whatever expenses I pay out of pocket. In exchange, I want the property Harney left you; the cabin, and everything else that's rightfully mine. And one other thing"—her eyes locked onto mine—"it's not important to me, but my citrus expert is the obsessive type. He's convinced you know the location of a very special orange tree. The mother tree, he called it. Is that true?"

This is what I'd been waiting to hear. "I knew it," I said, pointing a finger at her. "You hired a crazy man to follow me. He almost killed me the other day. Is that what you want?"

The woman started to get up, then decided it was wiser to stay where she was. "What in the world are you talking about? This is business, for god's sake. Calm down and listen. I don't give a damn about orange trees or some damn disease, but I do care about my financial security. When an expert I'm paying talks about millions in potential profit, I'm going to take his advice. You should, too."

"Answer my question," I said. "You hired Larry Luckheim to bully and intimidate—"

"Larry *who?*" The woman shook her head as if confused. "If you're being followed, it's because the word's out, Hannah. People in the citrus industry talk. I guarantee, Kermit's not the only one willing to steal your idea, or anything else, if there's big money in it. How many people you think are combing this state right now, looking for some damn old tree? And not just your tree. Keep that in mind. There have to be others."

I maintained eye contact. "Are there?"

Lonnie and her icy smile—I could picture her practicing in front of the mirror. "The two most dangerous animals on earth," she said, "do you know what they are? I'll tell you: stupid men and smart women. Hannah, the smart thing for us to do is to cooperate, join forces. You and your mother will never see one goddamn cent of Harney's money if you don't. Is that what you want?"

Her phone, which she had turned back on, rang. She looked, and said, "Oh shit, I've got to take this. Do you mind?"

She wanted privacy. Fine. The temptation was to put the ledger and the notebooks under my arm and march out the door. I could've done it. How would she stop me?

I didn't, but she stopped me anyway by stepping in front of my SUV as I was leaving.

"Reggie's dead," she hollered, the phone still to her ear.

My window was down. I heard her plainly enough but demanded that she repeat what I didn't want to believe.

"One of our Mexican guys just found him," she said. "Suicide. He hanged himself. I thought you'd want to know." She covered the phone and demanded, "Hannah, come back inside. We have too much in common—"

That's all I heard before I drove away.

Eighteen

The gate to the Salt Creek Gun Club was open. I turned left on the dirt lane to Reggie's house but stopped when I saw emergency vehicles in the distance. I'd hoped Lonnie had told an outrageous lie to manipulate me, but it was true. I didn't want to see the chauffeur's body, or answer more questions from the police, yet I couldn't believe he had actually taken his own life.

I put my vehicle in park and stared at the flashing lights. It had been a little more than two hours since I'd spoken to Reggie on the phone. A man contemplating suicide might polish a cherished car as a farewell gesture, but he wouldn't encourage visitors, and he certainly wouldn't have said he preferred barbecue to homemade sandwiches for lunch. Unless . . .

In a sack on the floor was a slab of pork ribs and containers of coleslaw and baked beans. The smoky fragrance, otherwise pleasant, became a queasy reminder that there was another explanation. Reggie might have been in the process of taking his own life when I'd called. Perhaps, in his mind, by accepting my offer to bring lunch, he could die with the comforting assurance that a friend, a woman he trusted, would be the first to find his body.

It was a painful possibility to consider, worse to imagine happening. That poor, distraught, lonely little man . . . ·

I spun my car around but could not escape the despair that descended. It would have stuck with me had I not seen a familiar truck as I approached the gate. I slowed and watched the truck enter from the main road, then accelerate toward the log cabin and river. The driver remained oblivious to me, and the dirt lane that led to Reggie's place.

It was a white Chevy Silverado.

My despair made a welcome transition into anger.

I sat and waited several minutes. If Kermit Bigalow was willing to trespass on a late Sunday afternoon, there had to be a reason. Rather than listen to more lies, I wanted to find out for myself what he was doing.

Beyond the horse stalls and the equipment shed, a path led to a dilapidated greenhouse walled with Plexiglas. Kermit's white Silverado was parked among trees to the side of the building and out of sight.

I approached on foot. He wasn't in the truck, so I went to the greenhouse door and peeked in. Kermit, wearing jeans and work gloves, was busy loading a wheelbarrow with planting pots, some containing fledgling trees, others just soil. When the door closed behind me, he jumped, as if shot, and spun around. Relief registered on his face. "Geezus . . . thank god, it's you. What are you doing here?" He busied himself brushing dirt from his pants and gloves.

"I might ask you the same thing," I said from the doorway.

"What's it look like I'm doing? I'm stealing plants I grew and giving them enough dirt to keep them alive. Someone needs to look after them." He indicated the wheelbarrow. "Do I really have to explain?"

"It's sort of funny," I said. "Until this afternoon, I dreaded having to tell you. Now I feel just fine about it. Mr. Chatham left this property to my mother and me in his will. And Reggie. You're the trespasser, Kermit, not me. When's the last time you saw him?"

The man resumed selecting gallon-sized pots from a row. "Guilty as charged, Your Honor. He left you the citrus groves, too? That's great news."

"Half the grove. Did you hear what I said?"

"I'm happy for you—yeah, I really am. Anything's better than Lonnie inheriting a place she doesn't give a damn about. What are you going to do with it? I could see you living in the cabin; have a little boat on the river, maybe a dog or two. If I'd known, trusted Reggie enough, I would've stopped and asked to take these—

plants I grew from seedlings. I'm glad you're here. We have to talk."

"Do we?"

He looked up for a moment. "Let me guess. You're not mad about me trespassing. You've been talking to Lonnie. I warned you she'd make up some sort of lie about why she fired me. What did she say? I bet it was a good one."

"What about Reggie?" I asked again.

"I haven't seen him in . . . I don't know . . . a couple of days, I guess. What's he have to do with it?" The man's expression transitioned to concerned. "Hey . . . what's wrong? You're really upset about something. What did that crazy woman say?"

"It was more of a show-and-tell conversation," I replied. "When she brought out your notebooks, I accused her of being the thief. Has that ever happened to you, Kermit? Defended someone you wanted to trust, then it turns out they were making a fool of you?"

"So that's it." He stood and sighed in the tolerant way of a man who'd been wronged but was willing to talk things through. "What else did she say? You couldn't have gone through my notes very carefully. If you had, you wouldn't be mad, you'd be helping me. I'm doing this for both of us, Hannah."

I decided it was safe to walk toward the wheelbarrow, a dozen or so fledgling plants, and potting soil containers in neat rows. "You filed for a provisional patent on an idea that wasn't mine to begin with. And it sure as heck wasn't yours. You stole those seeds from my mother's property. Where's the tree you took? I should've asked that three weeks ago. Don't deny it. Loretta saw it in the back of your truck. I was a fool not to believe her."

Kermit, with his copper hair and cowboy tan lines, stood patiently, open to any accusation I wanted to make. "Get it off your chest," he said. "When you're done, I want to show you something." After a glance at the door, he added, "Don't take too long—unless this property's already deeded over to you. She'd put me in jail."

"Maybe that's where you belong."

"You don't believe that. You really think I'd risk hurting Sarah? Or you?"

"Leave your family out of this. And stop talking as if there's something between us, Kermit. There never was. It was just a stupid kiss, that's all."

"Bullshit," he said. "I remember that night a little differently."

"Bullshit yourself," I hollered.

We argued like that for a while. My accusations were delivered in anger. He responded calmly to each one. Only when he showed me the citrus tree he'd taken from our grove did I begin to soften. But I didn't soften much.

"How do I know that's really it?" I asked.

"Do you see any others around? I can't force you to believe me, Hannah. I admit I took the damn thing. Isn't that enough?"

The tree was a fledgling, barely knee-high, far too small to be grown from a seed my uncle had planted six years ago. Kermit claimed it was one of many seedlings on our property. This was true, but I refused to acknowledge it.

"I didn't think you'd mind," he said. "You did give me permission to take oranges from your oldest trees. But you're right, I did it in a sneaky way."

"Yes, you did," I said. "But not as sneaky as filing for a patent on an idea that doesn't belong to you."

"A *provisional* patent," he said, "that I never actually filed. What Lonnie took from my office was only a rough draft, but even in that draft—"

"I don't care, Kermit! I don't want to hear any more of your excuses. I won't tolerate someone who treats me or my family in a two-faced, lying way."

The man's tolerant manner vanished. "Lying? Is that what you really think of me?"

"You could've told me about filing for a patent," I said. "You didn't even bother to ask. There's no difference between an intentional omission and a lie, as far as I'm concerned."

He put his hands in his pockets and looked at the ground, but only long enough to control his temper. "How could I ask you? You told me not to contact you for at least a month. I called anyway, the same night. Remember? You didn't answer. For weeks, do you have any idea how many times my phone rang and I hoped it was you calling back? Then, this morning, you hung up on me before I could say a damn word."

Now it was me who stared at the ground. I evaded the hurt look on his face by saying our relationship was all wrong to begin with. Then added something suitably inane, which was, "Everything happens for a reason, I suppose."

"Depends on what you're willing to settle for," he replied. "I think I've apologized enough for one day. Wait here." He went past me, out the door, then reconsidered. "Come on, it's hot in here and we both need to cool down. I've got something in my truck that might change your mind."

What he wanted me to see was inside a weathered khaki bag. He handed me a sheath of papers. The cover sheet was headed with the logo of the U.S. Patent and Trademark Office, blue with white lettering, Washington D.C.

"Keep it," he said. "I have other copies. When you get home, take your time, go through it. I have no idea what Lonnie showed you, but you either didn't read it or she gave you something she printed herself. She called this morning, screaming at me, then asked for your address, but I didn't tell her. That woman's either crazy or desperate, I'm not sure which."

I opened the document, saying, "Kermit, just point me to the right page."

He found a section titled "Declaration for Utility and Design." There, at the bottom, on lines provided for the signatures of applicants, was my full name—Hannah Summerlin Smith. It had been typed above the name of a second applicant, Kermit L. Bigalow.

I stared and swallowed. News of Reggie's death had pushed me near an emotional edge, yet I was reluctant to let go of my anger. All I could manage to say was, "Sometimes I'm too quick to judge. If I'm wrong, I'm sorry."

"I'd prefer a smile to an apology. Come on, you'll like this." He reached, almost put his hand on my shoulder, then decided against it.

Back into the greenhouse we went.

It gave me time to recover what little poise I had left.

Nineteen

The greenhouse smelled of earth and fertilizer and the fruity odor of white-blossoming vines that snaked their way up a trellis. On a bench was a plastic pan with a Plexiglas cover. Snap locks suggested something important resided inside. Suspended above was a bank of LED grow lights. Kermit switched on the light, then popped the lid. Inside, on a growing mat, were a dozen seeds, several of which had sprouted. "These are late bloomers," he said. "I'd about given up on them."

"Everything inside here looks healthy enough," I said. "Someone's been watering, at least—or is it on a timer?"

Kermit shook his head. "Just me. I've driven past that gate a dozen times. It was always locked, so, every few days, I'd park and hike across the pasture to check on my plants. Always after dark, of course, and I'd take home what I could in a bag. Today was the first it was open, so I thought, What the hell? Dodging police couldn't be any worse than dodging that big-ass bull Mr. Chatham bought."

"Jessie James," I said, and smiled for the first time in a while. I moved closer to the sprouting pan. "Are these from our citrus orchard?"

"The oldest trees your great-grandfather planted. Use this."

He handed me an inexpensive magnifying glass. Beneath the lens, the seeds ballooned with detail. From each seed protruded three delicate, fleshy sprouts. Two of the sprouts grew in opposition on the pointed ends. From the belly of the seed grew a shorter, more delicate sprout.

Kermit said, "Oranges—it's weird the way they propagate. Trees in isolation, too remote to cross-pollinate, they continue to produce seedlings that grow into exact clones. A hundred years, a thousand: it doesn't matter, if conditions remain stable. The mother tree will continue to reproduce perfect genetic replicas of itself."

"Mother tree," I repeated in a murmur.

"You probably know all this."

"Some, but it's better than arguing," I said.

"Okay . . . These two sprouts"—he used a pencil to indicate the seed's pointed ends— "one is a root, the other is a shoot that will produce a clone. This one"—he indicated the fragile middle sprout—"doesn't grow, not usually, because it's a genetic mix. It only grows if there's a fertile tree near enough to cross-pollinate. The birds and the bees, you know how that works."

"Keep going," I said, "I'm interested."

"The third sprout is key. It's smaller and weaker than the clone sprout. It's the same with all the seeds from your oldest trees. That's not what I was hoping. My theory is, after a several hundred years in isolation, the weaker shoot should also produce a clone. A way of adapting to the inability to cross-pollinate. Or, quite possibly, split into twin shoots. It's a stretch, but one single seed might produce three perfect clones. Here . . . have a look at what came from your orchard."

In the wheelbarrow, in plastic pots, seedlings had broken through the soil. One seedling tree in each.

I said, "The seed stock you're after should produce triplets. That's quite a theory. I've never heard of such a thing."

"Twins at the very least, if I'm right. Either way, there has to be an older, purer strain of Spanish citrus out there somewhere."

I knew where the conversation was headed but remained silent while he selected a pot and held it close to his eyes. "I had a friend do the genotype by sequencing for known markers. I couldn't afford to have him run the whole genome, but I found out enough to know a couple of things. What your great-grandfather planted isn't an exact match of any citrus my friend's ever come across. It's close, though— very close, genetically —but different enough to keep me working on this project. A year or two from now, if you're willing, after I've experimented with various grafts, the combination might be more resistant to HLB disease. Who knows? Until then—"

I interrupted, "I get it. The trees in our grove aren't original Spanish rootstock. I know what you're asking me, Kermit, but I can't. A couple of my fishing clients are in the biotech field, and there's a woman I went to school with, a plant pathologist—"

"Roberta Daniels," he said in a matter-of-fact way. "I know. She's good, and she's smart. The biggest grove owner down her way is Elmer Ogden. He's a tough old buzzard, and his new wife's a talker. Hannah"—Kermit touched my arm and gave it a squeeze—"that's why I don't want you going back to that place alone. There's more to worry about now than just snakes. I heard a python, or boa—one of them—bit you. How bad was it?"

I retreated a step. "How in the world did you find out?"

"I just told you, Elmer's wife, and probably a dozen other people by now. I'm serious. Keep the seed stock for yourself, I don't care. I'm volunteering, or take someone else, but please don't go back there alone."

"That's what I do for a living, Kermit, drive a boat, usually by myself. You don't know anything about me to say such a thing."

"I know there's a race going on, Hannah. That's

what you don't understand. Big ideas travel fast, once they're loose. Not just in Florida. All along the South American coast, the Spaniards planted seeds; Mexico, too, and into California. Somewhere, the original rootstock exists. The Brazilian citrus people have more money than God; the Chinese, all the major producers, will get in the hunt just on the chance your idea has merit. Trust me, if a clone of those original trees exists, someone will find it."

"More power to them," I said, "as long as they leave me alone."

He removed his hand. "Why are you so damn stubborn? That's what I'm worried about. Some of those people are ruthless. They might see you as an easy target. That tailing you, or conning you, is the fastest way to jump to the front of the parade. You need to be careful."

I replied, "I'm not naïve. It's possible I have more reasons to be careful than you realize."

The man wasn't sure what to make of that. "Then you know about the GPS?" In response to my blank look, he added, "I'm talking about the GPS on the plane you and Roberta rented. I heard someone stole it or got inside and copied the numbers. You didn't know?"

"How long ago?" I'd forgotten that Roberta had saved the location.

"Yesterday, supposedly."

I almost did it again, asked a question that

was unfair to ask: *Why didn't you tell me?* A distant siren stopped me before I could.

Kermit's head panned toward the door, then to me. "Damn it. I'm not leaving without my plants. Will it be okay if you talk to the cops?"

I said, "That's not what you're hearing. There was a reason I asked when you last saw Reggie. He's dead, Kermit. Lonnie told me. That's an ambulance. Or the police."

"*Him?* Oh no . . ." The man turned, hands on his hips, and took a few steps. "This is bad, Hannah, worse than you think. How'd he die? In his own house?"

I was startled by the stricken reaction. The two men hadn't been close. "You didn't notice the lights when you drove in. I know because I saw you. I was in my SUV, just leaving. Lonnie said it was suicide, but I don't know for sure. The emergency people have been there a while. I couldn't bring myself to look."

"Suicide . . . Geezus, that's awful. How'd she say he did it?"

"That he hung himself. One of the workers found him. It had to be within the last hour or so."

He stood as if he hadn't heard, then came toward me. "Suicide, my ass. Hung himself from what? You ever been inside that little trailer of his? I had to duck to get in, that's how low the ceiling is." He began pacing. "No . . . no

271

way it was suicide. Lonnie had him killed. I'd bet on it. Come on. I'll get the wheelbarrow, you hold the door."

As he hurried past, I tried to grab his arm. "Tell me what this is about."

"When we're someplace safe to talk." He placed the young tree among the pots and rushed around, gathering more things. "She'll have us killed, too. It's possible. I think it's because of what happened the day we met. Of what you might have seen. Her screwing that guy in the boathouse."

"I didn't see anything. Reggie didn't see anything, either, you know that. If she'd wanted to kill me, I was just with her at the ranch."

Kermit, pushing the wheelbarrow, said, "Tell that to Reggie. I didn't believe she was crazy enough, my god. Or that damn vicious."

"You don't know that it's true."

"Nope, but I'll find out. Goddamn right, I will. Open the door."

I followed him out, where he dropped the Chevy's tailgate, then reconsidered. "Where are you parked? I'll finish loading this stuff once I'm sure you're off the property and safe."

The bed of the truck was empty but for the detritus of hay, straw, and tools typically seen in the vehicle of a working man. I'd already started placing gardening pots in a row. "This won't take long."

272

"What if Lonnie is up there, waiting, and locks us in?"

"Tell me why you're so sure about her? I don't want to believe it either, but Reggie had been depressed. Working for Mr. Chatham was that man's whole world."

Kermit took me by the shoulders in a way that was gentle enough to seem caring, yet my guard remained in place. "Stubborn," he said again. "It's dangerous, me even telling you about it."

"You'd better. If the police show up, you'll need help explaining why you're stealing a truckload of plants."

"Geezus," he said. "Okay. Lonnie and Mr. Chatham, they had an infidelity clause in their prenup. I don't remember all the details, but he told me one eyewitness, that's all it would take, and she's out of his will. I'd bet anything that's what this is about. Firing me was a way to get me off the property. One suicide could be explained. Not two. So she must have something else in mind."

"Mr. Chatham told you that himself?"

Kermit, looking into my eyes, confirmed it was true. "Text me when you get home. I'll stop by tonight and we'll talk. Around eight, but it could be later. I'm helping some local growers get their smudge pots ready in case of a freeze. Is that okay?"

"Call first," I replied, which came out kinder than intended, but it's what I felt. I was tired of fighting. I couldn't fault a man who was a good father and cared about saving his plants.

At my car, I gave him the barbecued ribs as a peace offering, and even acquiesced to his arms; a brief hug that might have lingered, had I allowed it.

I did not.

Halfway home, though, I was quick to answer when Kermit's name flashed on my phone.

"Something just crossed my mind," he said.

"Are you still at the greenhouse?"

"You'll think I'm an idiot. I went off and left those damn seeds. The late bloomers in the growing box. Guess I got flustered, seeing you, and everything else going on. Now the gate's locked, so I'll have to sneak in through the pasture. If Lonnie notices those pots missing, she'll padlock me out of the greenhouse, too."

It was nearly sunset. Clouds were glaciers of charcoal and rust on this, the eve of a cold front.

"I can try and talk to her," I said.

"Don't you dare. Stay away from that woman. But that's not why I called. I have an idea, if you're willing to listen."

I was willing.

We were still discussing the subject when I pulled into the shell drive, relieved to see that Loretta was not on the porch. Sit there with a phone too long, my mother's witching powers might divine the marital status of my caller.

Twenty

What Kermit wanted to discuss was the python that bit me—and the weather. It was an odd combination until he connected the two, saying, "When the temperature drops near freezing, reptiles hole up. *Dormant* might be the wrong term, but this cold front could give you a one-day window. Possibly, two, according to my weather service. If you're worried about snakes, why not go tomorrow? I'm not asking where, but I am offering to help. No strings attached, and whatever we find belongs to you. Think it over. No matter how cold it gets, you shouldn't go alone."

The idea had merit. Gators, as I knew from experience, become lethargic when the temperature falls below fifty. The same might be true of pythons.

Or was it?

I had two hours before Kermit arrived. I used the laptop on my boat and did research. A few years back, after a cold snap, "experts" predicted that more than half the exotic reptiles in the Everglades had been killed. Field surveys proved them wrong. Two years later, similar experts estimated the python population had grown to more than three hundred thousand.

Some theorized that gradual exposure to cold weather might have created a stouter, more weather-tolerant hybrid.

There was other information I scanned through.

Pythons are the world's third-largest snake, commonly growing more than twenty feet long, although a thirty-five-foot Burmese had been captured and killed in India. It weighed nearly three hundred pounds.

They were ambush hunters, equally at home on the ground or in trees. Excellent swimmers, too, which wasn't news to me, but I was unaware they could lie submerged for thirty minutes or more while they awaited passing prey.

This caused me to think back. Had the snake that attacked Roberta been underwater, hunting, when it heard her wild splashing? The monster python we'd seen later might have been hiding on the bottom, too. If not thirty-five feet long, it was well over twenty. And two hundred pounds, at least, judging from its girth.

An image came into my head I did not want to linger. I continued reading.

Pythons were voracious feeders. They chose ambush spots based on the size of their preferred prey but were opportunistic. Hungry or not, they would strike and kill anything they could swallow. Proof of this was in a 2012 report done for the Department of the Interior regarding the Everglades. In areas where pythons were well established, foxes and rabbits had disappeared. Ninety-nine percent of raccoons and possums had been destroyed, and the white-tailed deer population was down by 91.4 percent.

According to the report, the problem began in 1992 after Hurricane Andrew destroyed a python breeding facility near Miami. Also to blame were pet owners who, after tiring of their snakes, had released them into the Glades.

The results were catastrophic. It was as if a nuclear bomb had been dropped, said one field scientist. Pythons—apex predators—were running out of food, so they were moving north, or seeking new varieties of prey.

The only reassuring certainty I found was that hunters—men who actually knew the woods—agreed the best time to find and kill pythons was during a cold snap. The snakes were sluggish and slow-moving. Their reptilian hearts required them to find a sunny spot in the open if they were to survive a drop in temperature.

Choking Creek. The name had stuck with me. I'd hoped never to go back. After reading what I'd just read, I definitely didn't want to, but I had no choice. "The race is on," Kermit had said. The Gentrys had implied the same thing, as had Lonnie.

I phoned Roberta and explained the situation. "I'm not asking you to get out of the plane, but can you land there and wait for me and another passenger? It has to be tomorrow, or, possibly, the day after. This could be the last cold front of the season."

Roberta understood, but she had obligations at work. "It's too bad you can't get in there by boat."

"That's another option," I said. "I think I can, if I carry a saw, and some heavy clippers. Or"— I had a chart in front of me—"we could hike in from the bay side, but that's through a couple hundred yards of mangroves."

"I don't even want to think about it. As long as you don't try it alone. Who's going with you?"

I hadn't made up my mind about that. My first choice was Marion Ford, if he'd returned from wherever it was he'd disappeared to. His pal Tomlinson was another possibility, although I doubted the man's skill with firearms.

"I've got a friend who's a deputy sheriff," I said, referring to Birdy. "If not her—she usually works Mondays—there's someone else. Do you remember me mentioning Kermit Bigalow? He's offered to come along, but . . . I don't know him that well."

When I said this, part of me hoped Roberta would offer a glowing endorsement and thereby settle the matter.

Instead, she responded, "Take a shotgun no matter who you choose."

Good idea.

In the attic of Loretta's house, I found my

uncle's footlocker. I returned to my boat carrying a heavy pillowcase. Inside was a sawed-off double-barrel and a box of twelve-gauge shells I hoped weren't too old to fire, if needed. I made another trip and came back with Jake's ripsaw and the stout hedge clipper he'd used to cut the original tunnel. Behind a drawer was a lockbox containing another of Jake's treasures. From it, I took an exotic-looking pistol, a rare 9mm Smith & Wesson that had been customized by Devel. It had clear Lexan grips and a chromium stainless finish. Since shooting the man who'd attacked me, I'd fired several hundred of rounds through it at gun ranges.

The pistol and holster went into my shoulder pack. The other stuff went into a canvas bag that could be stored aboard my skiff. As I packed, I made phone calls, and also kept an eye on the clock. I was nervous about Kermit's visit and the decision I had to make.

The choice was quickly narrowed down. Birdy had to work. Tomlinson was en route to a Zen meditation retreat in Polk City. The biologist's phone went instantly to voice mail. Seldom do I leave long messages, but, this time, I did. Lots of details.

It was a safety precaution that only a man like Marion Ford would understand.

That's what I was thinking about—Ford's unwavering eyes, his competence on the water, when another competent man came to mind.

I checked *Previous Calls* and pressed *Redial*.

Earlier in the day, Sabin Martinez had asked insightful, sometimes pointed questions about Larry Luckheim's intimidation tactics. "I'll look into it," he'd said, which is the sort of help people often offer but seldom follow through on.

Not true of Martinez. This time when I called, he answered, saying, "Guess who I'm watching haul his boat out of the water? Yeah . . . your favorite stalker. At marinas, he goes by the name Buddy Luck. But his luck's about to run out, according to a source I have at . . . Well, the less you know, the better."

I was flabbergasted. "You found him already? You must be in Placida."

"Harney told me to look after you and that's what I intend to. You sound surprised . . . Captain Hannah." It was playful, the way he added my name, and his operatic voice was pleasing to the ear.

"I'm . . . I'm flattered. But I hope you don't think I called to pressure you. This has to do with a boat trip I'm taking. Tomorrow; early in the morning. It's supposed to be freezing cold, and it's not an easy place to get to. I'll tell you that in advance, but I'd prefer not to go alone. The reason is . . . Well, maybe you heard about Reggie. If you didn't, I've got some bad news."

"He was a good little guy," Martinez said. "I'd prefer to believe good men don't take their own lives, but I know better. On the other hand, I've got my suspicions."

"Me, too. That's why I called. Is there a chance you'd be willing to go with me tomorrow? We don't know each other well, but I'm good with a boat, and I know the area. I figure I can trust a man who was Mr. Chatham's confidant."

"Now I'm flattered," Martinez said. "Unfortunately, I have meetings all day, one in Orlando, then I fly to Lauderdale. I could use a tough trip, though. And you're right to think Reggie might have been murdered." He paused to think. "Give me the details. I doubt it, but maybe I can shift things around."

I summarized my plans, then mentioned Placida again. "Larry supposedly charters out of there."

"Nope, we're closer to Arcadia, some little waterfront dive. Don't ask me why, but he'll tell me soon enough. Same with whoever's paying him to harass you. We're meeting for drinks after his boat's trailered. See, I'm a wealthy developer who's interested in building a fishing resort on Andros. That was my pitch—I need an experi-enced pro like him to run the operation."

I said, "I hate you having to spend so much time on this. How'd you find him? Arcadia . . . he must have run his boat up the Peace River."

"Now, now, that's another delicate point. As a

private investigator, you're aware it's illegal to plant a GPS on someone's car. In this case, a bright orange pickup truck. You ever see *The Dukes of Hazzard*? Don't worry, dear, I enjoy this sort of thing. Especially the egocentric types. Did you know Larry has a marketing degree from Penn State?"

"I don't believe it. Not unless he means the state prison."

"Would a man who calls himself Buddy Luck lie? Claims he graduated top of his class. That's why ESPN wants him to host a fishing show, but only if he doesn't make the final cut for *Dancing with the Stars*. Until now, producers have failed to appreciate Larry's marketing genius."

After a riff of baritone laughter, Martinez became serious. "Your instincts were dead-on. The guy's a freak. And he is dangerous. I'd say either coke or speed. He sniffs a lot, and his bubba accent is atrocious. I don't doubt he's from Florida, but I'm thinking he spent a lot of time outside the country."

"I'm the same way. His accent, I couldn't place it. Germany came to mind. Harsh, you know?"

"Not harsh enough. Basque, could be, or Portuguese. That's guesswork, but I know for certain he's wanted for questioning in Pennsylvania. Actually, the cop term is *a person of interest,* but that might be all the leverage I need. It has to do with the disappearance of a teenage girl a few years back. The pattern makes me think that Larry Luckheim isn't his real name, either."

I told him what Birdy had discovered, then said, "He plays the role of a Southern hick, gets this wild look in his eyes. I wouldn't be surprised if he's killed more than one girl."

"Odds are good." This was said in a way that suggested Martinez knew more, or suspected more, than he was willing to say.

"Is that what you're going to do? Threaten to contact the police if he doesn't back off? I'd just go ahead and turn him in, if you think he's dangerous."

Sabin Martinez warned *me* to back off, saying, "Harney was smart in a lot of ways. He'd give me a project—protecting you, for example—and that was the end of it. He never said another word as long as I got the job done."

"Sorry," I said. "You've done a lot for my mother and me, and I appreciate it. I won't pry again, Mr. Martinez."

"Call me Beano."

"I don't think I can do that."

"Okay, Sabin will have to do. Tell you what"— he became confidential—"you've got your PI license. I never bothered with that, but I'll share a trade secret: I've been doing what I do for thirty years and I've never threatened a man or fired a warning shot in my life. Know why?"

I said, "Because it's illegal?"

Martinez laughed at that. "It gives the other guy an advantage. Do you stomp your feet before casting to a fish? If I'm not there by six a.m., that means I couldn't rearrange my schedule."

It took me a moment to comprehend his meaning. "That would be great."

"But don't count on it," he replied. "I'll either be there or I won't."

That evening, I was dressed, ready and waiting, but there was no sign of Kermit, who was almost an hour late. After a lot of seesaw indecision, I decided it was better to cancel than to spend another minute worrying I'd been stood up. We could meet tomorrow night, preferably some-place public. A dozen times I'd reached for the phone, intending to say this, but had lost my nerve.

I touched *Redial*. Kermit's phone rang and rang before it, too, went to voice mail.

"Hi, it's me. Are you still coming?" I heard myself say. "I'm open tomorrow night, if that's better."

I held the phone up, glared for a moment, then slammed it on the bed. If I'd tried, I couldn't have combined three more needy-sounding sentences, two of which seemed vaguely suggestive when I replayed what I'd said over and over in my head.

My bedroom is the bow on my boat: a V-berth,

with drawers for storage beneath, a tiny closet, and pleated curtains over the portholes. It was a poor choice as a place to contemplate being stood up by a man I shouldn't be alone with in the first place.

I strode barefoot into the main cabin, switching on lights. On the settee table was a long-sleeved blouse from Target. It was a size too large, made of earthen-brown cotton. Beneath was a heavy plaid pullover with welted pockets and three-quarter sleeves—the ugliest garment I own. I scooped them up and hung them where they belonged.

I was disgusted with myself. Reggie, whom I had cared about, was dead, yet I had spent the last hour changing in and out of clothes for a man I barely knew and was only beginning to trust. I didn't want to encourage his advances. On the other hand, I didn't want to look like a bag lady, either.

Now I was wearing stonewashed jeans, ankle-cut, which made me look taller, even in deck shoes. Kermit, who was an inch shorter, would notice. Over a collared shirt of utilitarian tan, my cardigan sweater only hinted at what my guest might be tempted to explore.

What guest?

At nine-fifteen, I flipped on the dock lights and went out to find that a cold north wind had settled beneath a cloudless sky and cold,

cold stars. My breath plumed. A bulkhead thermometer read forty-four degrees. This gave me an emotional boost. No wonder Kermit hadn't appeared. He was too busy. All over Florida, citrus farmers would be awake, using giant fans, or helicopters they'd hired, or old-fashioned smudge pots, to save their crops if the temperature dropped near freezing. Without clouds as insulation, or a strong wind to blow the cold front away, this was a possibility.

I felt better about the evening, and myself. Disappointment and relief are not an uncommon mixture, in my experience.

The question was, what about tomorrow?

Don't go alone. How many times had I been told that? Didn't matter. If Sabin Martinez couldn't rearrange his schedule, I'd find some-one else. Or not. What I'd told Kermit was true. I've spent much of my life alone in small boats, and it is the rare waterman whose knowledge exceeds my own.

A sense of freedom and confidence are a less common mixture. That's the attitude I embraced. I had a window of one, maybe two days. Come hell or high water, I would go. It was sixty miles to what I thought of as Choking Creek. The wind had settled, but the Gulf would still be rough. It was wiser to trailer my skiff, drive to Marco Island, and use the public boat ramp. I— or we—would have to be on the water by sunrise.

There was no guessing how long it would take to clear the tunnel my uncle had cut years earlier. The same was true of finding an orange tree on an island thick with catbriers and vines. By noon, the sun would be high. Reptiles would be on the move. I wanted to be long gone by then.

Such a trip required preparation. First, though, I needed socks and shoes.

My lord, it was cold standing there barefoot on that dock.

A little before ten, my phone beeped with a text. I'd given up on Kermit so was pleased to see it was from him.

> Sorry worked late, then home. I always tell Sara a bedtime story. U mad?

Not after reading his excuse. This began an exchange that felt oddly comfortable. Texting negated the tension of speaking face-to-face yet ensured privacy. Secrecy—another way of looking at it.

Back and forth we went after I wrote:

> Not mad. Sarah comes first, business second. Will it freeze tonight?

> Probably not. Forecast low is 40 degrees. U on for boat trip?

Think so. Seems smart what you suggested.

Is that a yes?

Yes.

Tomorrow morning?

Very early. I'll tell you how it goes.

Not without me. What time R U leaving dock?

Kermit had bypassed my indecision. He was also my only choice unless Martinez showed up. So far, not a word from him.

I wrote, I'm trailering my skiff to Marco Island. Hang on.

In the Marlow's galley, the propane oven was lit for heat. Atop the table was a nautical chart, a tide table, and a list of Florida boat ramps. The tide table provided information that I passed along.

Sunrise is 7:01 a.m. I want to be on water by then. You don't have to go.

I WANT to go. Meet U on Marco at 6:30? Will bring doughnuts and coffee.

There. It was settled.

I sent directions to the public boat ramp on

Collier Avenue, a mile inland from the Marco Island Bridge. There were a few things I suggested he bring: gloves, heavy boots, a machete, but omitted firearms. It was better he didn't carry a gun if he'd had no training. After a pleasant, easygoing exchange about the weather, smudge pots, and how pretty the stars were tonight, the man signed off abruptly, writing, **Sara is up. Bye.**

That was okay, too. Family first. Always.

Or was it . . . ?

I reviewed our texts. His daughter's name was spelled with an *h*. I'd seen it on her sketchbook, yet twice he'd spelled it *S-a-r-a*. Children, girls especially, were fickle about such things. It was possible she had added the *h* as an affectation. It was also possible that texting has made us all lazy and inarticulate. Kermit's many shortcuts proved it, as did my own.

On the other hand, an adoring father wouldn't do that. No . . . the *h* had to be an embellishment from Sara's imagination. It's what I wanted to believe, but the inconsistency nagged at me.

It was quarter after ten. Outside, my skiff was already trailered, secured with straps, and hitched to my SUV. Sandwiches, drinks, an emergency kit, were packed and stowed. My destination had been entered into a Garmin GPS mounted on the boat's console. A handheld VHF radio was charging. I needed fuel, but the tank could be topped off on the drive to Marco Island.

I went inside, bolted the cabin door, and showered. This took courage. The Marlow's "water heater" consisted of a few heating elements built into the cabin's AC. The system is impotent as a cheap toaster. I was shaking before I got my hair rinsed well.

Cocooned in sweaters, sweatpants, and a blanket, I checked the thermometer a last time.

Thirty-nine degrees. Already, colder than the married man had predicted.

I should have slept fairly well after seeing that, but I couldn't. After midnight, I was up again, the galley propane stove on high. The warmest spot on the boat was at the helm, where the cabin roof is elevated. Warm air rises. I sat in the captain's chair, lights off, looking at stars while more details nagged at me regarding Kermit Bigalow.

That afternoon, while helping load plants into his Silverado, my eyes had seen the truck bed as empty, save for a detritus of hay and straw and a few other things commonly carried by ranch hands. But Kermit wasn't a rancher. He grew citrus. He had no livestock to feed or stalls to muck. Straw might be useful around the base of a tree, but why had he been hauling hay?

My imagination moved to the Chatham ranch, where, that afternoon, I'd heard a truck start. The doors of an amber barn opened. Lonnie was there, straightening her collar as if she'd dressed in haste. Within was a hidden space, redolent of clover hay freshly cut. And freshly delivered, Lonnie had said.

The scene switched to the boathouse, the day I'd surprised Kermit swimming. This was only minutes after he'd witnessed Lonnie with a lover, or so he claimed. But it was Kermit's clothes hanging on the railing . . .

Stop it, I told myself. The prospect of a woman like Lonnie seducing a common citrus grower was absurd. Mean-spirited jealousy had launched my suspicions, not reality.

Jealousy.

There it was, the truth. I was jealous of a man who wore a ring and adored his daughter. Was that where my life was headed?

At the helm, the captain's chair is stabilized by a locking lever. I disengaged the lever and spun to see the star-glazed windows of the house my grandfather had built and where my mother lives alone. Always alone. Echoing within an empty porch, Loretta's claims about no regrets, of loving a man purely for love's sake, rang with the timbre of hollowed bone.

It was the way she was. A tactic. Loretta was not above manipulating me into an affair after pretending to warn me of the dangers. Guilt, like pain and loneliness, is more bearable if shared.

I slipped from the chair and went down the steps into the cabin. My phone was on the table. Next to it was the nickel-plated Devel pistol and a box of 9mm cartridges. Speer Gold Dot hollow-points. My friend Birdy had split the cost after a fun day at the range. They were expensive, highly rated for personal defense.

Staring at the phone, I released the magazine and cleared the pistol. Several times I dry-fired, pressing the trigger with a familiarity once reserved for the clarinet I played in high school.

How often, since those years, had I spared my hands the hazards of familiarity? And the allure of restless wanting; a longing to touch and be touched.

I could not deny it. For the same reasons, I could not continue a theater of innocence as if unaware of the outcome.

This was me, who I am.

Finally, my mind was made up.

I exchanged the pistol for my phone. It was late, too late to contact a man who was probably asleep beside his wife. I texted anyway, rationalizing Kermit could use smudge pots and the threat of frost as an excuse if his wife heard the ping.

Must cancel our business meeting tomorrow. Will reschedule when appropriate. Capt. Smith

The decision regarding how to sign the note took a while.

I hit *Send* and went to bed.

Twenty-One

An hour before sunrise, I exited Interstate I-75, toward Marco, on a road that darkened between islands of neon. My phone rang. The car's Bluetooth screen showed Kermit's name, so I touched *Accept*.

"You're up early," I said. "You saw my text, I hope."

A woman's voice demanded, "Who the hell are you? How do you know my husband?"

I was stunned. Guilt makes no concessions to fantasy or imagined events. It was several seconds before I could say my own name. "I don't," I said. "Not in the way you're thinking. I apologize for texting so late, but I had to cancel an appointment we'd made—"

The woman, Kermit's wife, said, "Where is he? For god sakes, if you know, tell me. I don't give a damn what he does anymore. Take him, for all I care, but my daughter cried herself to sleep last night. Is he with you now?"

In the background, I heard a man say, "Mrs. Bigalow, I asked you not to touch anything. Is that your husband's phone?"

Kermit's wife, speaking to me, said, "Tell me! I know you were together yesterday; that he called you in the morning, then again in the afternoon. It was after midnight when you sent that text, so don't pretend—"

"I have no idea where he is," I said, "I truly don't, but I'll help if I—"

A man came on the phone, saying he was Arnold-something with the sheriff's department, meaning Sematee County, not the department my friend Birdy works for. "Who am I speaking with?" he asked.

I told him, and explained I was driving. Could he give me time to pull off the road so I could concentrate?

"I'll keep it short. Are you the person who sent a text around midnight to a man named"— he had to check to refresh his memory—"Kermit Bigalow?"

"We had a meeting scheduled for this morning," I said. "I wanted to catch him before he left. Can you tell me what this is about?"

"Have you spoken to Mr. Bigalow since?"

"No."

"Do you know where he is?"

"No."

The deputy said, "I'll call you from another phone if he doesn't turn up," and we were done.

Doesn't turn up?

It was fifteen miles to the boat ramp east of the Marco Island Bridge. I spent the time ruminating over what might have happened. Kermit had been home last night when we'd had our lengthy exchange via messages. That was around ten. He'd already read his daughter a story, which meant she was in bed. So why had Sarah cried herself to sleep after I'd texted around midnight?

I got a sick feeling in my stomach. In my mind, a scenario played out. My text had awakened the wife. She'd gone through Kermit's phone log and messages. They had argued. Sarah awoke as her father stormed out, slamming the door behind him.

But his phone . . . Why hadn't he taken his phone?

Reggie came into my mind. Then Kermit saying, *Suicide, my ass . . . Lonnie had him killed . . . We might be next.*

If not his exact words, the meaning was the same. Lonnie was dangerous. All because of a prenuptial agreement that contained a fidelity clause. And her greed.

I slowed. My turn signal bounced light over a sign that read *Collier Boulevard Boat Park*. It was an elongated parking area adjacent to the road, water and mangroves on both sides. Six a.m. on a frigid morning is a poor time to fish. The lot was empty save for an RV at the south end and a van parked close to the ramp. A mile away, the Marco Island Bridge a blazing silver arc. Here, only a few sodium lights provided pools of visibility. I'd hoped to see the white Lexus owned by Sabin Martinez. My disappointment added to the gloom of a frigid winter morning.

I turned in, parked in the closest slot, and got out to prepare to launch my skiff. The morning air had the sting of alcohol. My fingers numbed while battling ratchet straps. Inside my car, the phone rang again, and I rushed to answer. Heat spilled out when I opened the door. I stood there and warmed my hands as I spoke to the deputy, whose name I finally heard clearly. Arnold Nix.

He said, "Mrs. Bigalow shouldn't have called. Sorry about that. But, if you don't mind, there are a couple of questions I'd like to ask."

"Tell me what's going on," I said. In the background, I heard the whoosh of a semi passing by and pictured the deputy on a country road, in a patrol car, with the window down.

"How well do you know Kermit Bigalow?"

I said, "I know what you're getting at and you're wrong: there's nothing between us but business. Tell me what this is about, maybe I can help."

"Did you two have lunch together yesterday?"

It was a trick question that caused me to remember the barbecue I'd given to Kermit to take home.

After I'd explained, the deputy said, "You can understand why the guy's wife is upset. She checks the phone and sees you texting that late at night? It was signed *Captain Smith*. Some might assume you were trying to hide the fact you're a woman. You know, in case his wife happened to—"

I said, "Some might assume they should get their facts straight before making accusations. I'm a fishing guide. Fairly well known, which is easy enough to confirm. I can understand why she jumped to that conclusion. I don't mean to be rude, but—"

"Whoa, back up. You're not the one I read about in *Florida Sportsman*? The woman guide? You specialize in fly-fishing for tarpon."

"Tarpon and anything else. I only use *Captain* when it pertains to business," I added, which was a lie.

"I'll be darned. I didn't put it together. You know, because Smith is such a common name. The reason I noticed the article was because of your picture. We've met before. Well, sort of met; I shook your hand. About two years ago, you came into the courthouse with Harney Chatham. It was at the hearing after . . . after you—"

The deputy caught himself before saying *shot a man*. My guess was, he did so out of respect for Mr. Chatham, who still carried a lot of weight in Sematee County.

On Collier Boulevard, a pickup with giant tires flew past. Behind me, in the canal, the red-and-green running lights of a boat were noted by my peripheral awareness. Only a mullet fisherman or crabber would be out on a morning so dark and cold. The boat swung toward the seawall; lights blinked out, the engine still running.

I said, "Deputy Nix, I'm not asking for favors, but I would like to know what's going on. I've had maybe three or four conversations with the—"

"Hang on," he said. I heard muffled voices conversing, then he was back. "Sorry. Where were we?"

"I was talking about Kermit Bigalow. I don't know him well, but he seems nice enough; and he's a good father, from what I've seen. We'd arranged to meet this morning to discuss— well, actually, look for—a certain kind of citrus tree. I'm sorry his wife's upset, but I barely know the man."

It was another lie that went unchallenged. The deputy said he didn't doubt my story, then explained, "Domestic squabbles—that's how we spend half our time. I think Bigalow and his wife argued about something and he took off because he was mad. Around ten, she called him in as missing, then kept calling. I spotted his truck about an hour ago, and it took her a while to get here with the keys. What probably happened is—"

"Can I ask you something?" I said. "Where did you find his truck?"

"Bigalow's? On a fire trail off Bermont Road. Near the entrance to what Mr. Chatham called his gun club. Do you know the place?"

"The frontage is all pasture," I said. "Yeah, I've been there, but it doesn't make sense. Kermit was home at ten last night. Why would his wife say he was missing?"

The deputy's friendly manner vanished. "How do you know he was home?"

"Check his phone; the same text I signed *Captain Smith*. He mentioned his daughter, that he was home and read her a story every night. His first text came in before ten, I'm fairly certain."

"Nope," the deputy said. "I'll look again, but all I saw was the one you sent after midnight."

"That's odd. Maybe he deleted the earlier messages."

"Maybe he had a reason to delete them. If it was before ten, why were you texting? Most people do business over the phone."

The deputy was right. Kermit didn't want his wife to know, nor did I, but I said, "Find our texts, read them, you'll understand. Most of it had to do with citrus trees and the chance it might freeze. Or you're welcome to see my phone. What worries me is—"

"Hang on," the deputy said again. The creak of leather suggested he was walking with the phone at his side.

My peripheral awareness wandered to the boat

that had just arrived, engine still running. I couldn't see the hull, just the elevated helm—no one at the wheel. I'd been so focused, I hadn't noticed anyone step ashore. I wondered about that until, in my ear, I heard the deputy yell, "Hey! Where you're shining the light, see it? Doesn't that look like a boot sticking up? That could be him . . . yeah, by that big-ass bull." A moment later, another man said something about needing the property owner's permission or just shoot the damn thing.

I pressed the phone hard to my cheek and was ready when Deputy Arnold Nix returned. "Don't hang up!" I said. "What's going on there? Did you find Kermit?"

"A detective will call you," he replied, and was gone.

I felt dazed. Yesterday, on the phone, Kermit had said he might have to hike across the pasture to rescue the orange seeds he'd left behind. This was in the afternoon, shortly after I'd left the greenhouse. Why would he return to the property late last night?

A couple of plausible answers flitted through my mind—the threat of frost, an argument with his wife. Both made sense. But why had she reported her husband missing at the exact time he and I were exchanging texts?

It took her a while to get here with the keys, the deputy had told me.

Two scenarios emerged: Kermit had texted me from his truck, then left without his phone. Or . . . a person posing as Kermit had sent those messages, then deleted them before locking the phone in the truck.

Who?

Someone knowledgeable, that's who. And strong enough—or sufficiently charming—to keep a loving father away from his home.

Kermit might be dead.

The word *shock* accurately describes the electric jolt that radiated from my spine upward. It sharpened my senses and narrowed my focus.

I did a slow turn. Beside the boat ramp was a van, windows dark. Nearby was what I had assumed was a mullet boat, engine running. No . . . the boat had twin engines, which my ears confirmed. Only the elevated helm was visible. It wasn't a tower, but this was no guarantee it wasn't Larry's over-powered cat boat. Hinged towers can be removed.

I stepped backwards into my SUV, locked the doors, and removed the pistol from my shoulder pack. It was in an old Galco holster; soft saddle leather designed to be concealed by a jacket or shirt. I slid it onto my belt and positioned it comfortably against the small of my back. As I fitted the pistol into the holster, headlights panned the windows, and a car pulled in beside me.

A white Lexus SUV.

Thank god, Sabin Martinez.

As relieved as I was, I waited until Martinez was walking toward me, smiling through his Hemingway beard, before I got out. I held up a warning finger. "We have a problem," I said.

"Not if you're worried about Larry." He motioned to his car. "Come on. I'm freezing my tail off out here."

"It has to do with Kermit Bigalow. Do you know him?"

"The citrus expert Harney hired about four months ago. Yes, he's a good man. Harney trusted him. What's this about?"

A good and trustworthy man—the words caused me to wince.

I said, "A deputy just called. Kermit didn't go home last night. They found his truck near the gun club, off the main road. His wife reported him missing around ten."

"That's not like him." Martinez, wearing a hooded parka, blew into his hands for warmth. It gave him time to think. "There's probably a simple explanation, but don't count on it. First Reggie, now this. It was around ten?"

"That's when his wife called the police," I said, then explained about Kermit's phone; that maybe I'd exchanged texts with someone else.

"Damn it . . . I didn't anticipate him going after anyone but you."

"Larry?"

"That's one of the names he uses. I left him at the bar last night around seven. Everything was all set, I thought. In fact, I was sure of it until just now."

I nodded toward the seawall. "That might be his boat. I didn't see him, but he could be behind that van, for all we know."

Martinez shook his head in a dismissive way, which freed his gray ponytail from the hood. "Impossible."

"How can you be so sure? You believe he has something to do with Kermit disappearing. Maybe Reggie, too. You just said as much. There's something you're not telling me."

A sharp look reminded me that questions were not welcomed. "You don't want to know, Hannah. Just take my word for it." He blew into his hands again, and found the eastern sky. "The sun won't be up for half an hour. How about we sit in my car, with some heat, while we talk?"

"The place I'm headed," I said, "I need to trust the person with me. I'll leave you here, Mr. Martinez. I'd hate to do it, but I will if you don't tell me the rest."

"My, my . . . Captain Hannah," he said in a musing way as if thinking back to his days with

Harney Chatham. "Okay. Yes, I think Larry got his hands on Reggie. Maybe Kermit, too. Larry's real name—you wouldn't recognize it—but, years ago, Lonnie had a thing for him. Lonnie had a thing for a lot of football stars. This guy—Larry—he's the only one she cared enough about to help after he'd killed somebody. It's a long story. Point is, you don't have to worry about him anymore."

I remembered Birdy say she had found zero information about the man prior to his twenty-fifth birthday. "Good Lord . . . Larry . . . he's actually Raymond Caldwell," I said. "That never crossed my mind."

"Reggie must've told you about what happened," Martinez said. "No one else could have. Well . . . Lonnie, of course, but she wouldn't. She's paying him to screw up the project because she hates you and your mother —wants the orange tree patent, and everything else." As he spoke, a pair of rough-looking teens appeared from behind the van. They wore yellow rubber coveralls, as commercial fishermen often do, over layers and layers of clothing. They stopped to light cigarettes, then got into a boat whose name I didn't recognize when they pushed off.

Now Martinez's expression asked, *Convinced?*

"Orange trees can wait," I said. "If you've got proof that Larry has something to do with

Kermit, or what happened to Reggie, you have to call the police."

"That would be unwise."

"We've got to! Kermit might still be alive." I said this with more emotion than intended. It did not go unnoticed.

The man repositioned his ponytail while studying me. "You and Kermit, yes . . . I can see that happening. A strong guy with a sense of humor. You'd be a good match, you two. But there's nothing we can do now. Besides, I told you, I was in a bar with Larry last night. People saw us together. He's a talker. He might have told someone I booked his boat for this morning."

"You didn't. You chartered Larry's boat?"

"Buddy Luck," Martinez said, nodding. "Tell you what, if you won't get in my car, how about we sit in yours—at least until there's enough light to check for frostbite."

He started toward my SUV but stopped when he realized I hadn't followed. "Look . . . Caldwell disappeared years ago. He's presumed dead. Forget ever hearing this, but he might disappear again"—Martinez considered the sky, then his watch—"if he shows up for our charter on time."

"Where are you supposed to meet?"

Off Cape Romano, the man informed me. It was an uninhabited island to the south. "In about an hour," he added. "Seven-thirty, give or take. The guy's not very punctual."

There wasn't much light. I moved just enough to observe his reaction, before saying, "You're using me as bait, aren't you?"

If he lied, I would leave him there and drive home. No . . . I would go straight to Salt Creek Gun Club, seeking the fate of a good man I had wrongly treated with suspicion.

Martinez, reading me, too, said, "Yes . . . exactly. As bait. Why else would I stand out here trying to reason with a woman I promised to protect?"

Twenty-Two

Sunrise was a gray intrusion, slower for the frigid weight of darkness and stars. I stopped south of the Coon Key light to let my face thaw and watched a gloom of silhouettes brighten into islands. Already, we'd stopped twice because of the cold.

"I should've asked before we left," Martinez said. "Did you bring a gun? In my glove box, there's a Glock compact. I went off and forgot the darn thing."

"Someone like you," I said, "I figured you always carried a gun."

He sensed this was another test. Maybe it was.

"Never admit you're carrying," he said, but patted his hip to confirm he was. "I brought that Glock along for you. We should both be armed. I don't care how cold it is—and it's pretty blessed damn cold—your story about those pythons scares me."

At the boat ramp, we'd sat talking in my SUV for half an hour, the heater on high. Some of what he'd shared I'd found truly shocking, but Sabin Martinez had yet to give me a reason to doubt his good intentions. Even so, I was reluctant to answer honestly about the pistol holstered at the small of my back. I'm not sure why—particularly after ruining my chance to trust Kermit, a man who actually believed me to be beautiful.

"In there"—I pointed to the duffel bag stowed forward—"I've got an old sawed-off double-barrel, probably too short to be legal. I don't know if the shells are any good or not."

"Twelve-gauge? That's what I should've brought. We can test-fire the thing, if you want. There's no one around."

That was certainly true. I asked, "What time is it?" Behind us, Marco Island was a bluff of lighted condos. To the southwest, a navigation marker flashed off Cape Romano, a lonely intersection of sand and space. "I don't see any boats—none that're on fire anyway. Did Larry say where he was putting in?"

"I never said anything about his boat catching fire."

No, he hadn't. But Martinez had described how he had shorted out a voltage regulator on one of Luckheim's motors. He'd also caused a pinhole leak in a hose that fed the carburetors.

"You knew what would happen or you wouldn't have done it," I said.

"Don't expect an answer to that one," the man replied, taking off his gloves. "So what? Caldwell, why do you think he agreed to be here? Just you and him, that's what he expects.

It's because he plans to kill you. That wasn't clear? Not kill you right away, of course. He'll want to have some fun first. You researched the man. You should know." His head turned to face me; eyes so dark, they reflected light. "Lonnie might enjoy that sort of sick, kinky business. In fact, I'm quite sure she does. But not you."

I asked again for the time, then looked for myself. It was a little after seven.

"Hannah . . . don't tell me you're feeling remorse. What happens to the guy is all on me. Your only mistake was asking questions I shouldn't have answered. I know better. Not that the cops will find anything. I'm good at what I do."

Harney Chatham's "Lysol man" took out his phone and formulated a test of his own. "Tell you what, I still have one bar showing. I can call. Tell him to shut down his engines; that I think someone's trying to kill him. Or make up some cockamamie story that's convincing. You know . . . a warning shot. We talked about warning shots. Say the word, I'll do it." He gave me time to think before asking, "How many women did Caldwell assault before he disappeared? I bet you have the number in a file somewhere."

I turned away from the man's hard stare. "Sun's up," I said. "Get your gloves on. I don't see the point in waiting around here until it's warmer."

Martinez said what sounded like *I thought as much* as I jammed the throttle forward.

Off Camp Key, we flew across a tendril of sand. The bottom fell away, and I turned my skiff in the direction of Choking Creek.

In a labyrinth of oyster bars and islands, a GPS is no more useful than a compass. My eyes, my hands, did the steering while my mind reviewed something else I'd learned in the warmth of my SUV.

What happened that New Year's Eve, more than twenty years ago, was a sordid story that diminished my respect for the late Harney Chatham. As Martinez had reminded me, however, most of the "facts" had been provided by a drunken (or drugged) college cheerleader.

Long before midnight, Lonnie, in hysterics, had taken Chatham aside, desperately in need of help. She'd been assaulted by a drifter, she said, who followed the college holiday crowd, selling drugs. His specialty was a date rape powder known as Devil's Breath. Lonnie claimed she would've been raped if her boyfriend—who was already in trouble with the law—hadn't come along and beaten the man to death.

The drifter's body went into the gator pool where Reggie and I had seen crocs. A confession, written by Lonnie, went into a cement capstone atop the concrete weir. The next day, her boyfriend, Raymond Caldwell, fled the country. This required the assistance of a powerful man who could pull strings and owned a boat that could make the crossing to Mexico.

When I asked, "Why would Mr. Chatham willingly participate in such a crime?" I received the answer I expected. He didn't. Not willingly.

Martinez offered two explanations, the first provided by Lonnie.

While a junior in high school, she had volunteered to spend the summer working for Chatham's election campaign. He'd tried to seduce her. After weeks of being charmed and pressured, Lonnie finally gave in. By the time their affair ended, she had photographs to prove that the soon-to-be lieutenant governor was guilty of statutory rape.

Martinez didn't believe it. He knew that photographs of some type were involved but had a different theory. Lonnie had done the seducing. Either that or, during the campaign, she had photographed Chatham with another eager volunteer who, as some suspected, often slept in the great man's bed.

Chatham had never confided the truth about which version to believe. Not even to Martinez, a man who claimed to be Chatham's only confidant.

This oddity troubled me, but I let it go. Nor did I ask for names or dates. There was no need. That summer, I'd spent my tenth birthday helping my uncle hack a tunnel to a secret spot—the very place to which I was returning on this dismal winter morning.

Loretta, the eager volunteer, had been generous about granting me free time during my childhood years. Now I understood why.

Martinez, of course, knew all about my mother. He'd asked, point-blank, if Chatham had died in her arms. This gave me an opportunity, once again, to invest my trust in a man I barely knew.

I answered him honestly. Yes, Chatham had died in Loretta's bed. Lonnie wasn't the only one who had breached the fidelity clause in their marriage contract.

How smoothly I shared a truth that was not mine to share. Sometimes, trust must be awarded before it can be granted. Angst and self-recriminations regarding Kermit had also played a role.

You are a beautiful woman.

As I was speeding inland toward the sun, the married man's words chided me from a world I had seldom dared stray. Only once, in fact. Yet, over and over, they hammered at a wounded reality within.

Finally, I conceded, *I'm a fool. Yes, a goddamn fool . . . but* I am my own *goddamn fool!*

After that, I refocused on the task, which was avoiding oyster bars, and shielding my eyes from the glare. Martinez hunkered down beside me, a man who was as wide as a bulldozer yet nimble for his age and size. Articulate, too. He was using a pencil to mark our course on a chart he'd brought along. Occasionally, he made remarks or asked questions that confirmed his experience as a navigator. Watermen don't travel as passengers. They pay attention, aware they might have to find their own way home.

Smart. Few would have bothered to obtain the correct chart on such short notice. I would've done the same. To believe otherwise would have redoubled my doubts about the man beside me.

My hand moved to the small of my back. The Devel pistol was there beneath a jacket and layers of clothing. Not easy to get to, but still a comforting weight.

South of Tripod Key, an unmarked channel appeared as a swath of green. It traversed a sandy shoal. Never had I seen the water in this area so clear. The cold snap had killed all murky microscopic plants and sent them to the bottom. A few fish lay stunned there, too: ingots of silver that might revive as the day warmed.

The air was warming now. The numbness of my nose and cheeks suggested otherwise, but the change was palpable. The channel narrowed. Islands crowded in; long bars of mangroves, trimmed like Japanese hedges. The insulation they provided seemed to generate heat.

Far to my right was Faka Union Bay, where we'd stopped to visit the Daniels cemetery. Ahead was an opening that might have been a gate. I used the trim tabs, tilted the engine, and threaded my skiff through. Air temperature climbed. It was as if we had breached the mouth of an animal and were being shunted toward its radiant heart.

"Shouldn't we turn southeast fairly soon?" The pencil in Martinez's hand tapped the chart, our exact location.

"We could," I said, "it's doable, but we'd have to climb through a quarter mile of mangroves to reach the mound. There used to be a shorter route."

He consulted the chart, then considered the wall of islands that blocked our way. "There's no opening . . . none that I see here . . . and this chart's up to date. God knows how long that river's been landlocked. That's what I think it is, an archaic river. If there are Indian mounds, it would make sense. They had to have access."

"More sense than hiking through mangroves," I agreed.

The man squinted at the chart. "Wouldn't this be simpler?" He pointed to a river half a mile east that ran parallel to Choking Creek. "The entrance is tricky, but it deepens once you're in.

We tie the boat and blaze a trail, so getting back will be easy. Give it some thought. By this afternoon, it'll be in the mid-sixties. You know what that means."

There was no need to confirm I did.

"Are you sure you're willing to waste time just on the chance of saving time? Personally, I don't mind a tough hike."

I motioned to the front storage hatch. "There's a saw and hedge clippers, a machete, and some other stuff in a bag. If you don't mind, go ahead and get ready."

The man's bushy beard parted to show a friendly, bearish smile. "You plan to cut our way in?"

I replied, "It's been done before."

The confidence I wanted to communicate did not reflect my doubts as we drew closer to that wall of green. I dropped off plane and idled along a shoreline where there was no shore, only the tangled claws of prop roots beneath a curtain of waxen leaves.

"Impossible," Martinez said.

A few minutes later, I lifted an awning of branches, switched off the engine, and nudged my skiff ahead. There it was: an opening, where blunt stubs of tree limbs walled a channel. Over the years, new mangroves had bridged the space, but it hadn't changed much. Watery daylight was visible on the other side.

"I'll be darned," the man said. There was admiration in his tone.

I found that reassuring. I'd begun to fear there was a reason Martinez favored hiking in from the next river.

"We'll have to do some cutting," I said. "Keep low; watch your eyes."

I pulled the skiff into the cut. Tree limbs sprung back into position and hid our presence. Overhead, waxen leaves interlaced to form a shaded cavern. Spiderwebs glistened like ice crystals in the fresh sunlight.

"Listen." Martinez held up a hand, his head cocked. "A boat. Hear it?"

From somewhere in the distance, miles away, the whine of an outboard motor vacillated like gusting wind. A bumblebee sound that came and went . . . then grew steadily louder.

"You're the expert. Think it could be him?"

"Shush," I said.

A minute or more passed. In my mind, a black catamaran hull was attempting to cross a flat too shallow for twin, oversized engines. Then, as if influenced by my anxiety, what I hoped would happen *happened*.

The sound of a fast boat plowing itself high onto a sandbar is distinctive. Familiar braying notes reached my ears, a series of staccato thuds that ascended into the howl of engines starved for water. The driver refused to concede. After several pointless attempts, the howling became a sustained scream that, abruptly, went silent.

Wrong. The engines were silenced by what we heard next: a gasoline whoosh, then the faraway thump of an explosion. The soundless void that followed suggested images of smoke and flames.

Martinez was forward, hedge clippers in hand. I was on the stern casting deck, holding the skiff steady. We looked at each other. I felt dazed. Not him. "That stupid damn hick," he said, pleased with himself. "I told you there was no need to worry. Well . . . at least he's not freezing his ass off anymore."

Hick? Luckheim had only posed as a redneck, if what Martinez had told me was true.

Humor, in this remote place, and under the circumstances, strained my patience. The laughter that came next struck me as bizarre. It was a while before I could speak. When I did, what the man heard me say was, *"Raymond . . . ?* Hand me those clippers."

"Of course it was his boat," was the response to a question I had not asked.

What I'd said was, "Raymond . . . hand me those clippers."

Although still uncertain, I felt a chill when the big man did.

Twenty-Three

Martinez—if that was his name—didn't say much until we exited the tunnel into the bay where Birdy had nearly died.

"Beautiful," he said. "What'd it take, about forty minutes? Worth it, to see something like this. That Harney, he was right about you knowing your way around a boat." His eyes settled on me. "About some other things, too. Don't get mad. That's a compliment."

He had read my reaction accurately.

I said, "Closer to an hour . . . but it is pretty, I suppose—if you've never been here before."

The Garden of Eden might have been as deceptively idyllic: a crystal basin rimmed by palms that shaded clear water, and rivulets that dropped off, black and deep, near the bank. Gumbo-limbo trees sparkled with amber sunlight. They were elevated by mounds creating a sawtooth ridge.

"How'd you ever find this? Even with GPS numbers, it would be darn near impossible."

I lowered the engine, saying, "It's already almost nine. The tide's falling and I don't want to get trapped in here. Take a seat."

My terseness was intentional. If the man wasn't who he claimed to be—Caldwell, perhaps, a rapist and killer—now was the time to find out. There are many ways a good boat handler can rid them-selves of a passenger. I started the engine and throttled toward the first bend.

Martinez, with his beard and gray ponytail, remained standing. When he turned to face me, his weight caused the skiff to list. "Was it something I said?"

I feigned ignorance. "If we hit a snag, you could fall overboard. That's all I meant."

"Come on, now. Suddenly, you don't trust me. Which test did I fail? There've been so many." Amused, he took off his parka, a red turtleneck sweater beneath. I got a glimpse of a holster when he knelt to stuff the parka under the seat. When he straightened, the pistol was in his hand; not pointed at me, but there. Like a magic trick, that's how fast it happened. He continued talking, unaware that, reflexively, I reached for a holster not easily accessed.

"Maybe this will convince you." He released the magazine and locked the slide back. A chambered round was ejected, which he caught before it hit the deck. It was something I'd seen experts do. With the same professional ease (after I'd confirmed the chamber was empty), he presented the weapon to me. A heavy-caliber Beretta; a .45, possibly, that was not smooth to the touch, unlike my Devel Smith & Wesson, but held far more cartridges.

"Stick it in that bag or carry it, I don't care. When we get onshore, you take the shotgun. Check my billfold, too, but we both know how easy it is to fake IDs. Here, if you want—" He reached for his back pocket.

"You don't need to do that," I said. "I'm nervous, I admit it. I should've come out and said what's on my mind."

"Nervous is bad. Being careful, though, is smart. Hannah, every scenario you've considered; believe me, I would've done the same. Already did, in fact, back there while cutting our way through. Here's the way it went—tell me if I'm close. Larry actually *is* Larry—or was." His face tilted toward the skyline, where there might have been smoke if not for trees. "Lonnie and I could have cooked up the whole scheme, me in the role of Harney's old pal Beano. After I'd killed him, of course, and fed his body to the alligators—that's something Raymond Caldwell knows how to do. Lonnie gives me a list of three witnesses who saw us doing the dirty deed. Would a guy like Caldwell hesitate? Nope. Not if it involves money. Or keeping his kinky old girlfriend—"

"That's close enough," I said. "Isn't it scary, how our minds sometimes work the same? There is one thing you left out—"

"No pictures on the Internet. Am I right? Not of Sabin Martinez. If there are, the ages didn't mesh, or they didn't look . . . well, sufficiently intimidating? But, then, you figured a man in my line of work would avoid broadcasting his—"

"Take your gun back," I said. "This is just silly. You don't need to convince me anymore."

That wasn't true. But we were here, now, in this remote place, and I had to cloak my doubts with confidence or risk a meltdown between us.

The man refused my offer in a convivial way yet was serious enough to say, "Keep the gun until we get back to Marco with oranges, or orange trees, or whatever it is you're after. Under one condition. You test-fire that shotgun before stepping foot onshore, I don't care how cold it is, I'm not kidding. Your story about giant snakes was convincing."

When he again refused to take the Beretta, I placed it atop the console. The magazine went into my pocket, along with the bullet—after he'd turned around.

We had entered the serpentine bend. I motored along the concave edge, where water was deepest, then pointed. "See that spot just ahead? My last trip, we saw an orange floating, but it floated under the trees. We'll pull in there. After I get an anchor set, and we're tied up, I'd appreciate it if you tested the shotgun."

"A show of trust," Martinez said, not flattered but willing to make peace.

I, too, wanted to smooth things over. "You're

welcome to think so, but it could be because the darn thing kicks like a mule. Go ahead, open the duffel bag. It looks like the shotguns they carried on stagecoaches."

Finally, a real smile: broad, white Teddy Roosevelt teeth framed in a bushy, graying beard. "I'd be honored," he said, then, with the gun in his hands, amended, "If it doesn't blow up in my face. This thing's ancient."

"My uncle got it somewhere. Or maybe it was handed down through the family. I don't know. The last time I shot it, I was"—ten years old, I realized, *here,* while camping, but only said— "too young to ever want to shoot it again. The shells worry me. Don't they go bad after a while?"

He snapped the gun open, tilted the walnut stock, saw twin triggers and high-ridged hammers on a barrel set only twenty inches long. "An old side-by-side coach gun. The best home-defense weapon there is." He inspected a couple of shells. "Buckshot. Exactly what we need if it warms up."

Snakes, he was referring to. It was impossible to scan the water without imagining a monster lying on the bottom or a python tracking us from the trees. I tested the temperature by exhaling as if blowing a smoke ring. My breath did not condense. I'd already unzipped my windbreaker; removing it seemed infidelity to my fears, but I took it off anyway. "Get the bowline ready," I said. "You'll need gloves. And watch the trees—they might be up there, getting sun."

"Snakes?"

"Lay the shotgun on the deck," I replied, "until we're tied up."

As I throttled closer, I dropped an anchor off the stern, then fed line until Martinez got his hands on a stout limb. I snubbed the anchor; he tied a flurry of half hitches. Soon, the boat was secure, bow and stern, on lines as taut as springs. On a falling tide, I didn't want the engine to drift under the trees.

"Give it a try," I said.

Martinez loaded the shotgun and fired twice into the water, the rounds spaced like signal shots. The results were mood-lifting, but the shells didn't eject properly.

"Old Remingtons," he said after prying them out. "Paper casings. They must have gotten damp over the years."

He handed the gun to me. "Carry extra shells so you can get to them quick. A breast pocket or your right pocket. If it misfires, you need to be ready."

I said, "Why don't you take it? I'll go first with a machete. You don't know what it's like, how thick the brush is."

"Because you're younger, I suppose, in better shape." He smiled, viewing the scenery. "That's true of some old guys, but this one might sur-prise you. Or are you trying to prove a point?"

"I have no doubt you've yet to reach your peak," I replied, "but someone needs to clear a path. That way, you'll keep both hands free if we—wait . . . You didn't see this." I reached for my phone and opened a gallery of photos.

Martinez, shaking his head, said, "If you were my client, my advice would be the same. Never give the only weapon to a stranger—especially if he's walking behind you."

"*You* are carrying the shotgun," I said, then showed him the photo of the python.

That settled the matter.

Twenty-Four

There is no solid ground in a mangrove swamp, only a gauntlet of rubbery roots and muck. "Give me a minute before you start," I said, and headed into trees with a shoulder pack and the same machete I'd used before.

Martinez understood. Even with the leather thong, the machete might slip out of my hand. Low branches were also a problem in dense cover. Follow too closely, they could slingshot back and put an eye out. A shotgun, fired accidentally, could do worse.

No one walks through mangroves. You climb, and straddle, and monkey-bar your way through. Twenty yards in was an elevated area comprised of big whelk shells and horse conchs, all bone-white with age. A thousand years ago or more, Florida's first people had lived here. They'd feasted on the meat and shaped the shells into tools.

At my feet lay a whelk the size of a gourd. Four symmetrical holes had been drilled through the spire. Nearby were whelks with similar patterns. I'd seen many shell tools, but none like this. I knew it was wrong to disturb such an artifact, but I picked it up anyway. The holes didn't serve any obvious practical purpose. Perhaps it had been used in religious ceremonies; a vessel to sprinkle incense, like a censer used by priests. If so, it might bring me luck.

Absurd, the hopes we cling to when afraid.

I made a place for the shell in my pack, and continued on.

"See any oranges?" Martinez called to me. While securing the boat, he had reasoned the tree must be near the water if we'd found a floating orange.

"It might take a while," I hollered back. "You'll understand when you clear the mangroves. There's a shell mound here . . . really steep, from what I can see. You can come on now."

Behind me, I heard the splash of a big man kicking water. Ahead, the pile of shells angled upward into a curtain of vines. I cut my way through. Every few steps, I slashed a trail marker on the landward side of a tree so I could find my way out.

"Mosquitoes," Martinez grumbled. I couldn't see him but guessed he wasn't far behind. "Cold as it is, you'd think these bastards would give us a break."

Without my bug jacket, insects were tormenting me, too. They hovered in a frenzy as if mammalian blood was a rarity here.

No doubt, it was.

Up a steep embankment, through a coil of

catbriers, I saw the remnants of a game trail: an earthen indentation that tunneled through the brush. No tracks, no animal scat, no signs of recent use. The report I'd read about the Everglades came to mind. Pythons had killed ninety-nine percent of wildlife, from raccoons to white-tailed deer, in areas where they were "well-established." This evoked more details. The snakes were ambush hunters that chose hiding places based on the habits of their favorite prey. On land, in water, or in the tree canopy.

I looked up (not for the first time) and saw a rare patch of winter sky. That's how dense the trees were. No nesting birds, just a lazy pinwheel of vultures circling high above. I patted my bag to communicate with the ornate whelk. Hopefully, the birds had scented a monster python that lay dead on a distant part of the island.

This is insane, I thought. *At the first sign of trouble, I'm out of here.*

For a moment, I hoped an excuse was provided, when, somewhere downhill, I heard branches crack, then the stumbling crash of Martinez falling. "Hell's blazes . . . Shit . . ."

"Are you hurt?"

"Damn mosquitoes; I'm sweating like a pig. Does it thin out up there?"

"Sabin, answer me. What happened?" It felt okay using the man's first name. "I heard you fall."

"Just tripped a little . . . Don't worry . . ."

"If you're hurt, just say so. It's not going to spoil my day, if that's what you're thinking. Did you sprain something?"

"My ego . . . Is it as thick up there as it is here?" Before I could respond, his voice dropped in pitch. "Hey . . . you hear that?"

"What?"

"Probably nothing. Yeah . . . there it is again."

Backcountry silence is a shrill subtext of cicadas and frogs and wind. Not here. Aside from hearing mosquitoes, my ears strained in a vacant abyss. I held my breath for as long as I could, but no results.

Martinez said, "My imagination, I guess. Thought I heard limbs breaking; something coming through the woods, but a long way off. Guess it could have been a boat . . . maybe a plane. You know how sound plays tricks."

"From which direction?"

"Hang on, let me catch up. Wish to hell I'd've brought some water. You were right about these —ouch—these damn mangroves."

I cut a walking stick and waited. When I got a glimpse of his red sweater, I continued up the mound, trying to avoid the game trail. On both sides, though, briars were so dense, I was forced to follow its course. Every few steps required effort. Ficus trees grow by dropping vertical limbs to expand their radiuses. The limbs were

328

spaced like latticework and dominated the lower regions where gumbo-limbos towered. Again and again, I swung the machete, advanced a few yards, then swung again. The air was crisp but warming. I, too, began to sweat.

The mound leveled off. Ancient shells breached a carpet of loam so thick, it was spongy. Over every square foot of earth, plants or moss or saplings competed for sunlight. None flourished, but all reproduced in a relentless effort to prolong the struggle.

The game trail curved inland. Movement in the low branches caught my eye. I stopped. A patchwork of colors created a slow, gelatin spiral that rustled among the leaves. I approached cautiously. It was a snake, no longer than my arm. A checker-board of buckskin yellow and brown told me it was a young python. I did a full turn, concerned something bigger was watching, then moved close enough that I could have prodded the snake with my walking stick but didn't. Better to wait and confirm the creature had been affected by the cold snap.

It had. The python moved as if anesthetized onto a branch. The branch gave way and the snake thudded to the ground. I feared the impact would awaken the thing. Instead, it lay motionless for several seconds, then muscle contractions began to spiral its body into a slow coil.

I used the walking stick to poke it a few times. The python did not respond. It might have been dead.

After one swing of the machete, it was . . . or soon would be.

Whether fish, fowl, or reptile, I am reluctant to take a life. This was different. The animal I'd just killed was killing the Florida I love, choking the life out of her, one native species after another.

If not for my doubts about Martinez, I might have called him over, let him see that my confidence had ballooned after the encounter, which was true. If a small python was comatose because of the weather, a snake with a much larger body mass would be the same, or more so.

The game trail became a more comfortable path but no easier. It curved inland, where I stopped again. In the distance, a dusty column of yellow light suggested there was an opening to the sky. Suddenly, I craved air. Using the machete, I hacked my way toward it, so fixated I almost failed to notice what lay on the ground nearby.

An orange.

I made certain of what it was before hollering, "Found one!"

"You found the tree? That's . . . Shit, I can't keep up with you. Give me a minute. Geezus . . . these bugs."

Downhill, to the right, the muted crackle of branches told me he had lost my trail. I yelled, "Follow my voice," and said it again as I knelt to pick up the orange. Its skin was knobby, which was typical, and the fruit was firm. Juicy, too; deliciously sour when I split it open.

I looked up, scanned the canopy but saw only a cavern of leaves. My eyes moved toward the column of dusty light. It drew me like a magnet. The machete provided the means. When I was closer, I stopped and marveled: there, suspended in a high haze of green, clusters of oranges asserted their right to sunlight. They glowed above a darkened stage. More lay on the ground near the trunk of a massive fallen tree.

I laid the walking stick aside and began to gather the windfall while Martinez homed in on my voice. The area was so thick with ficus roots, logs, and walls of saplings, I dealt with the absurd problem of singling out the actual citrus tree.

Bizarre. Overhead, just out of reach, dozens of oranges, some ripe, some green, proved the tree existed. But which tree? Of the many dozens, bound root to root, none appeared sufficiently mature to bear fruit. Most of them, their trunks were no thicker than my wrist.

When Martinez appeared, I was standing on the giant log, moving from one sapling to another, giving each a shake. Sometimes fruit fell to the ground. Often, it did not. Because of my vantage point, peering up at the oranges, it was impossible to tell which branch was connected to what.

"I'll be damned . . . you're right again. Found the mother lode, by god." His excitement was unexpected. He shifted the shotgun to his other arm while staring up. "I figured you imagined the whole thing as a girl, but, by god, here we are. Is that the tree you were looking for?"

"There must be more than one," I said. "The tree I remember was full-grown. It was in a little clearing, and closer to the water. Lord knows, there's not enough space here to turn around. Step back a little and see if you can tell which limbs move." When he was ready, I chose a sapling and used my weight to rock the thing back and forth. No oranges broke free. The timber on which I stood was so wide, I used it as a walkway, and tried another young tree.

Three oranges fell . . . then a fourth.

"I think this might be it."

Martinez murmured something I didn't hear and backed away to get a broader view. "Try again, a different branch. I want to be sure before I say something stupid."

It was an odd remark. I moved a few yards along the log and selected a thick one. A lone orange plopped on the ground. "It must be the other tree," I said.

"Nope. You found it."

"This one?"

"All of them."

"What do you mean?"

"The orange tree. You're *standing* on it," he said, which was even odder given his tone of disbelief. "Those are branches you've been shaking. Some anyway. The others, I don't know what kind of trees they are. Come over here and see for yourself."

I jumped down and did. It took a while to reassemble an overview of what I'd mistaken as a fallen tree amid a forest of saplings. The trunk, massive and gray-splotched, was a living giant. It had won the battle for sunlight by growing parallel to the ground and shooting branches skyward. Each branch bore leaves healthy in appearance—although some were freckled with psyllids—and most were bowed by weight and the endless production of fruit.

"Amazing," I said, "how nature finds ways to survive."

"Nature, yeah," Martinez replied, his energy suddenly improved. "What I see is my retirement. This could be worth a fortune. How many people know about what you're doing?"

I stared too long. He sensed he'd slipped up. "Now what? Oh . . . you're wondering how I know about the biotech patent. Larry told me. I admire your vigilance, but, come on, enough tests for one day. I would've said yes to this trip anyway. I proved that back there. But now that it actually seems to be panning out—"

"I have three partners," I said agreeably. "It's only fair you're the fourth. You took the risk, invested the time. They'll sign on, I'm sure. Oh, and a friend, a marine biologist, he came up with the idea. That makes six."

The man appeared unfazed. "Who owns this property, or whatever it is—an island? The feds or the state, I suppose."

"Mostly. A few are privately owned."

"We need to check that out. All righty, then. For now, we've got the place all to ourselves. I bet there are smaller trees around somewhere, small enough to carry home, wrapped in towels or something. They might be worth a ton, if things work out."

"There's a procedure, when it comes to collecting samples and DNA," I said. "It has to be followed."

"The correct protocols, of course, I'll leave that to you. Did you bring a shovel? We need to take what we can before word gets out."

There was a trowel in my bag, and a folding shovel on the boat, which I told him about.

"We should've brought it. One of us will have to go back," he said. "Hang on to this for a sec, would you?"

He handed the gun to me. I levered the breech open and confirmed both barrels were loaded, while he took off his gloves. When he stooped to retie his boots, his back was to me. By the time he was standing, I had snapped the barrels closed.

"Why don't you carry the shotgun for a while?" he said. "That sun's warming up fast."

I said, "You take it. Don't stray too far. I want to get pictures and video first."

The man was limping a little when he walked off, the shotgun under his arm.

I snapped photos with my phone, and took more as I cut my way to a ridge where the tree had first taken root. Long ago, a storm had knocked it down, but the roots had survived by re-anchoring themselves in higher ground. They looped away in various directions, as clever as the tentacles of an octopus.

I paced the tree's length—almost fifty feet tall, if stood upright. The trunk was so thick, I couldn't get my arms around it. A dinosaur's neck, I imagined. I also gathered samples of leaves and bark, as instructed by Roberta. If I'd had satellite reception, I would've called to share the good news.

Never had I seen a citrus tree so large, and gnarled and lichen-splotched with age. How long had it survived here on the island? A tree in Tasmania, planted in 1835, was still bearing oranges—or so I'd read. A hundred years? Two hundred? Possibly, older . . . much older. North of Orlando was a famous bald cypress tree that had sprouted before Christ was born, and lived until 2012, when a woman crack addict set it on fire. More than three thousand years the cypress tree had survived, only to die at the hands of someone like that.

I backed up as far as I could and shot video; a slow pan along the mossy trunk, then panning the high canopy, bushels and bushels of oranges, bright as Christmas lights up there in dusty sunlight.

The mother tree.

I was thinking that when I heard the distant, rhythmic crunch of something moving, then heard Martinez, from the opposite direction, calling, "We've got company. Come look."

I drew the pistol, chambered a round, and adjusted the holster for easier access.

Twenty-Five

Martinez, studying the game trail, said, "An animal of some type. Anywhere else, I would assume it was a bunch of pigs—a horse, maybe—if I even bothered to notice. What do you think?"

I had approached with caution until then. "Something's coming our way. I heard it, too. From the south, I think, but it's hard to be sure."

He turned. "I didn't hear anything. Not since that plane, or whatever it was. I found two little trees; maybe orange trees. You're the expert." With the shotgun, he pointed at the ground. "And this."

It was animal scat, shaped like a football, but pillow-sized. I poked at it with my walking stick. Chunks of bone, hide, and scales were revealed; the skull of a very large snake . . . then the jaw and eye sockets of an alligator, medium-sized, but big enough for me to say, "It's time to finish up and go. They've run out of food here. They're eating themselves until something warm-blooded comes along."

"Pythons," he said, "I didn't even know they pooped. You think it's fresh?"

"There're no flies on it. Maybe it was too cold for flies earlier."

"Clever girl. Yes, get moving, but first I want

to dig up a couple of trees. It won't take long. Besides, I doubt if what you heard was—" He stopped when I held up a warning hand.

In the distance, muted by foliage, branches snapped, then snapped again after a long period of silence.

"Could be the wind," he said. "It's still chilly enough, reptiles wouldn't be moving. Know what I hoped for? A big, flat rock, somewhere, and a bunch of snakes sunning themselves. That would make it easier, but there's not a damn rock around for—"

Again, I motioned for quiet.

He listened a bit, then lowered his voice. "Yeah, just the wind. I don't see your hurry. I mean, think about it. In a week, it'll be like summer. Do you really want to come back another day and risk winding up like that?"

In a pile of animal scat, he meant.

It was true the wind was freshening; occasional balmy puffs from the southwest. I listened for noises a while before following him to a pair of saplings he'd found. They were scrub or water oaks, not citrus.

I thought for a moment, then said, "You know who would've been useful to bring along? Kermit. He knows as much as anybody about citrus."

Martinez, not interested, replied, "Yeah, too bad about him," then realized he might have slipped again. "Let's face it, first Reggie, then Bigalow. You've got to assume the worst."

"Two hours in a bar with Larry," I replied. "He's a talker. Did he say anything you might have missed?"

"About what? Oh . . . not about Bigalow, but, yeah, he couldn't say enough about getting his hands on you. Seems his ego took a bruising; a love-hate thing." Martinez's eyes wandered; a smirk there, maybe, with a suggestive edge, as he painted me up and down. "I'll spare you the graphics, but let's just say he admires the cut of your jib."

Jib?

I ignored that by settling into myself. *Kermit's dead,* I thought, *and this man might have killed him. Or helped.*

There was something else, if I was right: once we had the boat loaded with oranges, and a tree or two, I would no longer be of use. Martinez— if that was his name—might kill me, too.

"Something bothering you, Captain?" The smirk had vanished and, with it, possibly, the identity of whoever lived inside the man's head.

I started away. "Keep looking, if you want. I've got a bag full of oranges to take to the boat."

"That's the problem, obviously. I can't tell the difference between oaks and citrus; you can. Give it another half hour and let's do this right. Come on . . . don't worry"—he gestured with the shotgun—"I won't let anything happen to you."

I watched his reaction when I replied, "Sabin, I'm not the only one you need to worry about."

That didn't faze the man, either.

I was wondering: *Who's the fool? Him, for thinking I'm harmless? Or me, for pretending it's true?*

The most likely place to find seedlings, I reasoned, was to the northeast, or southwest of the mother tree, for they were opposites of the prevailing winds.

My theory produced results. I found a fruiting tree too big for a truck, let alone my boat. Possibly, the same one I'd picked oranges from as a girl. It provided more DNA samples, which I stored in separate Ziploc bags. Hopefully, it was a clone, a pure descendant of seeds planted many hundreds of years ago. By then, my shoulder bag was overloaded, including the whelk shell, which I didn't need but kept anyway.

Martinez stuck close by and offered encouragement if he noticed me checking my watch or pausing to listen. I often did both, aware the island was beginning to stir. Occasionally, something big crushed a branch too far away to pinpoint. Maybe the wind or tide. If not, it was an animal that moved slowly, very slowly . . . or it was intelligent enough to be cautious.

We'd been ashore nearly an hour. Shadows retained an icy chill while the sun drifted higher and warmed the forest canopy.

I snapped off a leafy orange branch and handed it to him. "This is what you're looking for. Let's split up. I'm leaving at ten, no later, and I mean it. Do you have a watch?"

He tugged at the sleeve of his red sweater. "That's less than fifteen minutes."

For a moment, I thought he might offer a test of his own, ask if I'd pull anchor without him, but he was as uncertain about me as I was about him. Whether my suspicions were valid or not, it was better to maintain an illusion of trust. He was doing the same.

"Not that I'd go off and leave you," I added, "but you have to understand something. You only saw a picture of that snake. It's different seeing the real thing, being there in the water, and knowing how it feels. That's why I'm anxious."

"Leave a person *here?*" he chuckled. "It would take one coldhearted bastard. Gives me chills to even think about it." He paused, then nodded as if he'd made up his mind about something. "Tell you what"—another glance at his watch—"let's keep looking. And if you don't find a tree by quarter after ten, I'll race you to the boat."

That wasn't going to happen. I didn't want him

around when I got to the boat. There was something I'd left behind that might alleviate or confirm my concerns.

"Deal," I said.

With Martinez walking several lengths behind, I angled away from the mother tree, hacking vines and briars. The gloves I wore were elastic mesh and leather, made for fishing, not a machete. My right hand was beginning to blister. I switched to the left and looped the lanyard over my wrist. Gradually, I worked my way toward the water until we intersected with the trail I'd marked. My boat was to the left, screened from view. I continued onward.

The mound sloped into a valley, created by a second, much higher mound, where the bark of gumbo-limbo trees filtered amber light. The air was musky with the odor of white stopper trees, too. Near some saplings about as high as my waist, I waited for Martinez to catch up.

"Will these do?"

Luckily, he had dropped the orange branch I'd given him. "Perfect size. Nice job. Aren't you glad we stuck around? All I need now is a shovel and some kind of bucket. Yes . . . this looks like a good area. A perfect place to camp because"—an amused look brightened his dark eyes—"no one would ever find us. Say . . . what's that smell? Smells like a skunk."

No, it was the scent of white stopper saplings,

so named because, in Old Florida, tea made from their leaves was used to stop diarrhea.

I opened my pack, intending to give him the trowel but pulled out a bottle of water instead. "You said you were thirsty, take this. I won't be long. Do you know which way the boat is?"

"Over there." He pointed in the wrong direction, which surprised me. Or did it? This was an articulate man with an orderly mind.

"That's what I thought," I said, and set off on the course he had indicated until I was out of sight. Soon I looped back toward the mother tree. The blaze marks I'd cut weren't as obvious as I'd hoped. It took a while to get my bearings. My concerns faded when, atop a vacant tortoise mound, I stumbled past three little trees clumped together, all about a foot tall. *Treelets,* more accurately. The easiest way to identify young citrus is to tear a leaf and sniff. I did. Tangy; a hint of lime and orange.

After chopping some vines away—a nearby ficus was in the process of strangling the treelets—I joined them atop the mound. Viewed from above, their leaves formed another triad. They sprouted in groups of three, not unlike a certain crest worn by Conquistadors. Each tree was a mirror image of the other; delicate, on trunks no thicker than my thumb.

Three identical trees.

Kermit had applied that phrase, or something

similar, to his theory about citrus trees in isolation. After an unknown period of time—"hundreds of years," he'd guessed—each seed might produce *three,* not two, clone sprouts.

The strangest feeling came over me. Kermit might be dead and here I was marveling at something he should have been a part of. I didn't know the man, had no right to and probably never would beyond what I had imagined. With Sarah, however, I shared a bond. In myriad ways, all daughters are kindred, linked by a parent they worship—imaginary or not.

My sense of sadness faded with the reality of what the girl might have lost. I became furious on her behalf. If Larry had actually died in the explosion, his fate was out of my hands. That left Martinez, *if* he'd played a role. When I got to the boat, I might finally discover the truth about him. An apology is what I hoped he deserved. If not, I would turn him in to the police.

It was nearly ten a.m. My focus returned to securing the treelets. I dumped some oranges from my pack to make room, and, with great care, used the trowel. I trenched a circle, then lifted them out, their roots systems mingled in a clump of sandy loam about the size of my hands.

To keep the roots covered, I needed some-thing more stable than Ziploc bags. The ancient whelk finally had a use. The roots slipped easily into its columned chamber as if by design. Then I filled the shell with loam; didn't pack it but instead opened my last bottle of water and soaked it good so the roots would settle.

Strange how awareness blurs when focused on a task. Only when I was finishing up did I notice a pile of fist-sized rocks lying inside the tortoise hole. Using the machete like a hook, I fished one out. It was brownish white, as leathery as a turtle egg but much larger. I held the thing in my hand. It was dense with embryonic weight. I turned it . . . then yanked my hand away as if it were a hot coal.

I got to my feet, heart pounding while my senses returned to a normal state of high alert. I had been digging around a python den! Where there were eggs, there would be a mother—a big one, judging from the eggs' size. Had I not been so spooked, I would have destroyed them all. *Maybe.* It was a decision I didn't have the time, or the courage, to make.

I grabbed my pack and backed away. Nearby, three larger juvenile citrus trees were now visible in the foliage. Another detail I hadn't noticed.

I wished them well, as I had enough to carry and needed to move fast.

Once I found the first blaze mark, getting back to the water didn't take long. To see my skiff waiting, floating high and secure with its gleaming white deck, was a wonderful image. I climbed aboard. The first thing I did, even before stowing the treelets, was look under the steering wheel at the ignition switch.

The key was there.

I checked under the console. The .45 caliber Beretta was where I'd left it.

The relief I felt was considerable. Out here alone, just the two of us, a man with sinister intentions would have taken both, given the opportunity. That's why I'd told Martinez to linger before coming ashore. True, I carried a spare key in my pack. It was also true I'd pocketed the Beretta's magazine, but a Lysol man, a true pro, would have an extra mag somewhere.

Sabin Martinez, it appeared, was who he claimed to be.

I plopped down for a moment to rest. A breeze off the water was icy, but the deck, gleaming white, was already hot to the touch.

A flat rock in the sun.

The phrase came back to me, a comment Sabin had made to illustrate the improbability of reptiles stirring on an island cloaked in shade.

I stowed the oranges and my treasured treelets, then grabbed the shovel.

Sabin wouldn't need it to dig white stopper

trees, but it might provide a segue to an explanation.

What would I say?

I hiked back through the mangroves, up the mound, and was still mulling it over when the man I owed an "apology" to stepped out, shotgun raised, his eyes framing me over the barrel. "I might not know anything about orange trees," he said, "but guess who does?"

Larry Luckheim, in tattered clothes, and his face charred, stood beside him.

Twenty-Six

I said to the man with the Hemingway beard, "You better think twice before using that gun. Larry has reason to bend it over your head once it's empty. Don't you, Larry?"

It was tough to speak pleasantly to the former bass pro or even look at his face, but I did. "Sorry about your skiff; I know you were fond of that cat hull. What happened is, he shorted your voltage regulator and poked a hole in the fuel line."

Larry looked at his boss, Raymond Caldwell—for that's who the man had to be. "She'd better be lying."

"Have a look in her bag, then search her."

"*Say it*—tell me she's lying. Getting blowed out of my boat was enough without being hacked by a machete. How well you know this girl?"

"Use your head. How else would she know what caused the explosion? She's still pissed about what we did to her boyfriend."

I understood what that meant, but Larry wasn't so sure. "What's-his-name, the guy the bull tromped last night?" When it was confirmed, he turned to me. "You're quite the sassy package, but, yeah, them cat hulls are a good ride. I'm gonna miss that boat more than I hate calling insurance agents. You ever"—he slapped a mosquito—"you ever have an engine blow when you were hard aground? When you land, there's not as much water as you'd hoped. I'll kill the joker who did it."

The bass pro sounded crazed but was in much better shape than he looked. The left side of his face had been scorched black and half of his mustache with it . . . or was it mostly oil and soot? I didn't want to get close enough to find out. Aside from a blistered left hand, he'd been strong enough to hike through a quarter mile of mangroves. That much was certain.

Larry whispered something to Caldwell, who nodded; said something else, then offered his boss a bawdy smile. "Seriously? Screwing that little dweeb? So that's what this is about." Again, he focused on me, having fun with the subject. "Kermit didn't seem much of a man, staked-out, waiting for that bull to charge. Bet there was times you had him begging for mercy, too. But wasn't he a married man? That's what he claimed; he was married and had a kid who—"

"Shut up! Search her pack," Caldwell told him.

"Not 'til she admits who she paid to futz with my engines."

I couldn't form words, my jaw was so tight, yet I heard myself say, "Wish I had done it, you bastard. You might not be so lucky if you keep talking like that."

"A wildcat," Larry said, and grinned. "I planned on the two of us taking a spin. You know . . . get us some naked time out there where"—he slapped another mosquito. "These goddamn bugs . . . shit. They'll take some fun out of my dance card, but what the hell? I aim to get my money's worth."

He came toward me; Caldwell followed. I steadied my shoulder pack and moved to maintain distance, the machete in my left hand. The shovel was on the ground somewhere. No idea where. It seemed a long minute or two since I'd dropped it.

We'd been going back and forth for a while. This was after they'd surprised me, and after Caldwell, with sly insinuations, had also made his carnal intentions clear.

"If you don't cooperate," he'd said, "and try to relax a little, none of us will enjoy what happens next."

Meaning he would shoot me.

Caldwell was determined to leave with a couple of citrus trees, too—another reason to tolerate my defiant attitude, which, under the circumstances, the ex–football star found puzzling. Instead of running, I'd stood my ground, backing a bit, or sliding away, when they tried to get too close or slip behind me.

Finally, the man with the Hemingway beard inquired, "What's going on in that pretty little head of yours? I bet I know . . . You took my Beretta off the boat, didn't you? Now you're hoping this shotgun misfires, or maybe that you'll surprise me somehow, get the gun out of your backpack, before I shoot. My dear Captain, that's not much to hang your star on. You don't seem to understand who you're dealing with."

"Beretta?" Larry asked. His silly grin vanished, and he retreated as if to use Caldwell as a partial screen. "Dude, for what you're paying me, all you had to do was ask. Or do some reading. If this woman's got a gun, she'll *use* it. She's freakin' nuts."

"What is the final tally, Raymond?" I asked, and for the first time stepped toward him. "I bet you got a pretty good laugh by asking me how many women you've assaulted. Know what the answer is to that? *None*—starting today."

"See!" Larry said. "Stop screwing around and shoot her in the foot, or something, to put her down."

Caldwell's attitude: calm; amused by my temper; this mouthy female hick too pissed off to be afraid. In a way, he was right. Since thinking about Sarah, I'd been getting madder and madder. Anger was elevated to fury when he said to Larry, "She's a fool. The Beretta won't

351

fire. I took out the slide spring before I came ashore. Here, watch."

He looked at me. "Go ahead, open your pack and get my gun out. See what happens. When you're convinced, drop the machete and humor us by explaining why you've been kneeling in dirt." His eyes moved to the knees of my pants. "A woman so damn anxious to get to her boat, that tells me you found an orange tree. Where is it?"

I removed my right glove, stuffed it into my back pocket, then placed the shoulder pack at my feet. "The tree's too big for one person to carry. That's why I got the shovel and came to find you."

Caldwell laughed at this obvious lie. "Came to find the idiot who doesn't know what an orange tree looks like, huh? Okay, I'll let that pass—as long as we leave here with at least two or three healthy ones. Afterward, when we're in the boat, out in open water"—he glanced at Larry to communicate his true meaning—"we'll stop and have a little something to munch on. I'm hungry. How about you?"

"Make her open that goddamn pack," the bass pro said, "to be sure she's not carrying. I've watched her grab treble hooks out of the air, and the bitch didn't even flinch."

Caldwell angled the shotgun toward my ankles and got ready. "Dump the bag on the ground, please—if nothing else just to shut him up. *Move.* I mean it, I'll blow your foot off just like he suggested."

I'd had enough. I kicked my pack toward them and followed it. "Is that how it's playing out in your head, Raymond? Shoot me before you've had the fun of scaring me so bad, I'll do any damn thing you tell me?" I reached back for the glove but changed my mind. "What about you, Buddy Luck? My guess is, you've been down this road yourself. Ever strip the pants off a girl whose

foot has been shot off? She wouldn't be much of a dancer." I kicked my pack again. "Know what I'd like to see just once? Someone with the grit to make cowards like you strip their clothes off first." We were separated by ficus streamers and ten yards of rot. I stepped over the bag and walked toward them, my hands at my sides.

The bass pro gulped. Caldwell stared. Neither knew what to make of this, but then Larry decided, "Maybe we should talk this over before she gets the wrong idea."

Caldwell said, "Fuck that," and told me to stop, not to take another step.

I did as he said; dropped the machete, then reached behind me as if for the glove. Then, as if isolated in a tunnel, I watched the man's expression change when my hand reappeared holding a silver 9mm pistol, not his useless black Beretta.

Caldwell, startled by the suddenness of it all, stumbled back and pulled one of the shotgun's twin triggers.

CLICK! The gun didn't go off—a failure to fire, not a misfire.

I took aim, my knees bent slightly, right leg back: the Weaver stance had been comfortable at the gun range. Automatically, I squared myself for balance. With both hands on the grips, a push-and-pull adjustment steadied the pistol. Beyond the front sight, the man with the Hemingway beard pointed the shotgun at my face and tried again.

CLICK! Another failure to fire.

Caldwell's eyes widened as I advanced toward him; a touch of wild panic there that reminded me of Lonnie Chatham's rearing horse. Larry hollered, "Shit!" turned, ran . . . tripped and sprawled forward on his face. My left eye tracked him over the barrel when he got up; my index finger, light on the trigger, but not light enough because of adrenaline pumping through me.

BAAP! The pistol jumped in my hands, startlingly loud. I hadn't meant to fire; could not bring myself to shoot a fleeing man, which is why I'd aimed above his head.

Larry looked back in shock, his skin paler

beneath streaks of soot. After an instant of indecision, he bolted away, his progress through the brush similar to the noise an elephant might make.

The pistol's front sight was an iridescent white dot. It pivoted toward Raymond Caldwell's forehead, then located center mass on his chest. I watched him snap open the shotgun, stare up at me, then look again in disbelief at the gun's two empty chambers.

"You . . . *bitch*," he said.

"An unarmed dumbass shouldn't call names," I replied. "The shells are in my pocket, Raymond. I did it while you were tying your boots." The pistol's front sight led me forward— slow, measured steps to keep the barrel from bouncing. "Run, if you want. I'll aim for your legs, and finish up after I've asked you a couple of things."

"You don't have the nerve."

I stopped and took aim.

"Hey . . . whoa, now. Ask me anything. That's what I'd prefer to do . . . yeah, talk this over." He tossed the shotgun on the ground; his big hands came up in partial surrender. "I wouldn't've shot you. You know that. What? Face a murder charge?"

"*Another* murder charge," I corrected him. "You would've done something worse. That never crossed your mind, did it? How scared

355

those girls were. How scared they'd always be, the ones you let live. How many were there, Raymond? You never did answer the question."

He began to back away. "What's that matter to you?"

"Let's pretend it does. I'm waiting for a number."

Something in my tone, or my eyes, spooked him. "Uh . . . none. *Really.* None that weren't willing after the first few minutes anyway, and that's the truth. I can't help they got scared later. Seriously, what Lonnie told you was the truth. I didn't attack her, I *saved* her. Come on, Hannah, calm down." Using my name to remind me of the friendliness we had shared. Then raised a valid point, saying, "You know where Larry will head, don't you? Your boat. Hear him? He's looking for it right now."

In a peripheral way, I'd been tracking the bass pro through the woods. A huge man whose freakish quickness didn't mitigate the noise he made. It was true. Someone with Okeechobee experience might find the trail I'd blazed and follow it to my boat.

"What will we do if he goes off and leaves us? It's getting late"—Caldwell turned his wrist for me to see—"it's already eleven, almost. Tell you what. In my coat pocket, you'll find the Beretta's slide spring. The gun's all yours. But if that asshole tries to jump us, I'm willing to take your side if—"

I let the man talk. Made a show of my cold anger by finding the shovel and flinging it so hard that, had he not ducked, it would've clanked off his head.

"Start digging," I said.

"What?"

"A hole. It doesn't have to be deep. I'm your last victim. I already told you that."

The threat was a ruse but produced the reaction I'd hoped for. "Jesus Christ, you wouldn't . . . Okay, okay—how about this? Lonnie and I, we've already invested ten grand in your project. How does another half mil sound? In cash. No one has to—"

"Using Mr. Chatham's money, of course. Now you're trying to bribe me?"

"Hold on . . . just *think* about it. In my back pocket, there's a pair of handcuffs. I'll let you handcuff me. I promise, no funny business. We can talk this out on the way back to Marco."

Handcuffs? He'd brought them to use on me, no doubt.

I walked toward him and stopped seven paces away—a safe distance, but close enough I couldn't miss. "You were right about warning shots, Raymond. I'll never waste another. Are you ready to cooperate?"

Pathetic, the way he nodded.

· · ·

I left Caldwell there—him with his big hairy chest and ponytail, wearing only white boxers and a copper bracelet—but took the shotgun, the machete, his boots, and the handcuffs with me.

On a briar patch island such as this, it was worse to be barefoot than hobbled.

The boots were heavy. Caldwell was far behind but still pleading for me to reconsider when I tossed one into the bushes.

The other boot, after dealing with some guilt, I left in plain sight near the trail I'd blazed.

Maybe he would find it.

That was up to him, a man who had helped murder Sarah's father.

The other killer was still out there, but I had no idea where. I could no longer hear Larry crashing through the brush. Unless something had happened to him, silence suggested he was moving with intent.

Had he found my boat?

I hurried on, and didn't slow until I got to the mangroves. Cautiously, then, I worked my way over rubbery, knee-high roots and under limbs one quiet step at a time.

Patches of water appeared through the foliage, then a wedge of my skiff's gleaming white deck.

I stopped; my breath caught. Something foreign

was on the deck, an object that didn't belong and hadn't been there thirty minutes ago.

A few steps closer broadened the waterscape. Not an object—an *appendage,* it looked like— the bloated, hairless leg of a man with very dark skin . . . or skin that had been charred by fire.

If it was Larry, why had he removed his pants? And why was only one huge thigh visible? No, couldn't be. It was much too large to be a human leg.

Another quiet step, then another, I moved with the pistol ready. I watched hairless flesh expand to the thickness of a telephone pole, then slowly, slowly contract.

I knew then what had happened: a snake had found the only large flat rock available and was warming itself beneath the noon-bound sun.

The monster python.

Had to be . . . unless more than one monster existed here.

Twenty-Seven

Twice I started toward my skiff but lost my nerve, and walked numbly inland. Stood in the ficus gloom, trying to ignore the baritone boom of Caldwell's pleas echoing across the island. If I heard him, so did Larry . . . and so did every stirring creature for miles.

If the men reunited, I would become less of a threat. They would arm themselves with whatever they could find, then attack, or create a diversion, to draw me away from their true objective: my boat. There was no other way out of an area where muck was too deep to support human weight and water too shallow to swim. Never mind the reptiles that had feasted themselves into famine. Alligators, snakes, and saltwater crocs were all that was left here. Now apex survivors had only themselves to prey upon, but the sun would soon awaken their sensory organs to the scent of a new food source: mammals; three oddities that walked on slow hind legs.

The fact was, we were all trapped. Reptiles included.

I took out my phone in the pointless hope a transmitter on Marco had doubled its range. The GPS triangulated enough satellites to show my position, but this was not a satellite phone.

I put it away, and listened to Caldwell's pleas become threats.

"Hey . . . Hey! I know you hear me. My feet; I'm bleeding. I can't walk. Hear me? I CAN'T WALK. At least bring back my boots. Hannah! Goddamn it! Let's discuss this like adults or, I swear to Christ, I'll find you and cut off your . . ."

I ignored the rest but understood what I had to do. Seeking shelter on the island was no safer than confronting, maybe killing, the snake that had commandeered my boat.

I tightened my gloves, retraced my steps, and, like a child on tiptoes, stepped clear of the mangroves. Water seeped in and numbed my toes while I waited for the python's reaction. There was none.

I returned to shore; left the machete hanging with my shoulder pack and holstered the pistol in favor of the shotgun, which I loaded. To stumble and lose my only dependable weapon was unthinkable. Also, two barrels of buckshot had a better chance of taking off a snake's head—if the antique shells fired. If they didn't, the pistol was there at my side.

When I was ready, I moved along the bank to avoid sinking in muck. Slid closer and closer until I had a full view of what I was dealing with.

What awaited made me want to cry.

The bulk of the python lay out of sight on the

floor of the boat, but a six-foot tail section spilled onto the stern. This suggested the reptile had entered via the transom. Looped like fire hose over the forward casting deck was a much longer segment. I'd mistaken a piece of it for a human thigh, despite its massive girth and its buckskin-on-black scales.

Where was the snake's head? That was the question; potentially, a life-or-death question. I couldn't see it from where I stood. Not sufficient elevation. I would have to wade close enough to look *down* into my skiff. Only then might I find a vulnerable target to shoot.

Fear streamed a scenario to consider: peering up, when I poked my chin over the gunnel, was the snake, already alerted by its radar tongue. The fangs-on-bone crunch when Roberta was struck echoed within me until I winced.

Another possibility: the snake's head would be near the motor, or the console wiring, or over the fuel tank. Some component impossible to repair. Pull the trigger, I might be left with a boat that wouldn't start and a two-hundred-pound snake that was still alive, and agitated.

Caldwell's baritone rage offered guidance from far away. "Buddy . . . Buddy Luck! Hey, man, can you hear me? Goddamn it, find that crazy woman. Hear me, Buddy? KILL HER . . . TAKE THE BOAT."

Buddy Luck . . .

There was no alternative. I was dealing with two killers who clung to the pretense of their own fake names. I had to be bold or forfeit a chance to take control. Yet my feet would not move without conjuring positive hopes.

Overhead, the sun glittered in a high, blue sky, but the breeze retained an icy edge. Pythons didn't function well if the thermometer dropped below fifty. Twenty degrees colder—even ten—they had to regulate body heat by coiling or seeking shelter. Thermoregulation, it was called.

Or was it a process known as brumation?

I was so nervous, I couldn't remember what I'd read. Some of the data conflicted, or was undependable, because exotic reptiles had found ways to adapt. Surviving the cold required behavioral changes. The same with ambush techniques—they had to adjust to the habits of their prey. Nature was shrewd. Nature was relentless.

One example: a tree growing parallel to the ground, by shooting branches skyward, had produced an exotic fruit for an unknown span of generations.

All I knew for certain was, the day wasn't getting any colder. Factoring windchill, I guessed the temp to be low fifties. The sluggish snake I'd killed earlier gave me confidence enough to think: *Stop wasting time, take back what is yours.*

Courage forged from necessity is a tenuous, untested ally. But it was all I had.

I continued along the bank, my skiff tethered fore and aft like a hammock that cupped a sleeping giant. Separating us was an awning of mangroves. Too noisy to push my way through, so I ventured into deeper water. Not far, only up to my knees. I knew better than to trust the spongy bottom, yet it seemed the safest way. I slid along as if on tiptoe, closer and closer, focusing on the snake's tail.

The reptile had yet to stir.

The footing was iffy. My thighs pushed a mild wake. When I was too far from shore to turn back, the boat began to rock imperceptibly, yet I could not stop. The bottom might collapse beneath my feet. In slow motion, I shouldered the shotgun.

Five yards separated us, close enough that my nose scented a reptilian, uric musk. Yet, the sun pushed me onward, step by careful step, and soon banged the boat's hull with my shadow.

The python *moved*. On the forward deck was a massive-bellied loop of scales. I watched it contract abruptly, as if holding its breath; an ambush technique, possibly, to lure me closer. Playing possum was one of nature's most effective tricks.

I freed my left hand from the shotgun, and was reaching for the boat's transom, when a distant crash of foliage caused me to freeze. *Larry—it has to be Larry,* I thought. *An intentional diversion.*

I turned to look.

Turning was a mistake. My right foot sheared through the crust and was immediately suctioned deeper into muck. I struggled to recover, then vaulted forward because my foot was anchored. The shotgun nearly flew out of my hands as I went down and under. After much splashing and kicking, I surfaced and immediately panicked. The snake could not possibly sleep through so much noise. I clawed and stumbled my way toward shore, afraid to look around because I knew—*I knew*—the python would be sailing toward me, head high above the water like a dragon from a nightmare.

I was wrong. Didn't realize it, though, until I tripped again and landed on my butt in the shallows, facing the boat. My eyes zoomed in: the snake lay in glistening, docile segments. Its tail had become my warning flag, yet not so much as a twitch.

The reptile wasn't dead and it wasn't playing possum; I'd witnessed the billows-like contractions of its breathing. The python was hypothermic: not dead but only in a lethargic sleep until its body warmed.

As an experiment, I kicked the water a few times, then freed the bowline from the trees and let the skiff swing. I thumped the bow with the rope. No response. I did it again, as if cracking a whip. This created an animated seesaw motion that unseated the snake's belly section from the casting deck. Like a loop of overstuffed sausage, it fell as deadweight, vanishing from view.

I paused to think while I snapped the shotgun open and checked the breech. The shells, made of brass and paper, were soaked. They couldn't be trusted. The only option this left me was as dreadful as it was unavoidable.

Carrying just a pistol, I would have to get close enough to fire a round point-blank in the snake's head. If that couldn't be done without disabling my boat, I would have to climb aboard to find a safer angle. If there was no safer angle, I would have to . . .

Dreadful did not describe what would come next: with the snake sleeping at my feet, I'd have to drive at high speed and use a series of slalom turns to vault the reptile overboard. Or flood the hull, let the snake's buoyancy float it out . . . Or rocket away after looping the anchor line around the snake's midsection.

All scenarios were workable but terrifying.

It came to me then: a better solution. Why had I not thought of it immediately?

The machete.

Of course! I'd already used it to dispatch two

pythons. All I had to do was sneak up on the creature and cut off its head while it slept. If it took several swings, that was okay. The blade wouldn't do serious damage to my boat. Even the snake would benefit. Swing the machete hard and true, it would all be over before its reptilian brain sensed danger.

There was no need to retie the boat. I dropped the bowline in the water and hurried into the mangroves. I'd left the machete hanging on a tree with my shoulder pack, but which tree? I couldn't find it. Water had obliterated my tracks. I searched along the outer fringe, then returned to the area where I believed it should be. No luck. Trouble was, I'd been in such a frazzled state, I hadn't marked the spot. Here, in the tangled shadows, all limbs blended.

I wandered deeper, zigzagging, until a sickening possibility knotted my stomach. I stopped, listened to a gust of wind crackle through the trees. Only then did I admit what my subconscious knew was true: I hadn't lost my pack and machete. They'd been stolen.

Larry Luckheim had found me. He'd been watching from the shadows, or, possibly, had just now stumbled upon my things.

Either way, his next move would be to steal my boat.

Twenty-Eight

I drew the pistol and backtracked as fast as I could go, vaulting roots, ducking limbs. When the water came into view, I slowed before exiting the mangrove fringe—and was knocked sideways by a blinding impact.

When I looked up, Larry towered over me, his charred face grotesque beneath the silhouette of a machete that was poised to strike. Only one long bar of his mustache remained. The effect was surreal.

"The boat key?" he yelled. "Where is it?"

I scrambled backwards, and said, "In the boat!" because I was too dazed to invent a lie.

"Show me your hands! I'll cut your head off, damn you. Where's that gun? Pull your gun, I'll do it."

There was a panicked edge to his insanity. He was as scared as me, I realized, scared I'd shoot him, but it was more than that. Kill me now, he was doomed if I was lying about the key. Police would link him to my murder—if a snake didn't get him first.

I extended my hands, palms out, to prove they were empty. "Take it easy . . . I'm lying on it. There's a holster on the back of my belt where—"

"*Don't.* Don't reach for anything. And stop your

damn squirming. Spread your arms—not like that, dumbass. I want your hands away from your body; as far from the gun as you can get them."

I lay in a sodden crevice between trees. My shoulders were blocked by coiled roots and deadfall. I scanned the area around my head before threading my left arm through the tangle. Then, with exaggerated difficulty, I extended my right hand until it rested behind the roots. It was because of what I had just seen: a flash of silver. My pistol had landed there.

"What's your problem, girl?"

"It hurts. I think you broke my arm."

"*Good.* Your shooting hand. Tell me the truth. Where's that goddamn key?"

"It doesn't matter. There's a python on my boat. Look for yourself. It crawled up there to get warm." In a hurry, I added, "Don't—I was lying!" because he straddled me, moving as if to crush me with a knee.

"No more of your bullshit. Where is the key?"

"In my bag," I said. "There's a zipper pocket on the flap. The key's in there."

The man stepped back and went through the bag. As he scattered my things on the ground, a baritone voice called, "Hey . . . Buddy. Buddy Luck! Don't leave me, man. I'll triple what I paid. Are you there? Goddamn it . . . ANSWER ME."

Larry howled in response, "Kiss my ass,

Martinez!" and held up the spare boat key in triumph. Then, looking down, started to say, "Put on your dancing shoes, girl, because—"

That's as far as he got before he saw the pistol; me, sitting up now, my eyes staring cold, ready to pull the trigger. And I would've done it, shot him square in the chest, had he moved toward me. Instead, he backed away and dropped the machete as if in surrender.

It was a ploy to defuse my willingness. He waited until I was getting up, then sprinted toward the water, using trees as cover.

I followed. By the time I exited the mangroves, he was almost to my skiff, which had drifted a little but not far. A huge man with a charred mustache was easily tracked over the pistol sights, yet I didn't fire. His back was to me; he was slogging along, muck up to his knees. An easy target.

That's not the only reason I didn't fire. I wanted to see what happened. If he made it to the boat and climbed aboard, yes, I'd pull the trigger—better to wound an unarmed man than to be lost to a place like this.

It all depended on the python. Larry hadn't noticed what resembled six feet of fire hose stretched across the stern. The tail, my warning flag. That's all that was visible. It lay as motionless as a hose, too. The snake was still a lifeless lump due to hypothermia.

Larry doesn't know that, I thought. *When he sees what's in there, he'll panic again and run.*

If he didn't . . . ?

That decision could wait. I would let it play out, watching from the water's edge.

Larry stumbled, fell sideways. His bulk made a mighty splash, displacing a geyser that sprinkled the deck of my skiff.

I watched the python's tail twitch, then twitch again. Or was it an illusion created by waves rocking the hull?

The big man righted himself, tried to stand and fell forward, but this time lunged within a body length of the skiff.

I watched the python's tail slowly curl itself into a question mark. Or was that imaginary, too? When angry, I am often guilty of perverse hope.

Larry did something smart that Roberta and I had learned weeks ago. He closed the distance by belly crawling, then reached up and slapped a big hand on the gunnel so he could hang there and catch his breath.

My eyes swung, hoping for a reaction, but there was nothing to watch. The python's tail lay as immobile as a frozen chunk of pipe.

I'd holstered the pistol but drew it when the man noticed me for the first time. Immediately, he turned his back and hollered, "Once I get the motor started, you're welcome to come aboard. But not with that damn gun."

"Look what's on the deck," I said. "You might change your mind about me and my gun."

He swung his head around, still sitting on his butt in the water. "In here?" He rapped the hull with his knuckles. "I don't give a shit. All I know is, you won't shoot an unarmed man in the back. That would look real good in a magazine, the famous girl fishing guide . . ." His voice trailed off because of a sudden change in my behavior. He'd seen a swift shift in countenance, and I'd raised the pistol as if to shoot him in the head. "Hey, don't! I said you can come along. What the hell's wrong with you?"

"I warned you," I said, barely able to whisper. "Move . . . Get away from there."

The man considered the pistol's angle and looked up to see what I was aiming at. His brain had only a microsecond to process the image—a swaying lamppost with a serpent's head, a flicking tongue the width of a pitchfork.

I fired.

The python struck.

Larry screamed.

Twenty-Nine

More than a month after returning from Choking Creek, I drove Roberta to her obstetrician's office in South Fort Myers. We were unaware that March 30, a Friday, was considered National Doctors' Day until we entered to find baked goods on a tray in a room decorated with balloons. Fittingly, they were about fifty-fifty pink and blue.

I am not a bows-and-ribbons type of person, so could only pretend to appreciate their gaiety.

Roberta said, "See why I like the place? Only a woman doctor would feed me brownies before ordering me to lose weight. Not that she will"—my friend and business partner took a bite—"but she might if someone doesn't finish off that fudge. Get to work, Hannah, or I'll have to fight that skinny nurse for the tray."

I selected crackers and a wedge of cream cheese instead. Roberta felt betrayed until I opened my shoulder bag and produced a jar of marmalade, which I dolloped out liberally.

"Is that new?"

"Right off the stove. I made a fresh batch yesterday."

"Not that. *That!* I don't remember seeing it."

She was referring to the vintage leather bag I'd

placed beside my chair. Yes, it was new. A present to myself after, despairing, finally throwing away my favorite shoulder pack. Bloodstains are tough to remove from ripstop nylon. I associated them with Larry Luckheim, another form of stain. He'd bled a lot—not an episode I cared to revisit. An afternoon spent answering questions from police, then reporters, had taken the dazzle out of what happened after the python anchored its teeth in Larry's head.

"Try this," I said, and heaped marmalade onto a cracker.

With roots in 4-H homemaking, Roberta would not have faked her wonderment when she took a bite. "Oh my lord . . ." Her eyes widened. "You made this?"

I showed her the hand-lettered label:

Mother Tree
Sour Orange Marmalade

"Incredible. And so . . . *different*. I've never had anything that comes close."

"It's easy to make. Just sugar and oranges, then a lot of boiling. Separate the pulp, and the more sliced peeling you add, the better. That makes it gel—the natural pectin in the skin. You already know the real secret."

"Special oranges." She smiled, and reached for another cracker.

Special. Yes, they were.

In the vintage leather bag was my laptop. Through emails, Dr. Gentry and her husband had kept us updated on their campaign to make our efforts profitable. An application for a provisional patent had been filed. Every *t* and *i* crossed and dotted. According to their inside sources, ours was the first to claim a foothold in an important, esoteric niche.

Roberta got up to use the restroom, muttering something about "Even faucets get a break."

Pregnant women, I had learned, do love a good joke about peeing.

I watched her waddle away, then opened my computer and found Dr. Gentry's most recent email.

Ladies, I had a great conversation with Vern Norviel of Berkeley, one of the nation's leading legal experts on intellectual properties and biotechnology. I have good news. Sequencing of samples you provided last month suggest they are more closely related to original Spanish seed stock than any previously tested. Congratulations!

According to Vern, if the clones prove to be more resistant to parasites/pathogens, the beneficial DNA from your plants can be reproduced. This is done via a gene processing device, then inserted into the DNA of modern varietals. The technique is a genetic breakthrough, recently named with the acronym CRISPR. (See below.)

Vern is going to put me in touch with Harvard geneticist Dr. George Church (he was the first to do Neanderthal sequencing), who might be willing to join in as a partner for profit (and fun).

There was still a lot of lab work and experimentation to be done, of course. Various scion varietals would have to be grafted onto our Spanish rootstock, then nurtured to fruition— something Roberta looked forward to during her maternity leave. The process was daunting. It would be two years or more before any conclusions could be drawn regarding how resistant our hybrids were to citrus greening disease. Yet, at any stage of the process, Dr. Gentry had told me, I could sell my percentage of the partnership and walk away. She had an investor who'd already offered 1.5 million dollars for my share, and the Gentrys were confident the figure would double within a year.

Roberta returned from the restroom only to be summoned by the nurse. I shouldered my new bag and went out for air, focusing on the door rather than a room full of very ripe, rosy-cheeked women. How much champagne and backseat jockeying, I wondered, did their numbers represent?

My peevish attitude accompanied me outside to the parking lot, where I rationalized my mood. *Seduction* isn't a word, it's a drama. Implied are three components: an instigator, a willing participant, and an objective, although the participant can be just as eager; slyer, too.

I was also aware the *objective* might be a whistle-stop. Or a life-changing destination.

As the women inside might agree, the distance that lies between the two is incalculable.

Marion Ford was on my mind. Under the guise of awarding him a partnership, I'd hoped to meet him for dinner to explain the windfall he might share.

Pure optimism on my part. The biologist is a difficult man to locate, let alone pin down. I think it was only out of concern for my mental health that, a few days after my return from Choking Creek, he answered the phone.

"How're you holding up?" he'd said. "That was quite a story in the newspaper."

Ford didn't read newspapers, but the deception was a kindness. Because of recent headlines, I couldn't fuel my skiff without being gawked at or congratulated for courage I do not possess.

"Fine, just fine," I replied.

The biologist understood. He skipped to the reality of the matter, saying, "Yeah. It can take a while."

We'd met at sunset on Useppa Island, a small, historic resort that lies equidistant between his lab and my transient floating home. Dinner transitioned smoothly into a night in the Barron Collier Suite, on the second floor of the Collier Inn.

Champagne wasn't involved; several margaritas were. Ford is not an abstemious man, but he is disciplined. It took some effort to charm him into more than one drink.

Charming him into bed proved more difficult. The dangers were obvious, and my efforts had the flavor of desperation, which we both realized. With a less understanding friend, I would have felt humiliated.

With the big Victorian suite to myself, I slept alone.

Long after midnight, wearing a silken robe, I'd gone out on the balcony and counted stars. *Literally* counted them. It was a technique the biologist had suggested when overwhelmed by emotion or the horror of certain events.

"Do math problems. It's the only way to disengage the right side of the brain. You'll be surprised."

Ford, a left-brained pragmatist, was correct if I used a pencil and paper, but counting stars did not work. Details, odors, sounds—particularly sound—came spiraling back. All I had to do was close my eyes to relive events in present tense:

Larry Luckheim clings to my skiff, unaware of the monster elevating itself behind him. He says something defiant—the words don't register because my world has gone silent. The chrome pistol barrel is all I see until, there it is! the serpent's head, a mass of diamond scales wherein twin goat's eyes glow. Its mouth is stitched. In my mind, a flash association is made: a zombie; the way a zombie's lips are sewn.

The mouth opens. A tongue slaps out, two pitchfork probes taste the air. They taste Larry's skin, the heat of his flesh. The tongue slaps data back inside to a reptilian brain.

The python stiffens, alert. Its Doberman-sized head tilts toward the water. My gun sights are not wide enough to frame the distance between the two lucent eyes.

The snake sees Larry.

I attempt to shout but can only whisper, "Move! Get away from there."

Larry, looking up, screams. I pull the trigger once, twice, yet the python strikes, and the fang-on-bone crunch is sickening. Twenty feet of reptile has spilled itself into the water before I realize the screaming has stopped.

The man's head has disappeared inside the snake's hinged jaws. The man's body is aswarm with frantic scales and splashing while the python coils. A squealing noise escapes the chaos. It ascends to penetrating animal decibels.

I lower the pistol as I watch. I turn away, nauseated . . . then stumble toward the machete, unsure if I am willing to help.

I am not willing but do it anyway when I hear Larry moan, "Help me, I'm hurt . . . I can't see!"

The snake, in its death throes—and a bullet in its brain—has released the man who intended to rape me. This is something Larry will admit when he's out of the hospital and in a prison psych ward. He has lost an eye, and most of his mind, but a bit of his conscience will return.

On Useppa Island that night, more than a month ago, no wonder it had been impossible to sleep.

Now, alone in a parking lot, waiting for Roberta, the details had lost some of their sting but not all. Just as the biologist had counseled, it would take a while. A lifetime, perhaps.

Raymond Caldwell had proved that. A week after his "disappearance," a weary search party, while hacking through vines, found a giant loaf of reptilian scat. Inside were fragments of hair and bone . . . and one shiny, bright copper bracelet.

When detectives yet again challenged my decision to rescue Larry but leave Caldwell behind, I silenced them with a truth that was also a lie:

I only had one pair of handcuffs.

The obstetrician was a methodical woman—very thorough, Roberta had warned—so I waited in my SUV rather than a room full of balloons and cheery women who had not shared a smile when shuffling off to pee.

That was okay. I had work to keep me busy while awaiting appointments of my own. Inside my vintage leather shoulder bag, separated from the laptop compartment, was my checkbook, my wallet, and other business-oriented necessities. A folder containing documents relating to Salt Creek Gun Club was there, but no signed deed.

Not yet. Lonnie Chatham, not by choice, had entered a labyrinth known as the criminal justice system. In the cement cap of a weir that spilled water, police had found her confession written twenty years earlier. In the crocodile pond, they'd also found a femur belonging to the real Sabin Martinez, a professional "Lysol man" who, for reasons unknown, had fallen for at least one fatal lie.

That's what I suspected anyway. And what I intended to tell the district attorney later in the day—among other things, including my conviction that Reggie had been murdered, too. Dear, dear Reggie. In this life, there are people we meet too late to appreciate all that is good and loyal in them, or to benefit from what they have to teach.

I'd thought a lot about the little chauffeur. It is impossible not to cling to the past. And just as impossible not to move on.

My deposition was scheduled for four p.m. It was now one-thirty, which wasn't much of a cushion on a day that included a meeting with the Gentrys and, hopefully, the Friday-night party at Dinkin's Bay, where the biologist lived.

Maybe he would be there; more likely, he would not. A man on the run does not keep a calendar, nor is he likely to answer the phone.

Marion Ford *was* on the run. Before Useppa, I'd only suspected the motives for his sudden departures and long absences. That night, though, he'd told me just enough to spare my feelings.

As a seductress, I was a failure. As the friend of a man in danger, however, my desire to provide comfort was genuine. The next morning, very early, we had both found solace in a space that, only twice in my life, had I allowed myself the freedom to explore.

I had no problem admitting this to myself—unlike my first indiscretion. With the biologist, it was different. Once, we had been lovers. Like me, he lived alone. He would probably die alone.

Marion Ford would never have cause to say to me, "Please admit it was more than just a kiss."

Kermit Bigalow had said something similar. Just thinking about those words still caused me to wince with regret.

In my bag was a letter I'd written to Sarah, expressing my sadness about the death of her father. I'd gone on and on, about what a fine man he was and how much he'd cared for her, because I knew the letter would never be sent. It was my way of attending a funeral I had no right to attend.

I opened the letter now and reread a passage about fishing, and my boat, if she'd like to drive it, and the wealth she might inherit thanks to a project her father had been working on prior to his death.

That was enough. I couldn't send the letter, and I couldn't read it again without bawling, so I put it away and checked the time.

One forty-five p.m.

My appointment was at two.

I was still filling out forms when Roberta returned to the waiting room. "What should I put here?" I asked, and handed her the clipboard.

She shrugged and gave it back. "If you're not sure, leave it blank."

In a way, I was sure.

In a space provided for the name of my child's father I wrote, *A good man.*

Center Point Large Print
600 Brooks Road / PO Box 1
Thorndike, ME 04986-0001 USA

(207) 568-3717

US & Canada:
1 800 929-9108
www.centerpointlargeprint.com